Praise for *Firestorm at*

"An ominous, gripping, and thoroughly th

"New material and the best of the historical record make for an authoritative, fresh account of an overlooked epic."
—John N. Maclean, author of *Fire on the Mountain*

"[A] thorough historical narrative. A chilling, absorbing account of the hellish events."
—*Publishers Weekly*

"It closes what up to now had been a gaping void in the annals of American history."
—David Cowan, author of *Great Chicago Fires* and *To Sleep with the Angels: The Story of a Fire*

"An ominous and quietly thrilling account of the 1871 fire. Gess and Lutz restore it to historical memory with an operatic quality it richly deserves."
—*Kirkus Reviews*

"You do not just read this book—you experience the heat and fear. . . . Masterfully done."
—Philip Gerard, author of *Secret Soldiers: The Story of World War II's Heroic Army of Deception*

"A necessary act of recovery. A heartbreaking narrative history that captures the inferno's full horror."
—Robert Lalasz, *The News & Observer* (Raleigh)

"A gripping, thought-provoking read."
—Neil Hanson, author of *The Custom of the Sea* and *The Great Fire of London in that Apocalyptic Year 1666*

"Well-researched, absorbing and terrifying."
—Don Campbell, *The Oregonian* (Portland)

"Gess and Lutz have rescued a national tragedy from the the dusty attic of forgotten history. This is great storytelling and great history."
—Tom Powers, *The Flint Journal*

FIRESTORM AT PESHTIGO

FIRESTORM
AT PESHTIGO

A Town, Its People,
and the Deadliest Fire
in American History

DENISE GESS
and WILLIAM LUTZ

A HOLT PAPERBACK
HENRY HOLT AND COMPANY · NEW YORK

Holt Paperbacks
Henry Holt and Company, LLC
Publishers since 1866
175 Fifth Avenue
New York, New York 10010
www.henryholt.com

A Holt Paperback® and ® are registered trademarks
of Henry Holt and Company, LLC.

Copyright © 2002 by Denise Gess and William Lutz
All rights reserved.

Permissions acknowledgments in Notes

Library of Congress Cataloging-in-Publication Data
Gess, Denise.
    Firestorm at Peshtigo : a town, its people, and the deadliest fire
in American history / by Denise Gess and William Lutz.—1st ed.
    p. cm.
    Includes bibliographical references (p.) and index.
    ISBN-13: 978-0-8050-7293-8
    ISBN-10: 0-8050-7293-4
    1. Peshtigo (Wis.)—History—19th century.   2. Forest fires—
Wisconsin—Peshtigo—History—19th century.   3. Peshtigo
(Wis.)—Biography.   I. Lutz, William.   II. Title.

F589.P48 G78 2002
977.5'33—dc21   2002017279

Henry Holt books are available for special promotions
and premiums. For details contact: Director, Special Markets.

Originally published in hardcover in 2002 by Henry Holt and Company

First Holt Paperbacks Edition 2003

Designed by Victoria Hartman

Cartography by Jeffrey L. Ward

Printed in the United States of America

40 39 38 37 36 35 34 33 32

For United States forest-fire fighters
and fire meteorologists,
and in memory of all the victims
of Peshtigo, known and unknown

"From water to earth, from earth to air,

from air to fire and round again."

HERACLITUS

CONTENTS

DRAMATIS PERSONAE   XIII

PROLOGUE   I

Part One : False Prophets   3

Part Two : Eden Burns   63

Part Three : Revelations   127

EPILOGUE   221

AFTERWORD   223

NOTES   225

BIBLIOGRAPHY   243

ACKNOWLEDGMENTS   253

INDEX   257

DRAMATIS PERSONAE

WILLIAM BUTLER OGDEN: founder and principal owner of the Peshtigo Company, sawmill, and Peshtigo Woodenware Factory

ISAAC "IKE" STEPHENSON: owner of the Stephenson lumber company in Marinette; co-owner and president of the Peshtigo Company and the Peshtigo Woodenware Factory with William Ogden

LUTHER B. NOYES: publisher and editor of the *Marinette and Peshtigo Eagle*

BENJAMIN FRANKLIN TILTON: publisher and editor of the *Green Bay Advocate*

WILLIAM A. ELLIS: superintendent of the Peshtigo Company

FATHER PETER PERNIN: French missionary priest who built the first Catholic church, Our Lady of Lourdes, in Marinette; pastor of the Catholic church in Peshtigo

CLEVELAND ABBE: astronomer; weather observer at the Cincinnati Observatory in Ohio; maker of the first weather maps; head of the first United States Weather Bureau

GENERAL ALBERT J. MYER: chief of Telegrams and Reports for the Benefit of Commerce by the Army Signal Service, U.S.A.

INCREASE ALLEN LAPHAM: meteorologist, weather observer in Milwaukee; author of the book *Wisconsin, Its Geography and Topography*; author of the 1867 text, "Report on the Disastrous Effects of the Destruction of Forest Trees Now Going On in the State of Wisconsin"

GENERAL HENRY HOWGATE: assistant to General Myer

GOVERNOR LUCIUS FAIRCHILD: governor of Wisconsin

FRANCES "FRANK" FAIRCHILD: wife of Governor Fairchild; acted as governor in her husband's absence from Madison and heroically rerouted supply trains to Peshtigo to help the fire victims

ELBRIDGE WEST MERRILL: bookkeeper for Eleazar Ingalls's sawmill in Birch Creek

CHARLES "KARL" LAMP: German immigrant farmer from the Lower Bush

CAPTAIN A. J. LANGWORTHY: head of the relief committee; author of the official findings and relief report in the aftermath of the fire

MAGGIE WILLIAMSON: resident of Williamsonville on the Door County Peninsula; mother of Tom Williamson

PHINEAS EAMES: spiritualist; farmer whose letters to his brother following the fire hold the key to wind direction and velocity on that night

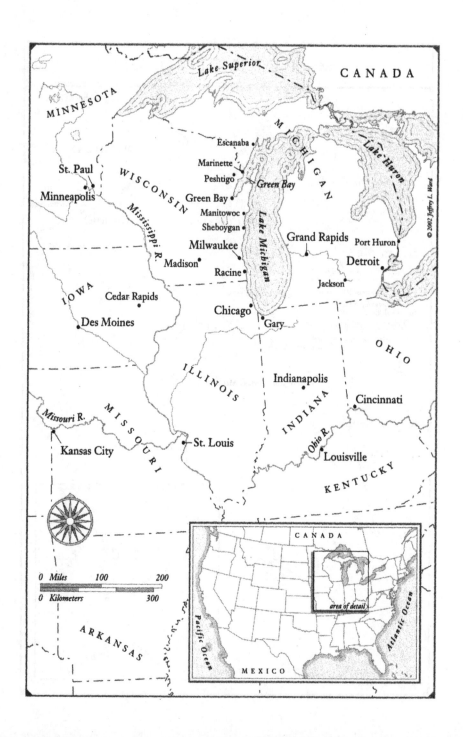

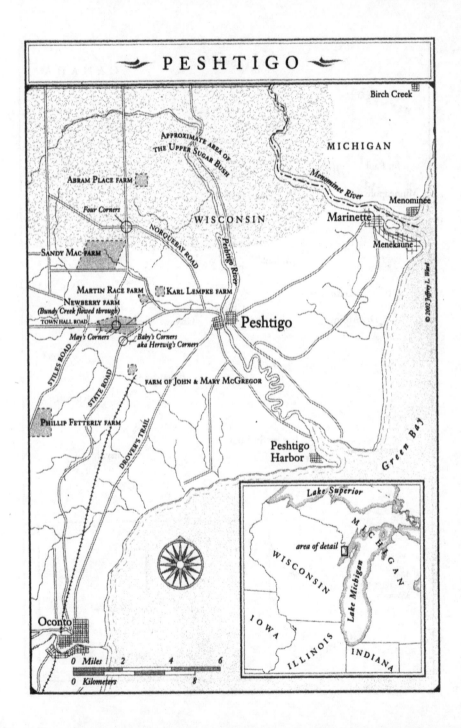

PESHTIGO

Birch Creek

MICHIGAN

Menominee River

APPROXIMATE AREA OF
THE UPPER SUGAR BUSH

ABRAM PLACE FARM

Four Corners

WISCONSIN

Menominee

Marinette

Menekaune

SANDY MAC FARM

MARTIN RACE FARM   KARL LEMPKE FARM

NEWBERRY FARM
(Bundy Creek flowed through)

TOWN HALL ROAD

May's Corners   Baby's Corners
                       aka Hertwig's Corners

Peshtigo

FARM OF JOHN & MARY McGREGOR

PHILLIP FETTERLY FARM

Peshtigo
Harbor

Green Bay

Lake Superior

area of detail

MICHIGAN

WISCONSIN

Lake Michigan

IOWA

ILLINOIS   INDIANA

Oconto

0 Miles   2   4   6

0 Kilometers   8

© 2002 Jeffrey L. Ward

THE FIRE ZONE

Triangle of Fire

WISCONSIN
MICHIGAN
CANADA
Port Huron
Detroit
Chicago
ILLINOIS

Escanaba

MICHIGAN

MARINETTE

WISCONSIN

Menominee River

Upper Sugar Bush
Birch Creek

Peshtigo River

Middle Sugar Bush
Menominee
Marinette
Menekaune

Lower Sugar Bush
Peshtigo

OCONTO

Peshtigo Harbor

Oconto

Oconto River

Pensaukee

Door Peninsula

Sturgeon Bay

Little Sturgeon
Williamsonville

Little Suamico

DOOR

Lake
Michigan

Green Bay

Tobinsville

KEWAUNEE

New Franken

Kewaunee

OUTAGAMIE
BROWN

Fox River

Extent of fire

Wind direction

Firestorm

0 Miles -10 20 30
0 Kilometers 30

Two Rivers

Manitowoc

© 2002 Jeffrey L. Ward

FIRESTORM AT PESHTIGO

PROLOGUE

September 13, 1871

Luther Noyes could feel the fires smoldering in the woods even when he couldn't see them, and at first light he could taste them: grit and burnt sap.

Noyes, publisher of the *Marinette and Peshtigo Eagle*, and his wife, Frances, whom he called Belle, were still relative newcomers in Marinette, Wisconsin. They had moved north from Sheboygan in March with their two children, fifteen-year-old Frank and nine-year-old Minnie. Instead of purchasing a house, they set up their home in the large, high-ceilinged rooms above Noyes's office in the Bentley Building. Unlike the squat, unremarkable pine-board stores and houses in Marinette, the Bentley was so boxy and out of proportion to Dunlap Square that it loomed, casting its shadow across the intersecting streets. People referred to it as the Bentley Block.

Belle was awake ahead of him that morning, already at work in the kitchen, her hair wound up in an amber comb. Frank and

Minnie were still asleep. As usual, Noyes did not take breakfast, only a cup of tea, then left his rooms to attend to his work, dressed in his stiff white collar, black frock coat, and hat. Outside, one quick breath was all he needed before he plucked a handkerchief from his silk breast pocket to cover his nose and mouth. People passing each other on the wood-planked streets were doing the same. Mr. John Belanger, proprietor of the Dunlap House, was pushing a crate of wine through the hotel doors with one hand, leaving his other hand free to hold his apron up to his face. A new sound had drifted in with the familiar chorus of whirring saws from the mills and the irregular beat of wagon wheels bumping along the rutted streets: the sound of muffled human coughing.

Noyes looked out at the masked townspeople and saw Mrs. Clark heading toward him, her skirts kicking up dust; she was holding a lace handkerchief across her mouth. Mrs. Clark ran a dressmaking and millinery shop in the Bentley Building; her husband, Charles Clark, worked at the Ingalls sawmill in Birch Creek on the Michigan side of the Menominee River. On a clear morning, Noyes would have tipped his hat and she would have smiled, and may have even today, but no one could make out a smile or frown behind these masked faces. In fact, this morning it wouldn't have been far-fetched to mistake Marinette for a community of tubercular patients, exiled to the forest. But there wasn't any disease here. The cloud cover was nothing like Ralph Waldo Emerson's description of the sky as the "daily bread of the eyes." There wasn't a syllable of poetry overhead for Noyes, the lover of Emerson and "Bobby" Burns. There was only smoke, a platinum gray scrim drawn down over the town.

Part One

FALSE
PROPHETS

1

The working day began before dawn in the gloom in the forest surrounding Peshtigo. Young chore boys, many no more than twelve years old, woke first in the logging camps. It was their job to kindle the fires and heat the water for the lumberjacks' morning tea. During the night, while the men slept and their axes lay still, the forest breathed, trying to blow off the accumulated heat of so many days of relentless smoke-filtered sun bearing down on its dehydrated foliage.

As the kettle heated up, the chore boys squatted on their boots, rubbing their damp hands together to ward off the chill from sleeping in their dirty clothes. Bent so close to the ground, they noticed a slithering around and between the bases of the trees. Snakes, maybe. Except these snakes were luminous, shimmery red-headed and golden-tongued threads, moving fast, coiling back on themselves before they disappeared again, darting under the cedar needles, burrowing down into a mole opening. In their wake the snakes left puffs of smoke that whirled as fast as grounded birds caught in a dervish even though the air was still. No wind for miles. Eleven weeks had passed without rain except for a shower so light on September 5 that the rain evaporated as quickly as it fell. The forest "panted," one survivor said later, while another claimed the entire landscape was ready for "suicide by fire."

The boys crouched in the clearing surrounded by trees so densely packed together that a person couldn't forge a trail through them; if he didn't cut them down, he was forced to feel his way along, touching each tree, trunk to trunk, to make a path.

Trees were currency here and nothing else offered as much money-making power. As Emerson observed, the "very look of the woods . . . the stems of pine and hemlock and oak almost gleamed like steel upon the excited eyes." A fairy-tale forest: blue-black, sun-blocked, and abundant with limitless stands of the great *Pinus strobus*, the most cherished and sought-after trees Wisconsin had to offer. A single tree was anywhere between 3 and 6 feet wide and grew from 120 to 170 feet tall. The hardwoods—oak, maple, ash, and birch—were also plentiful, but they were considered pine's inferior, regarded with the dismissive tolerance one reserves for an embarrassing relative. The white pine was breathtaking, bursting out in branches spanning 50 to 70 feet on the uppermost body of the tree. Otherwise the pine's fat trunks were branchless, clear and unpocked when cut, and easy to float once felled, qualities that made the white pine as valuable as gold. One tree produced enough wood to build a house. Many of them had already built the city of Chicago, the reigning Jewel of the Midwest.

—◆—

WHEN THE GABERAL horn sounded the call to breakfast, the chore boys took their cue and lugged the cast-iron kettles to the rows of plank tables. The lumberjacks ate in stiff silence; no one spoke of fiery snakes slinking along the forest floor.

After breakfast, they simply began their routine. First, the choppers, usually two to a tree, cut the trees down with their axes, then the barkers went at the trees, stripping them naked before they were sawn into logs that could fit onto the horse-drawn sled and sent out to the road for the drive downriver. The drive road was parched, but after rain came—they were certain it would—the men who spent the nights preparing the roads for the lumber sleds could wet it down, which would make the transport road slick and easy. Today transport would be a struggle; the horses would have to work doubly hard, dragging the sleds along the sandy road.

—

YEARS HAD PASSED since lumber barons from the East first turned their hungry gaze toward this settlement formerly called Clarksville, where geese gathered ten rows deep along the riverbanks, where the duck hunting was reported to be superior, where seven miles of marshes and cranberry bogs lay untouched, and where trout sped through the river. They renamed the place Peshtigo after the remarkable ninety-four-mile-long river that rose in "the highest land of northern Wisconsin"—an elevation of 1,620 feet above sea level—and then descended 1,040 feet before emptying into Lake Michigan. No one knew what the word *Peshtigo* meant, nor did anyone seem to care. It was enough to know the origins of the name were Indian and fine if people claimed the word meant "wild geese."

Despite the river's sharp twists and awkward bends and its small drainage area, the Peshtigo River had more and bigger rapids than any other river in Wisconsin. Speed ensured the one thing an ambitious lumber lord needed: natural, ferocious water power, which made the river's frothy rapid caps ideally suited to floating pine logs down to the sawmill known as the Peshtigo Company and to the Peshtigo Woodenware Factory. Both the mill and the factory were located in Peshtigo, by all accounts the brightest, most prosperous new lumber town to erupt between the town of Marinette and Green Bay.

A bridge joining the east and west sides of Peshtigo had just been completed. There were two new churches, Lutheran and Presbyterian. Reverend Edwin R. Beach's Congregational church had just received "a fresh coat of white paint." Another new church, Father Peter Pernin's Catholic church, was nearly finished. Oconto Avenue, once a nameless stretch of trees and sand, had become a wide street cut on a diagonal, flanked by stores. It sliced through the center of Peshtigo where there were two hotels, a sash-and-blind factory, a grist mill, the Peshtigo Company store, and T. "Tommy" A. Hay's new jewelry shop in Nick Cavoit's building on the northwest corner of Oconto Avenue and French Street. Hay advertised the lowest-priced and best-quality watches, gold-plated jewelry in the "latest styles," and a promise of repair "of every character."

So far Peshtigo did not have a fire company or a firehouse. If a serious fire broke out, people relied on the Black Hawk, a single hand-pumper fire engine that was housed next to the Peshtigo Company store on the east side of the river. Nor did Peshtigo have a police force or a jail, but just as new machine shops, dry goods stores, hotels, and houses were being built, so, too, were more saloons being erected. With close to sixty saloons spread out through the region and almost as many houses of prostitution, the town would eventually need professional law enforcement to keep the flow of lumberjacks, loggers, and railroad workers in line.

Peshtigo was a town split between devotion and indulgence. On Sundays the people filled the Congregational, Lutheran, Presbyterian, and Catholic churches. But on Saturday nights, the streets belonged to Miss Delia and Hatty Baker and to the men who frequented the saloons. Fights among the drunken loggers were expected and they'd use knives, ropes, guns, even the metal of their caulked boots to settle a dispute. Men were lynched for something as serious as a theft or as insignificant as a dirty look; if they freed their victim before the noose was tightened, it was apt to be more the result of intoxication and exhaustion rather than mercy.

Within a year there would be a vaccination for smallpox, and the first words out of a person's mouth would be, "Did you get yer vaccinate yet?" but in the fall of 1871 the only pox a man needed to be wary of was logger's pox, an affliction brought on whenever a gang of loggers stomped on their victim with their caulked boots. The caulking, consisting of sharp metal cleats that provided grip for the lumberjacks and railroad workers in the woods, became a weapon in town. Stomping a victim riddled the victim's back and legs with puncture wounds or bloody "pox."

Half wild, half civilized, Peshtigo was synonymous with progress. For the solitary lumberjacks who had successfully denuded the forests of Maine, New York, Vermont, and Pennsylvania before migrating west, Peshtigo promised steady work. The place was overflowing with trees—at least 1 billion covering more than 1 million acres.

For others, the outlying settlements of Peshtigo represented autonomy. Known as the Sugar Bush, the settlements were named for the stands of sugar maples that defined the geography. The Bush was divided into the Lower, Middle, and Upper Bushes and were fed by large creeks that emptied into the Peshtigo River. These settlements were the province of the immigrant farmers who had been purchasing land at the price of $1.25 per acre since 1866.

The immigrants hailed from Sweden, Germany, Norway, and Prussia, and they would have suffered any inconvenience, borne any burden, in order to be self-sufficient farmers on this new frontier. Many eagerly took jobs working at the Peshtigo sawmill in town until they'd saved enough for their grubstake, the money that would enable them to purchase eighty acres of their own forested land. Then, as landowners, the immigrants cleared their parcels. Clearing was an arduous process that required cutting the trees, hauling boulders and stones out of the way, pulling the stumps, then burning the stumps to prepare the acres for homestead building and farming. Since many of the immigrants had arrived in Peshtigo with little more than a trunk of belongings, a hoe, and an ax, clearing could take a man between five and ten years to complete.

Bands of hopeful farmers also migrated to the peninsula that jutted between Green Bay and Lake Michigan in Door County, Wisconsin. There, nearly three hundred Belgian families from Antwerp were building the settlements and sawmills of Brussels and Williamsonville. The Belgian immigrants brought their farming practices with them to Wisconsin. The jagged peninsula resembled an arthritic finger, a tract of land that had been cleared so successfully of trees, there were now shingle mills and sawmills but fewer and fewer barriers against storms.

People who did not choose to settle in Peshtigo often chose Marinette, located six miles north. Some purchased land across the Menominee River in Menominee, Michigan. Between them the towns of Marinette and Menominee boasted eight sawmills and as many man-made dams on the Menominee River where the Menominee Indians had once lived in thatched reed huts along the water. The hamlet of Marinette, which began as a lucrative fur-trading post run by a French and Indian woman named Marie Chevalier and her white husband, John Jacobs, was now in the business of producing 217 million board feet of lumber from its largest companies: the N. Ludington Company; Kirby, Carpenter & Sons; A. C. Merryman and Co.;

Eleazar Ingalls's mill; and the most well-known lumber mill, owned by Isaac "Ike" Stephenson and his brothers Robert and Samuel.

The story of Peshtigo is also the story of Marinette and Menominee. No one spoke of one town without referring to the others. Only five-and-a-half yards, or a rod, marked the line between the houses and the trees. One rugged road linked Peshtigo to Marinette; a wooden bridge across the narrowest and shallowest part of the Menominee River joined Marinette to Menominee in Michigan.

Wherever people chose to put down roots in the five thousand square miles of forests, lumber towns, farms, and prairies that comprised Oconto County, all agreed with the *Detroit Post* correspondent who had visited the area: "It is my humble opinion," he wrote, "that Wisconsin is the Eden of our country."

———

IN THIS NINETEENTH-CENTURY Eden, no tool proved more useful for transforming and taming the landscape than fire. Fire was

NEW JEWELRY
ESTABLISHMENT
At Marinette, Wis.

T. A. HAY
Would inform his old friends and customers that he saved a small Portion of his Peshtigo stock from the fire, and has now opened in **Ackrill's Block** on Main Street with a
New Stock of Watches & Jewelry
Of the Best and Latest Styles.
REPAIRING of every character, done neatly, promptly and WARRANTED.
☞ Call and Investigate. ☜

an ally. To hear its hiss and crackle, to feel its heat was as expected as the sound of the steamer *Union*'s fog horn as it approached the docks in Peshtigo Harbor out on Green Bay, six miles southeast of the tow, as ordinary as the sight of Adolph Kuchenberg's stagecoach making its daily runs into Peshtigo from the livery stable in Marinette.

2

Luther Noyes was a newspaperman. He knew that despite appearances that he remain an objective recorder of newsworthy events, his real job was to persuade loggers, farmers, and immigrants to move westward, encourage people to settle in Peshtigo.

Although Marinette's population was double the size of Peshtigo's, Peshtigo's two thousand residents were being joined by at least fifty to one hundred immigrants arriving by steamer each week, and Noyes wanted to cement the relationship between the towns. Noyes acknowledged the close association by changing the name of the newspaper from the *Marinette Eagle* to the *Marinette and Peshtigo Eagle* within a month after his arrival in Marinette.

"How do you like it?" Luther Noyes wrote in the first issue of the paper on June 24, 1871. "The bird is not full-fledged yet, but the pin feathers are of good stock and give some promise of a victorious future."

Noyes did not own a steam-driven printing press yet, but he had no complaints about his hand-driven Washington press, which printed on one side of the paper and produced 120 pages per hour on stock that was shipped in weekly from the Kellog Paper Company in Chicago. Requests for advertisement space were flowing in with each new business that opened, crowding out the familiar fire and weather reports.

In keeping with the general spirit of the three towns, Noyes maintained an editorial tone of brisk offhandedness in the face of any adversity. He made no exception for the extended dry spell that had left the Peshtigo and Menominee Rivers the lowest they had been in many years.

In the logging camps of Peshtigo and Marinette the camp bosses had been forced to bank their logs in tall piles after the drive from the woods. Until there was a drenching rain, it would be impossible to float them downriver to the mills.

The farmers from the Sugar Bushes who brought their goods into Marinette and Peshtigo for market said that the cranberry bogs they depended on to yield their winter canning and the creeks they depended on for their water supply were drying out. And earlier, on Tuesday, September 2, Wisconsin's indigenous southwest wind had kicked up so fiercely it broke down several telegraph poles, disabling communication between the north woods and the civilized worlds of Green Bay, Milwaukee, and Chicago. Before that dustup wound itself out, the wind tore down enough trees to block wagon passage between Peshtigo and the town of Oconto.

Still, Noyes knew, panic would not serve anyone. After all, the situation in the Sugar Bushes could be part exaggeration or pique or a combination of both. Regardless of the conditions, what mattered was boosting the town morale. In Green Bay, the same job fell upon the shoulders of Benjamin Franklin Tilton, editor of the *Green Bay Advocate*. Meanwhile, 262 miles south in the city of Chicago, journalists painted a similar portrait of prosperity.

Noyes took no small offense to the suggestion that his loyalty to the interests of the lumber lords bordered on propaganda, and yet his newspaper, like most newspapers in small towns of the time, was partisan. He and Tilton gave the public the information it needed while also promoting the public welfare as they saw it. As a devout Republican, Noyes was obliged to make the *Eagle* and what he printed in its pages synonymous with the agenda of the Union, with those patriots who had supported the Civil War.

———

LUTHER NOYES WAS born to Dr. Isaac Noyes and Minerva Osgood on December 17, 1830, in Chenago County, New York. A stout, round-faced, clean-shaven, small-shouldered man who was often praised for his erudition and integrity, he was known to all in Marinette as the Judge. In his forty-one years Noyes had worn many hats: teacher, lawyer, and county judge, appointed by Wisconsin governor Lucius Fairchild. He'd also been the editor of the *Eagle* in Sparta, Wisconsin, as well as the owner and editor of *The Sheboygan County Herald* before selling it and relocating in Marinette. Noyes had been a Union patriot, mustered in twice during the war, serving the 118th Regiment Wisconsin, Volunteer Infantry, Company C, before illness forced him to take leave.

After he had recovered, Noyes volunteered again, this time for the 36th Regiment Wisconsin, Volunteer Infantry, Company D, serving as first lieutenant during a campaign that tested all the fortitude and focus a man could hope to possess. Noyes had led his company in the assault at Cold Harbor, Virginia. The night before that battle, as the rain beat down upon them, Noyes's men, like all the Union soldiers who would attack the next day, removed their blue coats—a gesture of foresight or resignation—and wrote their names and where they lived on scraps of paper before pinning them to the backs of their coats. Upon their certain deaths, face down in the mud, they wanted to be identified. But Noyes and his men made it past the Confederate breastworks in the bloodbath that massacred seven thousand men in less than half an hour. Noyes felt blessed that he had sustained only a severe wound to his left leg.

Like so many other men who had survived battle and bloodshed, Noyes believed the worst of life was behind him, that his energy should be spent on the future. There was more work to be done in the lantern-lit warehouse where the bulky handpress, its long single arm raised, was Noyes's only companion until his son, Frank, who'd begun to show a natural flair for writing, came in to help him. The press stood ready, waiting to print whatever news Noyes deemed fit.

Noyes looked through the written submissions slated for the September 16 edition of the *Eagle*. Because the telegraph lines were not fully repaired yet, no weather bulletins had been sent north from either Increase Lapham, the weather observer in Milwaukee, or from Sam Brookes, the weather observer for Chicago's Register of Meteorological Observations. Even when Noyes did receive the telegraphed bulletins from the "weather prophets" of the Army Signal Service, he and others still regarded the infant weather agency with thinly veiled doubts.

"Do you think they can tell anything about it?" was the question most people in Peshtigo and Marinette asked regarding the weather. Although President Ulysses S. Grant had signed a resolution before Congress on February 9, 1870, to form an official weather bureau, here it was over a year later and still a full-fledged weather bureau was more fantasy than reality.

Newspapers were beginning to publish daily telegraphed weather records or "synopses" on a regular basis, but some people still agreed with President Lincoln's attitude toward meteorologist Frances L.

Capen during the Civil War: "It seems to me that Mr. Capen knows nothing about the weather, in advance," Lincoln wrote on April 28, 1863. "He told me three days ago that it would not rain again till the 30th of April or the 1st of May. It is raining now and has been for ten hours. I cannot spare any more time to Mr. Capen."

Noyes decided he would place the fire and weather reports where he always placed them, mixed in with the usual brief notices, without fanfare or bold headings. When the townspeople of Peshtigo and Marinette read their newspapers, they would not read anything especially alarming.

September 16, 1871

Heavy fires on the east of the village in the woods.

The potato crop is magnificent in the Sugar Bush this year.

We need a police and a calaboose for the benefit of drunken stragglers around nights.

Work will commence on the railroad bridge across the river at this place, now, shortly.

The Congregational Church of this place proposes to hold a series of revival meetings soon.

It has been a little quieter here Sundays and nights since the railroad gangs have moved further off.

Items from Peshtigo Harbor, intended for publication in our last issue, reached us last Tuesday noon. It was not Captain Moore's fault, however.

Fires are raging in the woods and on the marshes around Peshtigo. Considerable hay, and some fences have already been destroyed.

Dobyns is still boring for water at the harbor. He is 30 feet in the rock and 180 feet down, and still, the show is good for boring deeper.

> At 6 o'clock, A.M. of the 11th the fog and smoke were so thick and dense, that an object could not be seen at a distance of 30 feet on our streets.
>
> Some railroad bummer or dead beat got drunk Wednesday night and got licked twice for insisting on lodging at the dwelling of Mr. R. A. McDonald.
>
> Wednesday the wind blew so hard, and the dust flew so that one dare not open his mouth facing the wind for fear of being turned inside out like a parasol.
>
> The Peshtigo Company are erecting some very fine dwellings for their employees, and painting them beautifully. This is an attractive improvement. Success to the Peshtigo Company.

The Peshtigo Company and everything associated with it—a thriving sawmill; a new boardinghouse to shelter lumberjacks, mill workers, and their families; a company dry-goods store; the Peshtigo Harbor steam mill and its self-contained town of seven hundred people on the banks of Green Bay; the woodenware factory, which produced the nation's wooden products; and the town of Peshtigo proper—rose out of the forests of Peshtigo on the dream of two men: William Butler Ogden of Chicago and Isaac Stephenson of Marinette.

There had not been an unproductive moment in Peshtigo since William Butler Ogden purchased the small existing sawmill on the Peshtigo River in 1856. As an *Oconto Pioneer* reporter pointed out, before Ogden, "the shrill scream of pioneer progress—The Iron Horse—had not been heard way up amongst the swaying magnificent pine forests of Oconto County."

William Butler Ogden, or Mr. O as he was called, was born on June 15, 1805, in the town of Walton in Delaware County, New York, a mountainous region that offered both abundant pine forests and a river with great log-transporting capacities. Those who knew him recounted the story of a young Ogden who was so enthralled with the streams, river, mountains, and forests that he found it next to impossible to stay inside. His world was the open air and his passion for hunting and fishing became so excessive that his father, Abraham, decided to restrict his son's outdoor sport to two days a week. Ogden often referred to himself as an orphan, suggesting an early life of deprivation, but that was not the case. The most often repeated story about Ogden depicts him dispensing advice to a desperate mother who wanted to know, now that she and her family had slid from affluence to poverty after the financial crash of 1837, how her sons might earn a living.

Ogden's reply: "If I was in the position of your sons, if I could do nothing better, I would hire myself out to dig potatoes with my fingers, and, when I had earned enough to buy a hoe, I would dig with it, and so I would climb up . . . don't have the least concern. If your sons are healthy and willing to work they will find enough to do, and if they cannot begin at the top, let them begin at the bottom and very likely they will be all the better for it."

So many "ifs." Such a small word yet one filled with tremendous power when issued from the tongue of a great orator, and Ogden was nothing if not a compelling speaker. He knew how to construct an argument, plead a case, seduce and persuade with so much facility that in June 1871 Ralph Waldo Emerson listed Ogden with Henry David Thoreau, Oliver Wendell Holmes, and John Muir in his journals among the men he most admired.

No doubt Ogden's words inspired and comforted the desperate mother, but Ogden himself had never been forced to "dig with his fingers."

He went on to tell the woman, "I was born close by a sawmill, was early left an orphan, was cradled in a sugar-trough, christened in a millpond, graduated at a log-school-house, and, at fourteen, fancied I could do anything." But only the last part of his rags-to-riches speech was true.

The citizens of Walton on the Delaware, Ogden's father Abraham included, were among the most "cultivated and influential people in the early history of the State of New York." Books, teas, riding, and hunting for sport were part of Ogden's daily life as a young boy. He chose to study law while his father ran a very successful lumber and mercantile business. At the age of eighteen Ogden entered the New York militia and was made a commissioned officer the very first day of his service; on the second day he was made a member of the brigadier general's staff. But in 1820, when Abraham Ogden suffered a stroke, William Ogden took over the family business. After his father's death in 1824, Ogden began circulating with incredible grace among the heads of the land offices, the leaders of the New York legislature, and men of letters Emerson and Thoreau.

From the moment Ogden stepped in on his father's behalf, he began an ascension into the thin rarefied air of the affluent ruling class, and it appeared he could do no wrong. Even when he lost, he won. When he fell from grace (by 1836 he was financially "embarrassed, principally by the assistance he gave to his friends"), Ogden swiftly recovered those losses and landed on his feet. To hear his closest friend, Chicago attorney Isaac N. Arnold, tell it, Ogden embodied the qualities of a god:

"You might look the country through and not find a man of more manly and imposing presence, or a finer-looking gentleman. . . . He was a natural leader, and if he had been one of a thousand men picked, cast upon a desolate island, he would, by common, universal, and instinctive selection, have been made their leader."

His charismatic presence combined with his business acumen inspired trust and loyalty as he traveled through Philadelphia, New

York, and the towns along the Hudson River tending to the family business. President Andrew Jackson made Ogden postmaster of Walton. During the time he held this post, Ogden became so passionate on the subject of building the Erie Railroad that by 1834 he was elected to the New York State Legislature because of his zeal on the subject. The following year, during the legislative session of March 20, 21, and 22, Ogden made such a powerful speech before the legislature championing the Erie Railroad construction it was reprinted in full and demonstrated to the members of the session that an extraordinary and "visionary" young twenty-nine-year-old was in their midst. Every venture Ogden engaged in seemed fated for the extraordinary. His speech to the legislature was no less persuasive:

"Continuous railways from New York to Lake Erie, and south of Lake Erie, through Ohio, Indiana and Illinois to the waters of the Mississippi, and connecting with railroads running to Cincinnati and Louisville, Kentucky, and Nashville in Tennessee, and to New Orleans will present the most splendid system of internal communication ever yet devised by man."

To achieve his dream, Ogden needed four things: land, wood to build the rails, manpower to cut and mill the wood, and fire. Ogden called fire "the pillar . . . lighting the path of Empire on its westward way." That same year, after delivering his persuasive speech, his brother-in-law, Charles Butler, of New York City, who worked for the Land Office and had bought tracts of land from the Kinzies in Chicago, urged Ogden to make the long trip westward by horse to Chicago. Ogden's job was to encourage people to buy land and settle in the muddy tract that would eventually become America's "second city."

Ogden was disappointed by what he found when he first arrived in Chicago. He thought its wild growth of oak, mud, and general bleak appearance were horribly unattractive and not worth the

$100,000 the Land Office had paid for it. Nonetheless, Ogden quickly devised a public auction in order to sell the lots.

The auction was an ingenious idea. He knew he only needed several bidders; he banked on the belief that if several people found Chicago real estate desirable, others would want to own land there as well. His hunch proved successful and the auction provided him with at least twice the amount originally invested in the land.

Following the auction, the real estate business escalated in Chicago. He envisioned a city to rival New York and the railroad lines that would run through it.

Rather than follow the lead of most landowners, Ogden did not want to be an absentee landowner. He decided to make a permanent home there and founded a real estate company known as Ogden, Sheldon & Company. To those eager buyers who had caught the fever for land ownership but did not have the means to purchase land outright, Ogden offered a trust plan. Captain Redmond Prindville was a wary buyer; Ogden proposed a five-acre tract for $1,000, offered to trust the money for a year and accept partial payments. Prindville still refused the deal, to which Ogden told him: "Why, Redmond, that's not the way to get along. When you are dealing with Chicago property the proper way is to go in for all you can get and then go with your business and forget all about it. It will take care of itself."

Prindville never accepted the offer, but another buyer did and made $4,000 on his purchase within six months. Such increased land value at such a rapid rate convinced others to do the same. The financial success of those men who trusted Ogden was the only evidence they needed that Ogden was a leader who would guide them to great wealth.

Between the years 1836—when Chicago was granted a city charter and Ogden was elected the city's first mayor—and 1847, Ogden amassed a considerable fortune in the form of money and business associations. He then invested his profits to fund the building of the first Chicago railroad, the Galena & Chicago Union. At the time, William F. Weld of Boston was known as the railroad king, a title that would swiftly be ceded to Ogden.

The land yielded graciously to the hands of men like Ogden who sought to civilize and industrialize the wild forests and prairies. Land was cleared for farming at a breakneck pace, which meant fires were always burning somewhere in Illinois, Michigan, Minnesota, and Wisconsin. A city built of white pine buildings with roofs covered in tar paper literally rose out of the mud flats and marshes. The buildings were erected on elevated boardwalks, a protective measure against flooding and mud, which were common problems.

Ogden's own Chicago home, known as Ogden Grove, was the first house designed by an architect. A grove appropriately described the house that took up the entire block, 35, a section covered by maple, cottonwood, oak, ash, cherry, elm, birch, and hickory trees. On the northeast side of the house was a conservatory filled with fruits and flowers and beside it a forcing house in which he grew exotic grapes, figs, peaches, and apricots. "A drive around the house, and neatly-kept graveled walks, traversed the natural forest of noble trees, festooned with the wild grape, American ivy . . . and everywhere were ornamental shrubs, climbing roses and other flowers." In his notebooks Ogden wrote of the house: "I purchased in 1845, property for $15,000 which, twenty years thereafter, in 1865, was worth ten million dollars."

Mahlon D. Ogden moved to his brother's dream city by 1840 and became a judge. By then, the first swing bridge, which swung open on hinges to allow room for tall ships to pass into the harbor (another one of Ogden's visionary ideas), was in operation, and Ogden himself was admitted to the Chicago bar as an attorney in 1841.

The wood that supplied this growth of the west arrived by barge at Ogden's Chicago lumberyard. The board feet came from Peshtigo. Ogden owned over 200,000 acres of forest in the northern Wisconsin forest.

Ogden was seeing his dream flourish. He had more than enough money, which made it easy for him to travel in illustrious circles and to garner whatever support he needed from businessmen and government officials. He was well acquainted with the famous financier, Jay Cooke. Also, at this time Ogden had begun the construction of the Chicago, St. Paul & Fond du Lac Railroad; he was pushing for its completion with all of his energy. Ogden combined the Beloit & Madison, the Rock River Valley, and many other small rail lines into one, and with that move he laid the foundation for the shining moment of his career: the creation of the great Chicago & Northwestern Railroad, which would eventually become the Northwest Pacific & Union. The financial crash of 1857, followed by the Civil War, slowed his progress somewhat, but following these crippled times in America, Ogden's fortuitous meeting with Isaac Stephenson in 1864 accelerated his empire building.

❧

ISAAC STEPHENSON WAS the son of a lumberman from New Brunswick and Maine. The handsome, intelligent Scotch-Irishman was born on June 19, 1829. He knew wood better than a carpenter ant. Ike, as he was known in the twin towns of Marinette and Menominee, actually had risen up from the rough beginnings Ogden liked to appropriate as his personal myth. Isaac Stephenson was nine years old when his mother died; his father, also named Isaac, was "away in the woods" most of the time, leaving four sons and two daughters to care for themselves.

Stephenson was only a brash but optimistic sixteen-year-old when he first signed on with Jefferson Sinclair in a proposition that promised him a large financial interest in Sinclair's lumber business in Wisconsin. Stephenson worked hard for Sinclair to earn his promised partnership with the lumber lord, but Sinclair failed to make good on the deal. The betrayal did not deter Stephenson. Instead, with his zeal for success and his uncanny sense of timing, he took the soured deal on the chin and moved on. He spent several more years working in the brutal logging camps of northern Wisconsin and Escanaba, Michigan, enduring weeks of frightful cold in snow three to four feet deep with nothing more than the campfire and a thin blanket to warm him at night.

At the age of twenty-four, after having worked as a mast builder, lumberjack, mill worker, and logger, he finally settled in the small town of Marinette and put his stamp upon the settlement. He wrote home to his father and brothers in Maine, telling them of his plans to build a company of his own. In a letter dated April 2, 1846, Isaac Stephenson's father wrote, "Now, Isaac, be a good boy and I hope the Lord will prosper you." He took his father's well-wishes to heart and then convinced his brothers Robert and Samuel to join him there; each would have substantial holdings in the mills along the Menominee River.

To Stephenson, whose early life "meant little more than hard work," the mark of true achievement would come only after he was wealthy enough to "take tea" three times a day in comfortable surroundings. In Marinette, Stephenson joined forces with Nelson Ludington of the N. Ludington Company and for a period of several years acted in a supervisory position, learning the business and squirreling away enough money until he could buy out Ludington.

When the Civil War broke out, Stephenson was still working for Ludington, and although he was "by faith" a Republican, Stephenson did not fight. He claimed he was "anxious to go to the front," but other members of N. Ludington Company "contended that I would be of a far greater service to country by remaining where I was."

And so, Stephenson traveled to Green Bay where he paid $300 for his exemption, as was customary, and "raised" men suited for battle from the ranks of loggers and lumberjacks in his camps. In 1863 he convinced thirteen men to "join by paying them," and later induced another twelve men to enter service. Stephenson felt he was doing his part to support the war by contributing both men and funding.

Records indicate that Stephenson's lumber interests continued to prosper during the war years, although in his memoir, whether it stems from guilt or modesty, Stephenson claimed that during the Civil War a general lethargy and decline in prosperity prevailed. Yet in 1864, when Stephenson aligned himself with Ogden, the price of lumber, which had been only $12 per thousand board foot, had risen to $24 per thousand.

It was during this boom, in the middle of the dry summer of 1864, that William Ogden traveled up from Chicago to tour the copper mines in Upper Michigan with attorney Samuel Tilden of New York. For thirty-six hours the men stayed at Stephenson's Marinette mansion, an expansive Victorian with a striking widow's walk, its frontage on the Menominee River. During that time the men agreed that while the dried-out land made for hazardous fire conditions, the dryness also made the land ideally suited to laying rails at a fast pace.

Stephenson had spent several of his early years as a seaman and he was well acquainted with the dangerous Great Lakes. The unpredictable Wisconsin gales made transporting lumber by steamer or barge especially dangerous and time-consuming. Shipwrecks involving staggering loss of life and property were far too regular an occurrence and by 1869 a reported 1,914 shipwrecks would occur on the Great Lakes.

Stephenson, Ogden, and Tilden agreed that a railroad—particularly a line that passed directly through the pine forests—would serve everyone. The Peshtigo River had proved valuable because of its speed, but once the logs had been transformed into lumber and wood products, getting them to market was a slow and expensive process. So the three men decided to direct all of their efforts toward securing the extension of the Northwestern Railroad from the city of Green Bay to the Menominee.

Stephenson invested $50,000 in 1867 and with Ogden increased the Peshtigo Company's timber holdings. Ogden then rewarded Stephenson by making him a stockholder and vice president–general manager of the Peshtigo Company. Shortly after the transaction they began the construction of the first rail line north of Green Bay while the barge line that ran from the Peshtigo Harbor to Chicago transported 50 million to 60 million board feet of lumber per year. Stephenson chose his able right-hand men in Peshtigo: William A. Ellis, who was paid a sum of $525 every three months, to take charge of the woodenware factory; and Temple Emery oversaw the work at the mill. In the logging camps between Peshtigo and Marinette, Stephenson employed John Mulligan, an ex-boxer, to act as supervisor.

IN JUNE 1871 Ogden suggested to Jay Cooke that Cooke "bribe to the fullest extent possible" every journalist, politician, and Canadian fur trapper in order to ensure that the plans for the Northwest Pacific & Union not be interrupted. In September 1871 he made his appearance in Peshtigo with General Moses Strong, a Civil War veteran and engineer, to survey the cranberry bogs that lay west of Peshtigo Harbor. As usual, he visited with Ike.

As a young boy Ogden made it his business to learn as much as possible about the earth and trees; the same unerring sense that fueled Ogden to turn the mud flats of Chicago into a city and to invest in the pine forests of Wisconsin must have told him that now more than ever, with the land dry as dust, it was essential to push for the railroad.

By September 21, under the canopy of smoke, the railroad crews were working.

Ogden was in New York at his eastern home, Boscobel, on the Harlem River. Even from such a distance, or perhaps because of it, Ogden maintained his image of the great benefactor who had "the interests of his employees at heart." Not only had he sold them land to farm, but as employees of the company they received shoes and clothing. The Peshtigo boardinghouse provided shelter for those who could not yet afford a home, and for those who could afford it, Ogden provided an inexpensive design—the balloon frame house. In September 1871, these frame houses made of simple pine board were being erected so quickly, Luther Noyes reported that it was "difficult to keep track of them." The people of Peshtigo revered Ogden. His newest plan, which involved harvesting the cranberry bogs, then shipping the produce by rail to other parts of the country, would provide at least five hundred more jobs for those who settled in Peshtigo.

At last, toward the end of September 1871, Stephenson and Ogden were turning huge profits from the industry in Peshtigo.

"But in our efforts to better our position," Stephenson later wrote, "we unwittingly paved the way for disaster. . . . When work on the railroad was begun fires were started to clear the right of way. The contractors carelessly allowed these to spread and they ran through the county with startling rapidity, feeding on the dry forests."

FURNITURE ROOMS
— AND —
CABINET SHOP.

—— o ——

The subscriber has on hand, and for sale, as fine and well selected stock of Furniture as was ever of - fered in this market, consisting in part of

CHAIRS,
  SOFAS,
    LOUNGES,
      BUREAUS,
        WASH STANDS,
          CENTRE TABLES,
            BEDSTEADS,
DINING TABLES,
  WHAT NOTS,
    PARLOR SETS,
      SLEEPING ROOM SETS,
        DINING SETS,
          MIRRORS, &c. &c.

Ready Made Coffins!

Constantly on hand or made to order to suit customers. Everything manufactured or sold from this establishment will bear the impress of superior workmanship, and be disposed of at the

Lowest Living Rates!

Rooms and Shop East side of the Bridge
• • MARINETTE WIS.

C. E. PETERSON.

3

Another week came and went without rain in Peshtigo, Marinette, or Menominee. Still, on the other side of the Menominee River, in Michigan, the most interesting news was the battle between the "Judge" in Marinette and the *Herald* editor, J. A. Crozer. Someone had written that the new *Eagle* editor, Noyes, was a "blockhead." The Judge seemed to think it was his competitor, Crozer. The only other "aching" to appear in the news was the vitriol of a disgruntled reader whose letter of complaint was a response to an article about the cost for improving a road that made travel out to Thunder River much easier. The author of the article was Noyes; he'd signed it "Plain John."

The response to the article from a "taxpayer" took Noyes to task; it began with a terse "Mr. Editor."

> The Little River Road, Mr. P.J., although a public road in name, is practically a private road. From eight to ten tons of hay and about two hundred barrels of fish is about all the products that pass over your road in a year. There are many

people in other localities who catch more fish, cut more hay, and produce much more in every way, who never asked the town authorities to spend large amounts of public money for their especial benefit and your Little River Road has never been used for any other purpose than that above stated.

Five hundred dollars would buy all the produce that has been raised on the land "P.J." says is susceptible to cultivation for the past five years, and there has been a passable road to Little River for a longer time than this. For all the money spent on this road, "P.J." cannot show one settler more, or an increase of one dollar in valuation of the property it passes through . . . where is the value to the community . . . from the expenditures of money on Little River Road? This road was built to satisfy you and your friends if I do not mistake your identity Mr. P.J. . . .

In reality, the roads in the isolated regions weren't much more improved than the old, winding trails blazed by the Menominee Indians, or the sandy, sawdust streets of Peshtigo, or the patches of corduroy road cluttered with slabs and logs. In Marinette the rubbish and underbrush were strewn to the west of the Bentley Building; the roads from the farm settlements and the woods that led into Peshtigo were littered with sawdust, stumps, and slabs, conditions that made it difficult for many of the farmers to get their crops to market.

When Elbridge West Merrill, bookkeeper at the Eleazar Ingalls sawmill in Menominee, read the verbal battle between Plain John and the anonymous reader, he agreed that the road conditions were important; news of the fires, though (at least one hundred burning simultaneously in as many miles), were as sketchy where he lived and worked as they were in Peshtigo and Marinette. Ingalls trusted Merrill and had given Merrill carte blanche to supervise the mill whenever he was absent. To everyone in Ingalls's employ, Merrill was the undisputed leader.

The Ingalls mill was situated about six miles from the village proper of Menominee at Birch Creek, which put Merrill and the workers six miles northeast of Peshtigo. Merrill was concerned because the usually moist sod was so dry it crunched under his boots when he walked, as though he were treading on splintered bones. He could not forget the incident that had occurred on July 5 when a hunter fired into a tree stump and walked off, thinking nothing of it. Under normal conditions the bullet and wadding would have lodged there, an extra wound to an already amputated tree, but instead the wadding from the shot ignited the stump. Before Merrill or the other men realized what was happening, a fire broke out that burned the stump and took with it three acres of pine.

It was drier and thirstier now than it had been during the summer; there was no word from the observers that rain was coming to set things right again. For these reasons Merrill decided to shut down the mill, to put the men to work cleaning and making necessary repairs to the equipment.

Cutting trees and milling logs was a dirty and dangerous mission. The lumberjacks worked in the woods six days a week from dawn to sunset in all weather—blistering heat, pouring rain, arctic cold—for wages of $12 to $15 a month, plus room and board. Men could be and regularly were killed; on average, one per day. The pevees, the loggers who walked out onto the floating logs with long lances to pry apart a log jam, often slipped and were crushed between the logs speeding downriver. Loggers were struck by widow makers, the dead tree limbs that fell while they were cutting the base of the tree. At the mills it wasn't unusual for a worker to lose an arm to one of the saws or slip and injure himself on the slick sawdust.

Sawdust was a given in Peshtigo and in every mill town, and people used every ingenious method possible to dispose of it. They shoveled sawdust over the village streets and roads, poured it under the sidewalk boards and the foundations of their houses and shops. They even stuffed bed-sized envelopes of coarse ticking fabric with it to make mattresses. Then, after those places were filled, they simply heaped it into mounds near the mills. Perhaps with one less mill in operation Merrill could do his part to cut back the risk of a flying spark igniting the sawdust. Better yet, he could cut down the amount of sawdust itself as well as the refuse—bark, tree limbs, stumps, and leaves—left in the wake of milling the logs and floating them.

Merrill told those who wanted to keep sawing that they could travel three miles and work the mills along the Bay Shore if they wanted; he was *not* going to stand in any man's way. To those who stayed behind he announced his plan.

"I want two men on duty. Day and night."

The recent fires were different from the fires they were used to fighting, those usually caused when a spark hit the sawdust or the hay. These fires were burning under the ground, out of the men's sight and ability to stop them. Fire was eating the earth from its depths long before it erupted into flames and charged up the trunks of the trees. By then it was too late. Merrill hoped that with a constant watch in effect, they would be able to intuit the sinister simmering and attack, to douse it before it devoured another three or four acres of their trees.

"How will we choose?"

Merrill said drawing lots was best and fair. They'd write their names, his included, on cards, then shuffle them up, cut the cards, and take their turns guarding the forest. The men thought that Merrill was acting as if he had been called to war, but they kept their opinions to themselves. Merrill talked about fire as if it had become the enemy.

Everything Merrill thought he knew about how a fire behaved

had stopped making sense and everything he had learned from the Indians about digging trenches to create a firebreak and setting backfires to alter the direction of a fire had proved useless. In their small settlement, people got news of things they'd never seen before. At first, Merrill ignored these reports as the rantings of men who had drunk too much commissary for their own good. As far as anyone knew, once a fire burned an area, that was the end of it. He didn't know what to make of the gossip that a fire had rolled over a prairie in the Lower Bush and charred it to black cinders, only to burst into flame again over the very same acre of land. It had to be a mistake.

But similar rumors were coming from all corners of Oconto County, and they were coming from sober, God-fearing people who were not the sort to fabricate. Merrill made up his mind that if, as he was beginning to suspect, fire had turned on them, he was *not* going to take any chances.

→

WHILE MERRILL INSTITUTED his daily fire watch, a vague, formless anxiety was chugging along on its own weak steam throughout the three Bush settlements. Every experienced farmer and logger, every experienced mill worker and pioneer, had lived with fire, but one of these men couldn't seem to shake off his edginess.

This farmer was called Charles or Karl and he lived miles away from Merrill's encampment. His last name was Lemke, Lem, Lempke, or Lamp, depending upon the census takers who spelled by sound, or scribbled out names sloppily, often misinterpreting what the German immigrants with only a sprinkling of English at their disposal tried to tell them. Sometimes the immigrants deliberately provided misinformation. A mutual mistrust existed between the census takers and the "foreigners," mostly the result of the immigrant farmers' fear that the men who were taking count of the household were also looking to increase the taxes on their land.

Toward the end of September, Lamp's animals were pregnant. Because of the dry spell, one of his cows had dried up, forcing him to sell her to a butcher in Peshtigo. The curtain of smoke appeared to be siphoning the vitality out of his family and his livestock. He wasn't sure what he should do except to stop clearing land, even though it would not be of much help if he were the only farmer who was willing to stop setting fires.

As a member of the Odd Fellows Lodge in Peshtigo, Karl was learning the meaning of community. The Odd Fellows was instituted in England in 1819 with the express purpose to "educate the orphan," but by 1871 it had grown into a fraternal order that brought "odd" men together to form a philanthropic network of neighbors. Any reason for genuine alarm regarding the weather would have been part of the gossip at the lodge, which met on the first and third Wednesdays of each month. William A. Ellis of the Peshtigo Company was the grand high templar of the Odd Fellows. Karl Lamp took his cue from Ellis. If Ellis was not fearful, no one else should be either.

↢

CHARLES LAMP CAME to Peshtigo by lumber schooner from Mecklenburg-Schwerin, Germany, in 1856. He had heard that in Wisconsin he could own better farmland than any estate in Europe and that after seven years as a landowner he could vote and run for public office. He could build a church if he wanted, free to worship as he pleased; his children would be schooled and a son of his would have an opportunity to become the president of the United States.

Unlike other immigrants who tried to persuade their relatives to follow them, Charles set off for Peshtigo and left behind everyone he knew. He took a job at the Peshtigo Company and began accumulating the money he would need to buy building materials and land. When the time came, Charles wanted to be ready to purchase the land he leased from Levi Hale in the western half of the northwest quarter of section 28 near Bundy Creek just east of May's Corners. In order to make sure that eventually Hale would deed the land to him, Charles agreed to clear the eighty acres and keep his job at the Peshtigo Company, where he met Fredricke Tackman.

Fredricke was drawn to the boardinghouse at Peshtigo for different reasons. Necessity had brought her to Peshtigo, where she served meals to the mill workers. The beautiful, tall blond woman had arrived in America already betrothed to a fellow immigrant, envisioning a life that included a garden and a spinning wheel, children and neighbors. But her fiancé abandoned her before their wedding and left her pregnant with his child.

When Charles first saw Fredricke he began talking to her as she slipped a tin plate of pork in front of him. Fredricke had come from Mecklenburg, too, a coincidence that opened up her reserved Baltic face and sparked a flood of questions in their German tongue. How many times had they passed each other in the streets of their native Germany? Had they brushed each other's sleeve in a butcher shop? Did he, Charles, know the Prestins, Fredricke's sister and brother-in-law out in the Sugar Bush? They had been in each other's orbits all along, eclipsed from each other until providence brought them together in the forest. When he discovered that she was pregnant, Charles felt sympathy for Fredricke. Soon he grew to love her and by December 1856, when Luise was born, Charles and Fredricke were married. The new world promised everything a man wanted—land, work, his own piece of heaven.

The Lamps learned early on that despite the strength of their marriage, loss would be their inextricable shadow. About two years into their marriage, Charles was nearly finished clearing the land where he planned to build a cabin. Fredricke was still living in Peshtigo, working in the boardinghouse while she also tended to their two children: Luise, who had begun talking and walking, and their son, Karl, who was still nursing. Charles had been splitting his time between the two places, working long hours at the company for a few weeks and then taking time off to go into the woods, carrying a whetstone, a spare ax, a clean shirt, and enough food to sustain him while he felled the mature trees, then set fire to them, saving only the cedar for a barn and a house.

One day just as he was ready to begin chopping down the maples, certain that within a year the land would be inhabitable, he saw a boy making his way through the carpet of cedar needles and stumps. Jesse Leavenworth, who worked in town at the Peshtigo Company, had sent the boy with a message: Charles and Fredricke's daughter, Luise, was dead. The little girl had "dried up from the inside," the boy tried to explain, some stomach infection that was snatching babies back in town.

Charles abandoned his work in the woods and returned to Peshtigo. Usually, after being parted from her, the sight of his wife's face brought him simple joy. Now, the young woman who stood holding a baby in her arms, her woolen skirts floating around her boots on the steps of the boardinghouse, was someone else, a woman with a heart numbed by the loss of her daughter.

They buried Luise and tried to bury their sorrow. Shortly afterward, in 1859, Levi Hale received the deed for the eighty-acre tract of land, and, as he promised, he sold the land full out to Charles the very same day. At last the Lamp family could be together in one place. The day Charles drove Fredricke out to their plot of land, she was impressed with the work her husband had done and thrilled that he had chosen a place with a brook.

"I want ducks—hundreds of them," she told him. Charles said she could have ducks and he'd build her a sheep shed from the cedar, a hog house, too, and a pen for them to root in. He had already built the zigzag rail fence from the pine a peddler had found for him.

"Geese?"

"Geese and chickens," he told her. "With a coop."

Charles provided each one of these things for his wife, but there was nothing he could do when their son Karl died at the age of one year four months. Again they drove out to the cemetery in Peshtigo. This time the loss of her child twisted something in Fredricke. During their childless winter, she began calling her husband Karl. Charles believed he would lose his wife to madness if he asked her to stop, so he took on his son's name, the name that stayed with him from that point on. A new child, Hanna, was born in May, but like the siblings she would never know, Hanna died a year later and was buried beside her brother and sister in Peshtigo.

Fredricke worked and banked on her faith. She watched with amazement as her gardens and everything she planted multiplied. The geese and sheep feasted on the green oats and her much-longed-for ducks guarded her cabin gate. Fredricke sold fresh eggs from the chickens and the butter she churned. Whatever she sowed in the loamy soil grew in abundance—strawberries, green peas, beans, and raspberries—which Karl brought to market in Peshtigo. And then, when the thought of children was the farthest from her mind, Fredricke did get pregnant again. In late May, a new baby girl was born on the lush farm. Fredricke and Charles named her Sophia, after Fredricke's sister.

Karl would not remember a happier Christmas. Fredricke was infused with energy, scouring the cabin floors one minute, sewing clothes the next, preparing meals. Her body thrummed and set off the thrumming in his own. He pulled all the stumps on their property and hauled them across twenty acres. He and Fredricke picked every stone, moved each boulder. Together they carried them in a stone cart, piling them near their house as though they were planning to build a pyramid. Another baby, Caroline, was born to them, and following Caroline, Emma was born, and a year later, Nettie.

There would never be another son, and Karl would never hear his birth name uttered from his wife's lips, but it did not matter. They had a home, a barn, crops; they had Mrs. Bakeman as their neighbor, the Job Place school where their children would learn, and August and Sophia Prestin living a mile and a half away.

During the smoky week in September 1871, Fredricke was pregnant again, due to deliver in October. More than once that week Karl asked her if maybe she would like to go and stay at August and Sophia's house.

"You're worried. What?"

Karl shrugged. They were standing on their small porch. Usually by this time in September the air at dusk crackled with a fall snap, but tonight the air was heavy. Several miles off tongues of flame shot up above the tops of the trees in sudden bursts, the fires from a farmer so bewitched with his land he was determined to burn his stumps past sunset.

"They look like they're touching the clouds," Fredricke remarked.

"What clouds?" he asked. "Are you sure you shouldn't go with the girls to your sister's?"

"I should stay right here."

Karl did not bother to answer or turn around to watch his wife disappear into the house. He was watching the sky and the flames in the distance.

F. J. BARTELS,

PESHTIGO, WIS.

Dealer in—

DRY GOODS,
  GROCERIES,
    PROVISIONS,
      BOOTS & SHOES,
        CROCKERY,
          HARDWARE,
            PATENT MEDICINES,
              YANKEE NOTIONS,

Gents Furnishing Goods, &c.
**Flour, Butter, Eggs, Hams, Cheese,
Lard,** and everything else in the Provision Line
down to the bottom of the market.

Teas, Coffees, Sugars
and Spices, AT THE **Lowest Rates.**

TRUNKS, VALISES, TRAVELING BAGS, and in
short, everything that can be usually found in a
first class country store.

**Store on Oconto Avenue,
Peshtigo, Wisconsin.**

4

On the whole, the residents of the three Edens believed there was more to be grateful for than there was to fret about. The smoke was uncomfortable and irritating, and it appeared to be worsening, but the residents of Peshtigo and Marinette reasoned it away as no more uncomfortable than a heat wave in summer or five feet of snow in the winter. No one who chose to live in Peshtigo came there expecting it to be easy. Those harboring fear of fire were not fearful of loss of human life. Instead they feared losing their possessions. Nearly every family that had traveled from Maine, New York, and Pennsylvania and every immigrant who had cleared a patch of land in Europe had also fought back fire. Likewise, at some point, nearly everyone had lost houses, rebuilt burned fences, repaired ruined barns, and buried dead livestock, but every story of destruction ended with a list of what was saved—their lives, their families, their faith, and the gumption to simply breathe deep and resume.

So it was quite natural for Luther Noyes to downplay fire in favor of publishing a humorous account of being mistaken for one of his heroes, the journalist Horace Greeley, who had lectured on "Self-Made Men" in Green Bay. He penned a rousing article about the upcoming Republican convention that was to be held in Marinette in mid-October at which Marinette's own Honorable Isaac Stephenson would be elected to Congress; and he wrote a passionate, stirring plea for the value of education, calling it "one of the fundamental necessities of life." He was pleased to print his friend Tommy Hay's announcement that he planned to move his jewelry shop from the west side of Peshtigo to the east side. Noyes reviewed the touring exhibition "Old Babylon," he praised the newly organized brass band in Menominee, and he advocated the appropriation of $100,000 to be spent on improving and enlarging the Peshtigo Harbor settlement.

In Chicago rain fell on September 16, but it was only a sprinkle, fleeting and unremarkable. The only place unaffected by the persistent dry spell was the city of Milwaukee, which had enjoyed a driving rain on September 11 and still another downpour with lightning, thunder, and hail on September 18. Unlike the rest of the region, Milwaukee, situated on the banks of Lake Michigan, was wrapped in a spray of consistent moisture. Then, on Wednesday, September 20, Franklin Tilton made special note of the conditions around Green Bay. In the *Advocate* he wrote that the "morning smoke was more dense than at any other time before; the air is suffocating and is filled with flakes of ashes. On the Bay the steamers have to navigate by compass, and blow their fog horns, the shores being invisible."

Fortunately, Green Bay was surrounded on three sides by the Fox and East Rivers, and the city had an excellent fire department, which had been organized in 1858. The Germania Fire Company was equipped with the Steamer Amoskeg and twelve hundred feet of hose; Wide Awake No. 2 was headquartered on Adams Street, and

Washington Hook and Ladder Company No. 1 also boasted twelve hundred feet of hose. At every intersecting street of the city there were large reservoir tanks connected to the streams.

By September 21 the smoke continued to billow upward above the trees in dense plumes before it dispersed and formed a stubborn canopy between the ground and the sky. Behind the smoke the sun bled outward as if it were leaking copper, smearing the sky with rust. At this point, Luther Noyes wrote that although the dry spell remained unrelieved, "at least the flies are gone."

No man, even when the gods favor him, can control the wind, and yet, the favored sons of Chicago/Peshtigo and Marinette—William Butler Ogden and Isaac Stephenson—were loath to admit their limitations. Neither Ogden nor Stephenson could have avoided noticing the threatening sky, and Stephenson had already been faced with the problem of stalled logs, but each man had more important things on his mind: how to continue making money and how to use that money to turn the best profit available. While it appeared these profits would continue to come from the Peshtigo Company mill and the Peshtigo woodenware factory, Ogden and Stephenson had begun to suspect that the real money and the real progress would not be in wood much longer but in the iron mines of Escanaba, Michigan, and in extending the railroad farther north and west.

Luther Noyes reported on Ogden's and Stephenson's plans. At the same time he seemed to miss the implications of the reports he wrote. He had printed the facts and figures in plain sight on August 26 within the *Eagle*'s pages: "It is calculated that the stock of logs is short this season and that many of the mills, will in consequence, shut down, as early as September." Noyes had also added a sidebar on the iron ore in Michigan, writing that "it is confidently expected that this extension of the Northwestern Railway through this section of the country, will, instead of going to Escanaba, be deferred farther west and cross this iron ridge near these discoveries, and consequently afford an outlet for the ore."

Ogden's gift was in recognizing the true profit potential in an enterprise. The real money was to be made not in selling the commodity but in controlling or adding value to the commodity. Ogden set out to do both with the lumber business. While other timber barons concentrated only on buying large tracts of land and then cutting the trees for lumber, Ogden went one step farther. Producing and selling lumber was a cutthroat business, so intensely competitive that profits could be elusive at times. Ogden shrewdly lowered the risks of the business and raised his profit margins. The woodenware factory was fed by the trees around Peshtigo and the items it produced—pails, tubs, ax handles, clothespins, broom handles—sold at a much better profit margin than lumber. Trees and lumber were both at risk as the month wore on; iron ore represented a new venture and more profits.

—

ON THURSDAY, SEPTEMBER 21, on the western shore of Green Bay in the settlement of Little Suamico, A. C. Conn of A. C. Conn & Company put his entire force of men to work hauling barrels of water and digging trenches along the edge of the timber. The "angry glare" behind the smoke was not the sun; it was the illumination from the fires that were burning in Oconto and rapidly making their way toward Little Suamico. Conn's profitable sawmill had caught fire and he was certain that unless they could wet it down he was doomed to lose everything.

Franklin Tilton wrote that "the flames would advance until some change in the wind drove them in a different direction . . . they would work their way into the swamps and here develop almost a furnace heat, actually burning from one to three feet into the ground and completely burning out the peat, roots and alluvial soil, leaving nothing but ashes and the sub-soil of sand."

In response to the danger, itinerant preachers suddenly began stalking the countryside, appearing in settlements waving their Bibles until they became as familiar as the smoke. By midweek, a preacher had made his way through the woods in the Lower Bush, showing up at John Mulligan's camp where Mary McGregor served food to the railroad crews. He came around noontime knowing the work would be halted for the big meal of the day and he would find a full house.

His message was not one Mary wanted to hear, especially after the struggles she and her husband, John, had put themselves through. Fifteen years of work and now this preacher was suggest-ing that it was about to explode before her eyes unless they all made a concerted effort to ask forgiveness. For what? Mary wondered.

In 1866 she had sat with her husband under the eaves of the boardinghouse room they shared in Peshtigo. The room was too hot in summer and deathly cold in winter, austere and meager, a mirror of the life they'd been living. They had a board-and-straw stick bed, and John owned a few iron tools he was able to buy from the Peshtigo Company: "a grubhoe, a splitting maul, two axes, steel wedges, a carpenter's hammer, a cross-cut saw and a set of whet-stones." Under the inelegant bed there was nothing but a box of wood files, a folded canvas, a frying pan, and an iron kettle. The rest of their possessions were kept in a brass-strapped trunk under the only window in the room and in it were the sheep wool, linens, china, and cooking utensils Mary had brought with her when they moved to Peshtigo from Canada four years earlier.

"I'm tired of this sawdust town and piling lumber eleven hours a day," John said. "Wouldn't you like to have a homestead where you could have a garden and a clean place to hang your wash?"

Of course she wanted those things, and he'd asked it before. Mary wished he'd stop asking because the reality of it seemed too far out of reach. They were both fifty-six years old by that time. Mary earned their bed and board at the boardinghouse while John worked in the mill. At their age she didn't see how a farm was within their reach.

"I don't know why we came here in the first place," she told him. They came, like everyone else, to find something better and better meant one thing: land. It hadn't worked out as they had planned, but John was determined and Mary knew it.

"I want to die with my own good earth under my feet or in my own bed in my own cabin," he told her.

They'd been together so long Mary knew this was not just idle talk from her husband; he had done some investigating.

"The Land Office has an eighty-acre tract up for homestead between four and five miles from town," he explained. A friend had told him this is where they planned to survey for a railroad. If he and Mary settled there it would not be quiet; they'd hear the locomotive's whistle, feel its rumble, but they could hop a train whenever they wanted.

"It'll be back-breaking all the way," he said. "You don't get virgin soil ready for crop by doing nothing." But he added that the eighty acres was one of the last tracts left and still close enough to town. Of course, there was not a real road to travel on, only the Oconto Drover's trail, and half of that was through swamp timber, but Mary agreed. There was only the matter of signing the affidavit for the land, which required a trip to Green Bay. The trip would mean spending some of their hard-earned money on a stage and hotel, so they decided to send a telegram to the Land Office, notifying the office of their intent to purchase. John said that they'd spend their summers clearing and the winters working in Peshtigo and they would do it until they had precisely what they wanted—a home and land of their own.

The McGregors got what they wanted and had succeeded by sheer hard work. Mary resented the preacher who invaded the camp to tell her that "God is very angry with some of His children in Peshtigo. He's is going to send doom of some sort."

The preacher spoke as if he had just returned from a private audience with God himself, and it was the conviction with which he spoke that frightened Mary more than the words themselves. She raked her mind for any possible infractions she and John may have committed against others. She could not think of a thing. The only infraction she could imagine was that they had prospered after fifteen years. They had a "log house and a barn, each 16 by 20 feet, a chicken coop, a hog house, and a sheep shed. A large garden was fenced with sapling pickets. Orchard and berry patches flourished . . . every surplus thing they raised could be sold at a profit in Peshtigo or to the crew building the railroad up from the south."

John had kept clearing that fall, burning land, although Mary asked him not to. Split maple lined the graded right-of-way that would cut diagonally through their property. Meanwhile she was selling eggs, milk, ham, and vegetables to the railroad workers rather than hauling the products into town. John's rush to clear the land was not borne out of recklessness; it was a race against time. By September John McGregor was seventy-one years old.

The day the preacher arrived with his message, Mary had already got word that there were brush fires in Peshtigo. She'd been breathing the smoke-polluted air so long she barely noticed anymore, but she was keenly aware of the flames dancing against the horizon in the west. Perhaps the preacher had a point. She wanted John to drive her into Peshtigo so she could attend the Congregational church that Sunday, but John told her she couldn't allow herself to be ruffled by a preacher who preyed on the nerves of good people doing a good job. This section of the railroad was nearly complete and the men doing the work needed food to keep them going. Providing sustenance was God's work. Feed the hungry. Mary couldn't argue with that.

The commonly held belief among the preachers was that after thirty years of clearing, burning, and building, a moral drama had been staged: man was the architect, not only of cities, farms, and mills, but of destruction, and wounded Nature would fight back.

⸺

ON SATURDAY, WHILE news of fires spread through Oconto, Noyes's *Eagle* contained an article about a meeting that was to take place on October 12 in Green Bay. It was to be an "ordinary meeting" in many respects except that it would include discussion of Ogden and Stephenson's plan to build the Sturgeon Bay Canal at the mouth of the Peshtigo River in the settlement known as Peshtigo Harbor.

The Harbor settlement was manufactured by Ogden and Stephenson and was situated six miles south of Peshtigo Village proper. There they had erected a boardinghouse, a schoolhouse for the children of the laborers, and a steam-powered mill. Lumber was transferred from the barges with tremendous difficulty as the barges and tugs had to navigate the long way around the peninsula in order to gain access to the harbor. The canal project would involve creating an artificial channel across the peninsula; if it were built, the detour through the existing vulnerable channel, called Death's Door, could be completely avoided. The Peshtigo Company had taken the initiative for the proposed plan, and Stephenson himself had completed the initial survey, but so far, Stephenson noted, "In Green Bay, the city which was to be most benefitted by it, the only subscription we obtained was five dollars from one of the prominent lumbermen."

Noyes encouraged his readers to view the canal project as a "necessity" and its eventual completion as a "mark [of] a new and important era in our commercial pursuits." As for other issues in Marinette and Peshtigo, September 23 appeared as normal as any other day. Noyes reported on a band of four Italian minstrels who had arrived with violins and were serenading the town at night. Their music, he said, was much better than what one generally heard from traveling minstrels. At the Harbor Mill, George Bazette was injured when his hand caught under the chain of the lathe machine. And Noyes was happy to report that "railroad work is progressing rapidly, but we cannot quite hear the whistle of the C. & N. W. R'y's locomotive yet."

❧

WHAT THE TOWNSPEOPLE in Peshtigo heard instead by Saturday evening was the one sound they feared: the mill whistle signaling a fire. On a night lumbermen and loggers usually reserved for drinking and dancing at the saloon, and the townspeople looked forward to entertainment by a traveling exhibition of players or lecturers, the alarm broke through, requiring every man—nearly two hundred total—to rush to its call. Father Peter Pernin, the French missionary priest who was building a church in Peshtigo so he could serve the Catholic parishioners there as well as in his church, Our Lady of Lourdes, in Marinette, said the fire he witnessed and struggled against that Saturday night "was a grand sight."

THE WIND DIRECTION had been erratic for nearly two weeks, sometimes veering in from the north, then shifting within an afternoon to the southwest. Just the day before, on September 22, Pernin had ventured out to the Sugar Bushes to minister to a family there. After visiting with a farm family, Pernin decided to go pheasant hunting and was accompanied by "a twelve year old lad" who had offered to act as Pernin's guide in the woods. The priest and the boy set out that afternoon, but as sunset approached and Pernin suggested they begin making their way back to the farmhouse, the boy could not determine which way to go. Pernin realized they were "completely lost in the woods." Night was falling and the forest, thick and otherworldly, fell into its nighttime silence except for the disturbing crackling sound of fire. Pernin noticed "a tongue of fire that ran along the ground, in and out, among the trunks of the trees, leaving them unscathed but devouring the dry leaves that came in its way, and the swaying of the upper branches of the trees announcing that the wind was rising."

It was at this point that Pernin and the boy began shouting, hoping someone would hear them and be able to track their voices and lead them out of the sizzling woods. Pernin fired shots in the air, a dangerous move, he realized afterward, had the wadding lodged in a tinder-dry tree. Almost immediately after the shots, Father Pernin and the boy heard a band of voices shouting in the distance. As it turned out, the voices belonged to the boy's family members and neighbors who had gotten worried when the boy did not return home before dark. Finally, Pernin and his young guide's shouts were on the same path as their rescuers' voices. But then there was a new threat.

"Fanned by the wind," Pernin wrote, "the tiny flames had united and spread over a considerable surface. We thus found ourselves in the center of a circle of fire extending or narrowing, more or less, around us." Pernin and the boy could not reach the men who'd come to fetch them and the men could not reach them; no one could broach the fire without risk of burning or being suffocated. One of the men began beating the flames with strewn tree branches, an awkward method of setting a backfire. The tree branches acted as a large matchstick lighted to divert the flames in another direction, allowing Pernin and the boy to make a quick passage to safety.

IN MILWAUKEE, ON September 23, weather observer Increase Lapham recorded falling barometric pressure with low relative humidity, two meteorological factors that affected the fire conditions. At around seven P.M. on the night of Saturday the twenty-third, sparks and cinders blew across the Peshtigo River from the northeast, igniting a pile of sawdust and wood slabs next to the Peshtigo woodenware factory. When they heard the whistle, every man—regardless of class or station—ran to the riverbank. The men formed a chain and passed water hand over hand to douse the flames that had not yet ignited the factory building.

James McGregor, the livery and stable owner, joined in the battle against fire with D. R. McDonald, a police officer. Achille Granger, a millwright, passed pails of water to David Henry, a farmer from section 9. The blacksmith for the Peshtigo Company, Charles Wenzel, who had learned his trade from his father in Prussia, stood guard with Peter Peterson, the Swede who ran a small boot and shoe shop. W. A. Ellis ran to the river and worked alongside J. W. Gould, the proprietor of the Peshtigo House hotel. Ellis told Gould that as soon as possible he would have to get to the grocery store, where W. C. Oakes operated the telegraph, and wire Ogden in New York telling him of the near disaster. The telegraph line ran along the railroad right of way, but Ellis, like the others, did not know that at the very moment they were fighting fire in Peshtigo, south of them in Oconto fires had already eaten up the telegraph lines, leaving a twenty-mile gap in communication between Green Bay and Marinette.

—◆—

THE FIRES IN Oconto, Big and Little Suamico, Fort Howard, and Manitowoc had erupted into flames about three hours earlier; barns, livestock, fences, houses, cords of wood, and mills lit up, but no one could point to a single source of ignition. Apparently the ashes that had floated over Green Bay the day before still had enough burn in them to ignite the dry landscape easily. The simplest shift in the wind whisked the separate infernos into fire devils that fed on each other with alarming speed and made a sweep through the settlements. The townspeople were shocked. These fires were abrupt, unpredictable.

In Peshtigo that evening, it took several hours to pour enough water over the flames to stop the fire in its tracks. Peter Pernin later wrote that after the fire was out, he and the others were disturbed by a sound from the west. The men turned in the direction of the sound only to see fire darting out of the treetops.

In Noyes's list of gossipy items for the *Eagle* he had included an anecdote about a deer that had come out of the woods four weeks earlier and taken up residence at Levi Hale's place next to Peter Pernin's church on Oconto Avenue. Both Hale and Noyes were charmed that the wild deer seemed to long for domesticity. But it would soon be made clear that even the wildlife wanted safety from the fires in the woods. Shelter from smoke and heat is what the deer was seeking and why it stayed, seemingly tame, at Hale's place.

That night, two hundred men watched as thousands of birds flew up out of the trees. The birds were shrouded in ash, their feathers bleached white. They were stunned and seemed to have lost their sense of direction. Pernin said that for a few moments the birds hovered over the fire, their instinct for flight impaired. The birds banged into each other, tangled in each other's wings as they screeched for their mates. Then just as quickly as it began, the scene ended. Instead of making an escape, the birds plummeted, sucked back into the burning branches before the tall pines turned into a column of fire, hissing and filling the air with more smoke; the pines fell toward them, crashing to the ground where the team of already exhausted men extinguished the flames.

◂

ON SUNDAY, SEPTEMBER 24, Green Bay was not burning, but many of the scattered settlements, logging camps, railroad camps, and towns north, south, west, and east of it were and had been since Saturday night. Much later Tilton would write, "Whether we were all unrighteous, or lacking in faith, or doomed to chastisement for our sins or for a solemn warning to the world, we leave to others to decide. Certain it is, that the scourge of fire increased."

The young widow Latour, mother of six children, lived about two miles outside of Green Bay. Her husband had died in the spring, leaving her the only provider for her family. She worked the many acres, kept the fences mended, fed the animals, and did all the work she had to do to keep the farm running. In the last two weeks of September she had lost an ox to the fires, and the following week yet

another ox. On this Sunday morning, all of the rail fences surrounding her property burst into flame. Townsmen came to her rescue and fought the flames, but even after they had extinguished the
fire her land was still in danger. She knew that if fire erupted again
her neighbors might not be able to come to her aid. As the fire
spread, every farm was in danger, and her neighbors would have to
fight to save their own homes, leaving her to fight the flames herself.

Even those who escaped serious damage to their properties were
hesitant to relax after a fire had passed. From the Wolf River in the
west to Lake Michigan on the east, which was a distance of about
seventy miles, and from north to south covering a distance of over
one hundred miles, the minute a fire was extinguished in one area,
another erupted just as quickly in the next settlement or town.
Sawmills in Little Suamico, Big Suamico, and Fort Howard were
completely burned. Lumber and thousands of cords of firewood fed
the advancing flames and fed the panic of the residents who began
collecting whatever personal belongings they could, strapping them
onto wagons before heading out in a mass exodus of prairie
schooners to the city of Green Bay twenty-five miles to the south.

As residents were fleeing, Older's Circus with eighty horses
pulling twenty wagons had just managed to cross over into Manitowoc when fire struck the bridge. But the circus would have no
audience that day; instead the people of Manitowoc were unsuccess-
fully fighting the garish circus of fire in their town, trying to save
their houses and barns while the taverns, fences, and trees burned
around them. All three bridges on the road from Green Bay to
Manitowoc located thirty-eight miles to the southeast caught fire.
When he made it to safety in Green Bay, Fred Scheller, a resident of
Manitowoc, said that the sound of "the falling of the burning trees
was like a continual discharge of artillery."

Without the telegraph to alert people in Green Bay about what was happening in Peshtigo, refugees straggled into the city and told stories of fires climbing trees, consuming stacks of hay, feasting on fences, homes, and livestock. These refugees were enervated. Some, especially the small children, were suffering from smoke inhalation. Many of the men had singed eyebrows and burned hair from beating back flames.

Franklin Tilton listened as the refugees told countless tales of destroyed mills, burned-out bridges, and charred settlements, but the most disturbing report came from farmers who insisted that the fires seemed to be burning beneath the ground. The heat had seared off the soles of their boots and the flames chewed up the railroad ties. They said the flames "gnawed at the roots of the trees" before rapidly curling up around the trunks and into the uppermost branches. The crackling trees crashed to the ground, sending up bright sparks in their wake.

DUNLAP HOUSE

Marinette, – Wisconsin.

—:o:—

This house is fitted specially to meet the wants of the

TRAVELING PUBLIC!

Good Rooms, good Clean Beds, Table as well supplied as is possible in this market,

STABLING

Of the very best order for teams, in short, all the Appurtenances and surroundings to this house, are fully up to the wants of the locality

TRY US AND SEE.

J. M. BELANGER, Proprietor.

5

On Sunday morning, in both Peshtigo and Marinette, every pew in every church was filled. The atmosphere outside was sickly, the smoke tinted a hue no one could name. The sawdust was piled in parched heaps. In Peshtigo, beneath the mill boardwalks, seventeen barrels of benzine were stored out of the way. The people still believed that a friendly rain would fall, that their faith and prayers would not go unheard much longer.

Reverend Edwin Beach, pastor of the Congregational church, had been holding special prayer meetings on Wednesday nights. He called them revival meetings and the tenor of his homilies was changing. No longer gentle, he now stood in the pulpit and read from the Bible. Those with stains on their souls, he reasoned, had only to walk through the streets to know that God was asking something of them, calling them to repent before he "rained down fire and heaven" on them. Had the McGregors been there, John might have been shocked to hear a minister they respected echoing the words of the itinerant preacher who had come pleading his case in their camp several days earlier.

In the Lutheran church at the ten A.M. services Reverend Charles Huebner was telling his parishioners much the same thing. Perhaps these fires were just punishment for those weekly Saturday nights of drinking and lust. Perhaps the congregation had expected too much, perhaps they had been greedy or negligent. Shunned a neighbor. Treated a child cruelly.

Father Peter Pernin stood at the altar of his newly built church. He held the host, a thin white wafer representing the body of Christ and His sacrifice on Calvary, between the index finger and thumb of each hand. He raised the host high above his head so that his followers kneeling behind him in their pews could see it. They were waiting to receive communion from his ciborium, to become human tabernacles for Christ. With their Savior inside them, the Catholics believed they would be protected from harm.

No one could mask their apprehension, not even Father Pernin. This morning in church no man could forget the pillar of fire they'd witnessed the previous night, especially now with Reverend Beach reciting the tale of Sodom and Gomorrah. At eleven A.M. Beach was still preaching, nowhere near the end of his sermon. The congregation was dressed in wool and linens, layer upon layer of it. The little girls especially wore underwear, thick stockings, pantaloons, crinolines, and dresses trimmed in lace or flocking. Their long hair hung loose to their waists. Ribbons trailed from their hair. One child's clothing could fuel a flame if it caught in her hair or skirts. The women were swathed in layers of clothing that could not be ripped off easily if it caught fire.

Beach continued, reaching his crescendo when the whistle blew, signaling another fire. Men told their wives to rush back to their homes with the children, to wet blankets and cover the boards of their houses to protect themselves against the fire.

Flying sparks had set fire to the sawdust near the factory again. The men were quickly able to snuff them out, but then the wind shifted. A gale blew in from the northwest, feeding the fires in the timbers, which, they realized, were advancing toward the river. William Shephard of the Peshtigo Company store instructed the men to haul out the Black Hawk. Peter Pernin joined the fight at the river. He said, "I have seen fires sweep over the prairies with the speed of a locomotive and the prairie fire is grand and terrific, but beside a timber fire it sinks into insignificance. In the timber it may move almost as rapidly, but the fire does not go out . . . nor is there the same chance to resist the advance of fire in the forests. It is as though you attempted to resist the approach of an avalanche of fire hurled against you."

At the same time the trees were burning in Peshtigo, a fire broke out on the south side of the Peshtigo Road to Marinette near the residence of Reverend Thomas Walker, where Luther Noyes watched "showers of cinders igniting combustible material in every direction." The new Marinette volunteer fire company took to the streets in full force. Ike Stephenson, his brothers Robert and Samuel, Dr. Jonathan Cory Hall, and Luther Noyes joined in the fight with shopkeepers, millwrights, and loggers. When the bridge from Menominee to Marinette caught fire, the fire company managed to extinguish the flames before they could do any serious damage. Stephenson ordered the men to begin digging trenches; he was certain that the fierce blaze six miles south would soon be upon them.

Late that Sunday afternoon, a second alarm rang out in Peshtigo. For the third time in twenty-four hours hundreds of men were called to fight the fire. The smoke was blinding, the air painful on inhalation. The only way they could continue to fight and stay alive was to periodically throw themselves onto the ground, dig a hole in the earth with their fingers, and stuff their faces into it, drawing enough fresh breath to resume the battle.

"The work," Luther Noyes wrote, "consumed the afternoon. Still the woods to the west of us were full of fire. It was concentrating near Henry Gregor's place, and if not checked would burn his buildings, rush across the street and destroy all of Oconto Avenue up to and including the Peshtigo Hotel."

The men managed to save both buildings, but as dusk approached, they were not much closer to beating back the flames. Luther Noyes, who had seen the destruction of vast areas of land and even entire cities in the war, could only comment that September 24 was "such a scene as we never witnessed before, and never wish to witness again." Noyes could not bear to see the panic on the women's pale faces as they clasped their children to their chests. Or to see his friend Tommy Hay struggling for breath, "bowed before the unequal battle."

Not before the wind shifted again and veered south did it sweep the flames away with it. In Peshtigo, Peter Pernin believed the wind shift was God's breath blown mercifully over the two towns.

On Monday, September 25, in an unprecedented move, W. A. Ellis suspended all operations at the Peshtigo Company and the woodenware factory. In Marinette, Ike Stephenson ordered the men to begin a cleanup of the debris-strewn streets. Both Peshtigo and Marinette breathed a collective sigh of relief and gratitude. The following week, in the September 30 issue of the *Eagle*, Noyes delivered a blow-by-blow narrative of the weekend of fire. He said the "fire fiend" that had been nourishing itself on the dried landscape for weeks had "at last come and gone."

New York
Triple Sheet
(New York Herald)
The Conflagration in Wisconsin
Milwaukee, Wis., Sept. 27, 1871

Later news from the fire raging along the coast of Lake Michigan, between Manitowoc and Ahnapee, state that the flames are lapping up everything and sweeping houses, barns, stores and piers in their course. Henry Marshall, of this city, who escaped through the fire at the risk of his life, and whose horses were badly scorched, counted twenty-two houses and barns reduced to ashes. The losses in Kewaunee county will reach a quarter of a million of dollars. The farmers are burying their household goods in the ground to save them. As all communication has been cut off the exact situation cannot be ascertained; but it is feared that unless rain sets in the damage and loss of life will be fearful. The wells are all dried up, and the lake is the only resource for water.

The compressed report made it seem as if the fires were limited to a small area along the coast; the report never hinted at the destruction west, east, and north of Ahnapee. If Ogden read the account at his Harlem River home in New York, he had no indication that the railroad camps or the Peshtigo Company had suffered. He had not heard any bad news from Stephenson or Ellis or from his brother Mahlon in Chicago. From his distance these fires would not have appeared extraordinary. Since the report cited only one man's account—a visitor's account at that—Ogden would likely have dismissed it.

In Peshtigo the townspeople now believed that the blackened trees resulting from the September 24 blaze could not burn again. Those trees were useless, but because they were still standing the people believed they would act as a barrier against any further threat of fire. Now that the branches had shucked their leaves, even if the wind shifted suddenly again, it would be unlikely that the charred timber could attract enough flame to do damage. What they were not considering was the high charcoal content of the maples the railroad workers continued to clear. The higher the charcoal content of a tree, the longer its burning capabilities. The sawn maples were still smoldering, rich with combustible fuel even though the rail workers and farmers would have sworn the stumps were cold.

❧

AGAIN, LIFE PROCEEDED as usual in Peshtigo and Marinette. Noyes reported that Tommy Hay had in fact moved his jewelry store from Nick Cavoit's building and reopened on the east side of Peshtigo in Captain Fred Bartels's new store. The railroad work was back in full operation. Noyes wrote that "the fires have nearly died out now in this vicinity."

On Thursday, September 28, J. G. Clements was not about to allow fire to interfere with love. He married his Menominee sweetheart. On October 1, Clements's mother-in-law, Mrs. Theodore Trudell, visited the newly married couple in their balloon frame house in Peshtigo. According to journalist Robert Wells, Mrs. Trudell felt compelled to give some advice to her new son-in-law.

"Take care of my girl," she told him.

Clements wrapped his arm around his bride's waist and assured Mrs. Trudell, "I'll take good care of her."

Before Mrs. Trudell could board her carriage, Clements added that he would, if necessary, die for his new wife.

Part Two

EDEN
BURNS

6

During the first week of October, Marinette and Peshtigo were bathed in unearthly light: by day, a mottled yellow that bore no resemblance to sun or wheat or gold; by night a glaring red that deepened to brass, then tarnished to bloody mist. Luther B. Noyes wrote: "Moonlight evenings of late have not been very pleasant. Pale Luna has veiled her face in smoke."

Noyes was suffering from what he called "red eye." He and everyone in town were complaining of itchy, watering, bloodshot eyes. The superintendent in the town of Oconto, south of Peshtigo, had closed the day schools because the children were lethargic. Many children had unexplained fevers and hacking coughs. If the newest immigrants to Peshtigo and Marinette were expecting lush green trees or earth glistening with fall frost and dew, upon arrival they were greeted instead with dry soil that blew across their shoes and boots in quick dusty whirls and a collision of smells: roasted salt pork from the logging camps, the musty scent of charred pine, the sharp tang of crisp cedar needles, the strangely sweet odor of burned hay. Yards of hay had been swallowed up in fires. Flowery perfume mixed from vanilla extracts and honeysuckle now soured in the cooked air. Nothing could mask or tame the stench of horse manure or the acid odor of horse urine oozing from the livery stables. It was the price for prosperity and still another new venture was about to commence full operation that fall.

Blast furnaces would soon begin operating in Menominee and Marinette. Mr. H. J. Colwell, an iron manufacturer, had made surveys and found Marinette and Menominee suited to iron manufacture as long as "assurance can be given that he can have the refuse of the mill to convert into fuel." As Noyes pointed out, "There are enough slabs and edgings on each side of the river wasted annually to supply a blast furnace at each place." The furnaces would be fed by the mill, and logging slash and the debris—two parts decayed leaves and twigs, one part the rot of dead animals caught in the underbrush—added the brutal odor of burnt refuse to the towns. Peshtigo and Marinette were fast becoming unchecked ovens. The ground surface was heating up. Ionized atoms of charcoal combined with trace methane from the dry marshes; gases blew into the upward flowing drafts of relentless combustion that gathered into clouds in the air overhead.

THE "COMBUSTION" BETWEEN Luther Noyes and J. A. Crozer of the *Herald* showed no signs of abating. The two editors continued to stoke the verbal fire between them in the *Eagle* and the *Herald* pages. The newest bone of contention was the issue of the blast furnaces. Both Noyes and Crozer were on the same side of the issue, yet it seemed that having found themselves in agreement about the revenue from ore mining and manufacture, they were determined to disagree about which one of them had shown the most foresight in the matter.

Crozer was firm: "We have never thought that there was the amount of money in the buildings that some other writers have imagined, for the time has gone by when furnaces could pay for their cost of erection in the first 12 months . . . it is owing to the course *this* paper has always pursued and the interest we have always felt and manifested in the matter that it has reached its present and very flattering condition."

Noyes shot back: "Well, who said that the time had *not* gone by when furnaces could pay for the cost of erection? We made a few calculations, and a few figures a couple of weeks since, which we claimed to be only an approximation to the results that could be obtained."

The point, Noyes wrote, is that furnaces would be erected, the plan was a go, which meant more jobs, and more jobs meant that more money would flow into the area.

Whether the sparring was sport or serious disagreement, it distracted the readers and served as a sleight of hand. As long as Peshtigo, Marinette, and Menominee kept their eyes on the future, which included the harbor improvement project in Peshtigo and the new iron manufacturing, readers would be less inclined to panic about the fires.

For instance, long articles about the coming blast furnaces diverted attention away from this item: "It is reported that the mill of T. Cole & Co. on Little River, commonly known as the Judge Ingalls Mill, was burned last Wednesday."

It was not true. Thanks to Elbridge Merrill and his mill workers, who had continued choosing lots and keeping up their twenty-four-hour watch, they and the mill were still very much intact and word was sent to correct the mistake. However, Mr. Merryman was not quite as lucky. The tramway at the Merryman mill had caught fire and the *Union*, which was docked at the time, "got up steam in a hurry" to avoid the flames that had taken off from the "fire-pen" where refuse from the mill was regularly burned. The damage was not extensive, but "had there been a strong wind," the mill would not have been saved.

At least Noyes could report with confidence that the sound they'd been anticipating—the whistle of the Chicago & Northwestern Railroad through Marinette—would definitely blow loudly by December 1, if not sooner. The railroad gangs continued working even though trees had fallen across the road because of a sudden high wind. Noyes wrote, "The whole country for miles along the Peshtigo road presents a charred and blackened surface," but he resisted the urge to issue a warning.

Two small notices referred to John Belanger. Noyes expected to see John Belanger every morning; he'd enjoyed Belanger's excellent meals at the Dunlap House. Belanger's absence from the place was sufficient cause for Noyes to write, "J. M. Belanger, of the Dunlap House, has been absent from his home the greater portion of last week." Noyes thought it unlikely that with so much invested in his extraordinary hotel Belanger would flee. However, in addition to Belanger's disappearance, Noyes had also discovered that a "tied up package" of the *Eagle* destined to go to Menominee by stagecoach "had been left at the Dunlap House the Saturday before, snugly stowed away in a corner." It was the issue of the paper in which Noyes had recounted the big fire of Sunday, September 24; only now did Noyes realize that his Menominee neighbors had read nothing of it.

A few residents had decided the threat of fire was a weight more oppressive than the air and they boarded the steamer or loaded up a wagon with their belongings and headed south toward Green Bay. Out near the railroad camp, John McGregor had no intention of leaving, but he did ask his wife, Mary, to begin gathering food and valuables. The week previous he had told her not to listen to the preacher's warning of fire and brimstone, but now he wanted to be prepared. He told Mary to secure their belongings in the root cellar he'd built on their property.

The Lamp family had not fled from their farm and Fredricke's newest child was a week overdue. Karl wanted her to leave, to go to Sophie's home or to at least have Mrs. Race nearby. Mrs. Race had helped all the women deliver their babies. Karl fretted that fire and birth would erupt at the same time. As usual, Fredricke took her husband's concerns in stride and convinced him that they should all remain exactly where they were.

Noyes was scrabbling around for shiny, heartening news. There was some. The McCartneys had a new addition to their family— eleven and a half pounds of "fresh, unadulterated humanity," a baby boy. Noyes said that the new parents were "ecstatic" and "who could blame them?"

Noyes was finally enjoying the personal success he'd only dreamed of when he arrived in Marinette that spring, but he wrote of this success in muted, humble tones. His beloved *Eagle*'s circulation had already "quadrupled" since the first issue and it now "had the largest circulation of any paper between Green Bay and Marquette, Michigan." Noyes was unaware that as he announced the *Eagle*'s success, General Henry Howgate was instructing weather observers to discontinue reports to Marquette, which made it unlikely that the *Eagle* would be delivered there if a telegram could not be put through.

Noyes gave voice to his musings: "What has become of our sporting fraternity?" "What has become of Stearn's livery stable at Menakaune?" Pickups to and from Stearn's had decreased in the past week. Perhaps more spot fires had made pickups and deliveries impossible. He knew that the swamps had never been drier and that the "very moss covering the lowest places will ignite readily."

Noyes had heard from a Marinette resident that an old man who lived "about four miles north of the city in the woods" was found burned to death and "lying by the charred embers of his dwelling." Noyes had just managed to digest that news when he was informed of a husband and wife who lived several miles south of Oconto and were forced to "retire" from their burning house when the fires caught in the timber. According to the report, the couple had traveled a small distance and then remembered that they "had left their money" in the blazing house. Noyes could not begin to imagine what madness made a couple think of money when they'd managed to escape a timber fire, and he was almost certain that if he were in such a circumstance, the only reason to rush into the burning Bentley would be to rescue his little girl, Minnie, or his son, Frank, or his wife, Belle. But not for money as that couple had, returning to the house to retrieve their trunk of cash. That's when the woman's clothes caught fire and before they were extinguished she was horribly burned. She died the next morning.

Oct. 3, 1871

6:15 p.m.
FROM: Robinson, S., Gen. Supt., Milwaukee
TO: Genrl Myer, Chf Sig Ofr

Extensive fires have been raging in forests between Green Bay and Escanaba, for more than a week and our line have [*sic*] suffered very much. Supt. G. H. Bliss of Chicago is doing his best, but so long as fires continue along the line, we cannot repair them.

The future was written on that thin leaf of paper, encapsulated in a single message: "forests between Green Bay and Escanaba." Robinson, the superintendent at the Northwest Telegraph office in Milwaukee, was trying to be clear, to let his superior know that fires were *out of control* on the timber stands in two states, a 107-mile stretch, but Robinson's use of the plural "forests" inadvertently deemphasized the seriousness of the fires and summed up both the vision and the attitude toward fire on the frontier.

Politics, personal ambition, and skepticism were working at cross purposes that October and had been for quite some time. Before and during the Civil War, weather was the province of the Surgeon General's Office with the aid of the Army Signal Service. The Civil War had brought with it a large expansion of the Signal Service Corps. Since 1854, Colonel Albert J. Myer had been in the army acting as assistant to the chief of the corps. By 1860 he was appointed to the position of Signal Office. Myer's special corps became a strong force during the Civil War and the Signal Corps grew as part of the volunteer army. The only tool as powerful—if not more powerful—than a gun was the telegraph. The elaborate system of heavy black wires sagging from leaning pole to leaning pole had become a pulsing network, the exposed veins and arteries of human communication, casting new shadows over the landscape. Myer felt entitled to its control and said as much, which offended Secretary of War Edwin M. Stanton. The whole matter resulted in Myer's being relieved of his duties, then sent off to Cairo, Illinois, to await orders that never came.

Eventually, Myer won his appointment back with the pay of colonel, but it was a pale victory since the Signal Corps had been mustered out with the volunteer army in 1865. The year 1869 found Colonel Albert J. Myer, a man with the title of chief signal officer, and an office that could not keep its name straight. Myer's office was known as the Signal Service, the Signal Corps, the Signal Force, the Signal Detachment, or the Signal Bureau, while Myer and his men worked and tested signals in abandoned forts using salvaged war materials.

Meanwhile, the study of soil composition, fire chemistry, cyclonic patterns, trade winds, eclipses, barometric pressure, and medicine met with equal parts excitement and skepticism.

Isaac Stephenson, who possessed the foresight necessary to create the Sturgeon Bay Canal project, a man who enjoyed "modern" improvements in his mansion, looked down on medicine and would remain suspicious of doctors until his death.

He firmly believed that doctors made people sick with their elixirs and rituals. "With the flood of doctors pouring out upon the country after a perfunctory university education," he wrote, "I have little patience. We succeeded in getting on very well without them. . . . Early experiences and close observation have led me to the conclusion that nature will work its own curative effects and that the elaborate formulae devised by physicians often times becloud the ailment, to the dismay of the patient but to the advantage of the druggist as well as the doctor."

Stephenson had lost two children in 1861: his firstborn daughter, Mary Elizabeth, and two days later his son, Samuel James. Both children died from scarlet fever despite the advice in the *Eagle* that "following a nutritious diet, exercising in the open air and keeping the extremities warm and dry" would help prevent the dreaded disease. The newspaper suggested that following these prescriptions and adding "a little proper medicine" would cure the fever. Nothing worked. In 1871, Stephenson's wife, Margaret, was suffering from an unnamed illness that had kept her bedridden since the spring. Stephenson concluded that he and the country could get along quite well without doctors—and without the slippery predictions of meteorologists too.

Fortunately, Congressman Henry H. Paine was more than a politician. Paine had studied with Elias Loomis, a forerunner in the field of meteorology, while he was a student at Western Reserve College in Ohio. Paine valued the new scientists, especially Elias Loomis and Professor J. P. Espy who had made exhaustive studies of storm structures and movements. If not for his prior association with Loomis, Paine might have ignored the letter that came to him in 1869. The letter was sent from Increase Allen Lapham.

> *Milwaukee, Wis.*
> *December 8, 1869*

Dear Sir:

I take the liberty of calling your attention to the accompanying list of disasters to the commerce of our Great Lakes during the past year, and to ask whether its appalling magnitude does not make it the duty of the Government to see whether anything can be done to prevent, at least, some portion of this sad loss in the future.

> *Yours very truly,*
> *I. A. Lapham*

Increase Allen Lapham was devoted to the earth, and was perhaps one of the most outstanding scientists in American history. An engineer by trade, he acquired this skill at the age of sixteen under the tutelage of Byron Kilborn, a real estate agent for the Land Office in Wisconsin. Lapham's hunger for knowledge and his voracious reading led him to the study of geology, botany, and meteorology. He was determined to know every grain of sand, blade of grass, culvert, forest, river, and lake in Wisconsin. A Quaker canal builder and engineer from Palmyra, New York, the thirteenth of fifteen children of Seneca Lapham, he was as fascinated with the outdoors as Ogden had been as a boy. Like William Ogden, Lapham was also a visionary.

Ogden saw what could be built in the way of railroads and cities *on* the land while Lapham understood the land from the inside. Lapham was interested in determining how Wisconsin's, Michigan's, and Minnesota's plains, lakes, and forests—or the profligate waste of these—related to and changed the climate and surrounding atmosphere.

In 1844, Lapham had published the book *Wisconsin, Its Geography and Topography*, a work of such thoroughness and magnitude in the worlds of geology, geography, and botany that it garnered him the respect of the famous botanist Asa Gray at Harvard University.

When Gray wanted plant specimens, the world-renowned scientist sought out Lapham and Lapham provided them from his vast collection. Louis Agassiz, the famous naturalist who shared a place on Emerson's list of great men along with William Ogden, consulted Lapham as well. The literate immigrants who wanted to learn about the soil and land they were moving to wrote to Lapham ahead of their departure. "Where might I buy your *Lapham's Wisconsin?*" one immigrant wrote.

Lapham's letter to Painė also included the valuable information that would have shed light on the encroaching fires. Lapham sent Paine his full-length papers on fire, forests, climate, and storms and their subsequent effects on soil, erosion, shipwrecks, and sea level. Lapham's work was extensive and novel. Paine could not ignore the alarming facts of Lapham's studies. Lapham recognized the importance of Loomis's work and Espy's Law of Storms, which identified the characteristics of different kinds of storms. Not only were Espy's classifications useful, but Lapham determined that Espy's careful explanation of wind direction and speed would do much to help divert ships on the lakes and seas out of harm's way. Lapham also understood the importance of accurately measuring wind direction and speed with regard to fire.

After reading Lapham's work, Paine obtained permission to reprint the Lapham documents then forwarded copies of the documents as the proposed bill before Congress to the heads of the small existing weather service, Surgeon General J. K. Barnes and Professor Joseph Henry of the Smithsonian Institution in Washington, D.C. Paine promptly received a letter from Colonel Albert J. Myer, chief signal officer. Myer boldly made it known to Paine that if the resolution became law and an official agency was formed, he wanted to become its executive leader.

At last, Myer, the wandering "bureau chief without a bureau," saw an opening that seemed tailor-made for him. Cleveland Abbe, who was a good friend of Joseph Henry and had been working with Henry for the past three months creating forecast bulletins and weather maps from his observatory post in Cincinnati, also saw an opening for himself.

After studying and working in both Russia and at the United States Naval Observatory in Washington, D.C., Abbe concluded that astronomers who wanted to improve their measurements "must investigate their local atmospheric conditions more thoroughly, and to this end must have numerous surrounding meteorological observations."

By 1870, Abbe had worked tirelessly in a three-month trial period, during which he composed the first weather maps. Abbe's maps, however, did not include isobars (the lines on a weather map that link equal points of atmospheric pressure) or isotherms (the lines that link equal or constant temperature). Abbe needed a scientist versed in meteorology in order to make his case that civilian scientists should head the weather agency—and he needed someone who could redraw the maps. Abbe wrote to Lapham himself.

> *Cincinnati Observatory*
> *January 7, 1870*

Dear Sir:

    I must write to express the pleasure experienced in realizing the energy with which you are pushing the matter of a telegraphic meteorological system of storm warnings.

    My own labors in this field have been not perhaps so much for the good of the country and the advance of meteorology as for the sake of astronomy. . . . It would, I think, have been wiser if the bill had recommended that Congress appoint a committee of three (Henry, Coffin, and a naval or army officer) to report some plan of action. And I am specially of the opinion that the money expended would do more toward effecting good results if it goes through the hands of meteorologists and not through the hands of Army officers . . . it would be a pity to see the country saddled with an inefficient meteorological office as it has already enough to do to carry on the naval observatory with its present objectionable system of management. Every such onus is a hindrance to the progress of science in this country. . . . The daily weather bulletin that I have been publishing stops temporarily but will be resumed. I have sent a short notice of it to the Bureau.

Very respectfully yours,
Cleveland Abbe

But things turned out differently than Abbe thought they would. He believed Congressman Paine would choose either Lapham or him to head the agency. Abbe had made his mistrust and disdain for the Signal Service clear in his letter to Lapham. Paine surprised everyone. Dollars won out over science. Paine wrote that "his decision, requiring the Secretary of War to execute the law was this: it seemed to me at the outset, military discipline would probably secure the greatest promptness, regularity, and accuracy in the required observations."

"Military discipline" had far less to do with Paine's decision than the fact that soldiers were already on the government payroll. Hiring scientists would inflate the budget like a hot-air balloon. Then there was the matter of equipment, observation towers, and a dependable telegraph service that would not squeeze the government for more funding. Myer, who had already done time in dilapidated forts with used-up equipment, had proved he knew how to make do and keep a tight budget.

Therefore, under the auspices of the Department of War in cooperation with the Smithsonian Institution, General Albert Myer and General Henry Howgate became the chiefs of the budding weather agency. Joseph Henry was wise enough to choose Cleveland Abbe as his top assistant at the Smithsonian and Abbe in turn called upon Increase Lapham to aid him in making uniform maps and to analyze the reports from the observers that came through Milwaukee.

The result of these appointments was that the men who knew the most were not in the power positions. But Myer was happy. He was busy organizing and hiring observers, buying instruments, and negotiating with the telegraph companies to keep costs at a minimum. If it were up to him, Myer wanted to do without the weather prophets altogether, even though the New York *Herald* had taken a genuine and sustained interest in the probabilities issued by the prophets, and that both France and England were far in advance of American meteorology. Myer wrote to his observers that the "official deductions or forecasts to be had from the mass of reports received at different centers involves so much of responsibility, that while it has been considered, the office is not willing to enter upon it."

Lapham wanted the most accurate measuring equipment, especially barometers and anemometers. When he requested anemometers, he was told to "place a flag in the wind" to measure direction. On the subject of barometers, Lapham was told they were "too expensive."

All it took, however, was an onslaught of severe storms in November 1870 before Myer changed his tune and asked Lapham to be his assistant, supervising forecasts on the lakes under the title of assistant to the chief signal officer, at a salary of $167 per month. Lapham accepted the offer.

But there was a hitch. Myer wanted Lapham to perform his forecasting duties from Chicago and not from Lapham's hometown of Milwaukee. Chicago was—like New York, Cincinnati, Philadelphia, Galveston, and Washington, D.C.—outfitted with the best and most sophisticated equipment. Just as Chicago boasted of its extraordinary fire department, a department light-years ahead of the "pass the pail of water" method of putting out fires in the small villages and forests, it was also where the barometers, wet/dry bulbs, and anemometers Lapham so desperately needed were.

Lapham did not know that Myer's budget of $50,000 for 1870–71 was rapidly evaporating; the public was demanding more service from the Signal Corps and the telegraph company was not willing to give its services away for free. Myer did not want to use up any more money than he needed to. In the meantime, General Henry Howgate had his eyes and his pilfering fingers on the funds in the government till. Howgate was embezzling money. Some estimate he'd made off with a total of $237,000 by writing "fraudulent vouchers" over a period of many years, beginning with his position under Myer's command, which partly explains why salaries were stingy and money for new and better equipment never seemed as readily available as it should have been. Lapham removed to Chicago and immediately and without complaint fulfilled the duties assigned to him.

After he completed his duties, Lapham requested that he be allowed to return to Milwaukee. His wife, Ann, his sons, and his daughter Julia were there in the cottage he'd purchased ten years earlier. He had other business dealings there as well with members of the historical society; he'd founded a lyceum for discussing important scientific discoveries.

Myer remained firm. Lapham took it upon himself to travel to Washington, D.C., to plead his case with Myer in private. After the meeting, Lapham wrote to his daughter.

> *Washington, D.C.*
> *February 3, 1871*
>
> *Dear Julia:*
>   I dined last night with General Myer at his home on I
> Street. Have arranged matters satisfactorily—am not to be
> ordered to Chicago anymore.

Somehow Lapham understood that it was fine with Myer that he
remain in Milwaukee now. From that post Lapham assumed he
would continue his duties and be given even more work. It never
occurred to him that Myer would begin to phase him out and make
Milwaukee far less important than it had been up to this point.
Lapham was too distracted to sense the undercurrent.

Lapham's defining work, titled *Report on the Disastrous Effects of
the Destruction of Forest Trees Now Going On in the State of Wisconsin*
and published in 1867, should have made Myer far more amenable
to Lapham's desire to stay in Milwaukee. He was a twentieth-
century thinker trapped in the nineteenth century, writing well in
advance of the development of the internal combustion engine and
the modern world's dependence on fossil fuels:

> On this question of fuel, we are to calculate by ages of the
> Earth, and not by the life of man. Fuel will be required so
> long as man shall inherit the Earth, for his comfort and for
> existence. Without fuel, humanity would cease to exist.
> Viewed in this light, the deposits laid up during uncounted
> periods of time . . . in the shape of coal, petroleum and peat,
> and which man is now drawing out and using for fuel or wast-
> ing, must be exhausted.

Lapham pointed out that there were important lessons in history's errors. "Both past history and present experience show that a
country destitute of forests as well as one entirely covered by them

is only suited to the conditions of a barbarous or semi-barbarous people."

Having Lapham happy and well-supplied in Milwaukee, or paying him enough to have made a permanent move to Chicago with his family worthwhile, might have helped alert Myer, Robinson, and Howgate to the fire's ravages. Or perhaps not.

Myer, Howgate, and Robinson were working out of the old order or paradigm regarding fire and weather. Unfortunately, in 1871, fire would have to define itself in a catastrophic way, be experienced or "conceptualized" differently before anyone sought to revolutionize their attitudes and practices toward it or meteorology.

Green Bay & Marinette
STEAMBOAT LINE.

The staunch little Steamer
U N I O N

Plies regularly, tri-weekly between Green Bay and
Marinette, touching at Pensaukee, Oconto, Peshtigo
and Menominee, during the season of navigation, as
follows:

Leaves Marinette, Mondays, Wednesdays and Fridays, and Green Bay Tuesdays, Thursdays and Sat-
urdays.

Her running time is as follows:

Leaves Hamilton & Merryman's Dock, Marinette,	6.30 A.M.	
" Kirby & Carpenter's Dock, Me-nominee,	7.00 "	
" Peshtigo,	9.00 "	
" Oconto,	10.00 "	
" Pensaukee,	11.00 "	
Arrives in Green Bay, at	1.30 P.M.	

R E T U R N I N G

Leaves Green Bay,	8.30 A.M.
" Pensaukee,	11.00 "
" Oconto,	12.30 P.M.
" Peshtigo,	2.00 "
Arrives at Menominee,	3.30 "
" Marinette,	4:00 "

THOMAS HAWLEY, Captain,
A. PINTO, Clerk.

HAMILTON & MERRYMAN, Agents at Marinette.

On October 4, 1871, Increase Lapham's Casual Phenomena Sheet (the appendix observers attached to their official reports noting any unusual atmospheric activity) reported: "Smoky. Great fires at the north for several days past." On October 5, Lapham added in his scratchy cursive, "Fires all the way from Lake Michigan to Dakota Territory." The temperatures were taken three times a day in open air and then taken again with wet/dry bulbs in order to measure relative humidity. On October 5, temperatures were within normal range, but Lapham left his wind direction and velocity columns blank. He did record the barometric pressure, however.

In Chicago on the same dates, Sam Brookes, the weather observer located at 53 Clark Street, did not include the barometric pressure in his readings, but he noted both the velocity and the direction of the winds. On the morning of October 4, the winds were coming out of the northwest. By late afternoon they had shifted and were flowing in a northeasterly direction. On October 5 they blew northeast but with steadily increasing velocity throughout the day and were clocked at 25 miles per hour by nine that night. A storm was brewing. Brookes described cumulus clouds on his accompanying phenomena sheet, but he did not write a detailed description of their shapes. Cumulus clouds, especially when they form the shape of an anvil, are associated with thunderheads and tornadoes. The atmosphere, Brookes wrote, was "warm and hazy."

Myer was headquartered in Washington, D.C., and Superintendent G. H. Bliss was in Chicago. From their vantage point the forest was still a wilderness full of slash, tamarack, and pine, an image that did not include houses, livestock, farms—or people. It's not that they didn't know there were families and busy lumber towns between Green Bay and Escanaba, and it was not that they did not care. For them, the fact that the telegraph lines were down took precedence over the weather and fire. To Myer and Bliss the woods were the outback full of inexhaustible acres of trees, a place where there were always fires, a place as remote and startlingly different from their respective civilized cities as another planet.

On the same evening Superintendent Robinson had first telegraphed his superior, General Albert Myer, a long, detailed weather report published on October 3, 1871, in the St. Paul *Pioneer.* The report appeared under this alarming heading: PRAIRIES IN FLAMES: ONE HUNDRED AND FIFTY MILES SWEPT BY FIRE—MEN, WOMEN, AND CHILDREN FLEEING FOR THEIR LIVES—IMMENSE LOSS OF PROPERTY OF ALL KINDS.

The Minnesota fires had begun on the western border of that state during the last week in September, at precisely the same time fires were worsening in Peshtigo and Marinette. According to reports, these fires were exhibiting similar behavior: leaping roads, burning underground, curling back on themselves, rolling along at frightening speed. The fires would have seemed a galaxy away from each other except for the fact that the "Big Woods" traversed the entire northern section of Minnesota, just as they did in Wisconsin and Michigan. At the time of the report, the Minnesota fires were being fed by winds from the west traveling in a northeastern direction. The *Pioneer* reporter wrote, "They did not calculate upon the force of the coming whirlwind of fire . . . the flames spread upward with the fleetness of the wind . . . and will probably sweep far northward unless a providential rain puts a stop to its ravages."

The weather report from Galveston, Texas, published October 3, 1871, expressed both delight and surprise that the weather prophets had been correct in predicting a violent storm with gg, or great gale, winds and voluminous rainfall. The "terrific" storm that had just subsided "was preceded by all three general premonitions and followed the general law literally and to the very letter."

The wind from the storm in Texas would make its way north toward Michigan, Minnesota, and Wisconsin. Topography, wind, and humidity in an unusual combination in a specific locale will create what is known as "atmospheric instability," which in turn affects the path and far-reaching trajectory of a fire in progress. Such instability can sweep separate smaller fires into one large catastrophic blaze.

J. P. Espy's Law of Storms defined the varieties of winds and their movement, and that week several newspapers had published part 4 of Espy's law, but Luther Noyes did not choose to publish it in the *Eagle*; Tilton's Green Bay *Advocate* published the abridged version of the law on October 5, 1871.

Espy divided storms visiting the United States into four types: cyclones, rainstorms, northern snowstorms, and tornadoes. The West India cyclones begin beyond the West India Islands, then move toward and pass across the Gulf of Mexico, and across Texas before traveling northward to the lakes and then eastward off the Atlantic coast.

Rainstorms of autumn, winter, and spring usually originate in the southwest plains across the Mississippi and move eastward across the lakes and eastern seaboard states.

Occasional rare disturbances characterized by snow succeeded by dry, cold weather occurring midwinter are caused by exceptionally strong northeast winds and high pressure.

And lastly, Espy classified thunderstorms, northers, and tornadoes as those storm systems generally confined within the United States. The important feature of these types of storms is that they are extremely limited in area and are dependent upon local currents. They originate in intense local differences of temperature, moisture, and pressure.

Lapham understood that Espy's second type of storm—the West India cyclones—and his fourth type—which included tornadoes—are not separate classes of storms. Both come under the heading of large atmospheric circulation systems, which include small cyclones, larger and fiercer tropical cyclones, and tornadoes.

A forest fire's behavior is connected to these storm systems. When a fire rages out of control its behavior will mimic the dynamics of this large circulation family. There is one important difference between the dynamics of a storm system and the dynamics of fire. Cyclones, hurricanes, tornadoes, and waterspouts are formed, maintained, driven, and defined by one source of energy: the latent heat produced by the amount of available moisture.

In a fire, the speed and force of the flames are driven by the release of heat during combustion, which is the *absence* of moisture. In other words, in a large fire there are two systems operating: the fire itself and the wind it creates. The bigger the fire, the bigger the wind; the bigger the wind, the bigger the fire, in a cycle that will not stop until all combustible matter in its path—trees, vegetation, houses, animals, people—is consumed.

Lapham later found fault with only one of Espy's theories, which stated that fire could produce rain and lightning. Espy mistakenly thought this weather phenomenon was possible because rain often followed a large blaze. What Lapham realized is that a storm and a fire could occur together and that a lightning strike, heralding a storm, could also ignite a dry forest. However, the rain Espy thought came *from* the fire was actually the rain being held in check and suspended inside the clouds, pushed up by the rising convection columns *during* the fire.

The irony is that while the railroad magnates, lumbermen, and loggers had little use for scientific theory, they did choose to believe this one incorrect point in Espy's law because it suited their purposes. They would not have to stop using fire; perhaps the more fire they made, the better the chances there would be rain.

A large fire creates its own weather in the form of winds, but a wildfire does not produce rain. Instead, in the absence of moisture, both the wind and the fire feed each other, growing more intense and creating an even greater unpredictable level of atmospheric instability.

And when this system encounters a change in topography—like the tall wooden buildings of Chicago or the towering trees of Peshtigo—the chemistry of the fire changes yet again. They did not know it then, but the fire sweeping along with amazing speed on flatland or prairie, as it was in Minnesota, would reach dangerous proportions when the terrain changed markedly from flatland to mountains, or from flatland to a sharp rise, or from flatland to a depression such as a culvert or canyon. The wind driving the flames converges with the wind coming in from behind a ridge or a dense stand of trees, so that when they meet, a vortex or multiple vortices are created. These vortices lead to fire whirls, fire tornadoes, and the most violent of all, firestorms. Of the three, the fire whirl rotates at 22 to 67 miles per hour. The fire tornado, like a true tornado, can average up to one thousand feet in diameter and rotates at speeds up to 90 miles per hour.

Wind's most consistent feature is its inconsistency; it is mutable, able to shift from a light breeze to a great gale when it encounters an unexpected front, shear, wave, or significant change in topography. Therefore, wind and fire are equal sharers in their infinite capacities to destroy.

Yet, two days after the report in the St. Paul *Pioneer*, regardless of the encroaching Minnesota fires, the smoke, or the storm system traveling up from the Gulf, General Myer's second in command, General Henry W. Howgate, sent a message to Superintendent Robinson in Milwaukee:

> Washington, D.C.
> October 5, 1871
> TO: Mr. S. Robinson. Supt., N.W. Telegraph Co.,
> Milwaukee
>
> Please discontinue sending reports from Milwaukee to Marquette until the line is in good working order again. Let the Marquette and Escanaba reports come this way as usual whenever they can be got through.
>
> H. W. Howgate, S.O.

Howgate then followed up with yet another more general message to the "observers." Presently there were a total of sixty-two observation sites, among them Cairo, Illinois; Galveston, Texas; Louisville, Kentucky; Omaha, Nebraska; Chicago, Illinois; and two of the most important, the observatory at Cincinnati, Ohio, and the site in Leavenworth, Kansas, not far from the town of Lawrence, which is the location in the United States where warm and cold fronts meet, making the United States singularly vulnerable to the widest range of weather patterns in the world. The warm front from Galveston was traveling northward as a cold front from Canada was moving south. Given their geographical location, Peshtigo and Chicago were especially vulnerable to the meeting of both fronts.

Howgate was brief.

Washington, D.C.
October 5, 1871
TO: Observers at Marquette and Escanaba

You will not receive any reports from Milwaukee until wire
is working well again. File your reports at the regular hours.

H. W. Howgate, S.O.
ASO and Asst.

Fire had eaten up both the railroad ties and the telegraph lines between Green Bay and Marinette, but Robinson never asked for help and Howgate did not even ask about the fire conditions. The first line of defense against the fire—telegraphic communication— had collapsed. Fire had successfully isolated the north woods from the rest of the nation.

N. LUDINGTON COMPANY

A. C. BROWN, Superintendent.

———o—o———

At their store in Marinette Wisconsin, keep a full stock of

DRY GOODS, GROCERIES, PROVISIONS, CLOTH, HATS, CAPS, CLOTHING, BOOTS AND SHOES, HARDWARE,

And in fact everything needed in a family, or usually found in a general supply store, and at prices as low as any dealers selling as good quality of goods.

———o———

Our stock of

CALICOS and DELAINES,

Ladies' Dress Goods, White Goods, &c.,

IS FULL AND COMPLETE,

All of which will be sold at the

LOWEST CASH PRICES.

8

By six o'clock on the morning of Friday, October 6, the towns of Peshtigo and Marinette were at full-throttle commotion. The mill at the Peshtigo Harbor spat steam amid the shouts of the workers and the deafening sound of the saws and the filers. The construction crews pounded the residents awake with their cutting and hammering. The sun was out, the day was warm but not unusually so, and everyone had their handkerchiefs ready to shield themselves from the smoke. A portion of the oppressive smoke was not Wisconsin's own, but the fast-moving smoke from the Minnesota fires, traveling eastward.

Although they'd been burning for more than a week, by Friday, October 6, the fires in Minnesota had not abated at all. Flames had hit the timber stands in the Big Woods "with unabashed fury" and had reached not only north but as "far south as the Iowa border, and eastward as far as the Minnesota River." High winds on October 5 had driven "the fire forward with lightning rapidity and it was burning fiercely in the Big Woods around Glencoe, Leseni, Mankato and New Ulm." The Minnesota reporter who was stunned by the scope of the fire and at a loss accounting for its intensity or strange behavior—hurling embers, leaping creeks, seeming to come in from two directions at once—finally just dismissed what he thought was incomprehensible. He wrote that these reports were "evidently exaggerated."

———

THE GREEN BAY and Marinette Steamboat Line was preparing to leave from the Hamilton & Merryman dock. The "tramway" was now repaired. The steamer, *Union*, navigated by Captain Thomas Hawley left the docks at six-thirty A.M. on Mondays, Wednesdays, and Fridays. It would reach Peshtigo by nine after it stopped at the Kirby-Carpenter dock in Menominee, so that by one-thirty that Friday afternoon, its horn would be sounding as it approached the smoky docks in Green Bay.

Luther Noyes placed an advertisement for help in the *Eagle* asking for a "good, smart, intelligent, industrious boy between 12 and 15 years of age to learn the Printing Business." Noyes's son Frank would be going off to Milton Academy in November and Noyes would need someone to fill Frank's place. When the paper found its way into the homes of Peshtigo and Marinette's residents on Saturday, the people would not find any warning that they should leave immediately, only that prayers for rain should be continued.

Father Peter Pernin did not want anyone's prayers interrupted, but they were going to be. He stood outside his church building where he and several men had removed the altar and all the pews and set them out in the yard. The workmen were scheduled to arrive on Monday, October 9, to spread a fine coat of white plaster across the new building's rough interior walls. "Marble dust and lime were lying ready in front of the building," he wrote.

Pernin had already informed his Peshtigo parishioners that because the church building was quite literally inside-out, he would not be saying Mass there on Sunday as he usually did. Pernin's plan was to skip services at Peshtigo and hold Mass in Cedar River. Cedar River was situated on Green Bay about four or five miles north of Marinette. Pernin had just finished building a new presbytery in Marinette next to his church, a building he planned to live in while he built yet another house there that would serve as a Catholic school. Like others who lived in Marinette and Peshtigo, Pernin also was enjoying Eden's prosperity. The priest's reward did not come in the form of money; it came instead in spiritual currency, from the willing Catholics among the scores of French-speaking immigrants and the French-speaking Indians who had abandoned their tribal rituals and converted to Catholicism in the north woods.

Pernin, a small, dark-eyed man with a faint smile and softness around the mouth, was born in France in 1825. He had arrived in Marinette in 1871, appointed by the archbishop of the diocese of Montreal, after serving in Oconto in 1870 and at parishes in L'Érable, Quebec, and Clifton, Illinois, from 1865 to 1869.

That Friday morning Father Pernin was waging an internal war between intellect and instinct. "On one side, the thick smoke darkening the sky . . . seemed to afford grounds for fear in case of a sudden gale." Instinct capitulated to reason. Pernin said, "Reason assured me there was no more cause for present fear than there had been eight or fifteen days before."

In Pernin's and nearly every other account of the two days immediately before the fire, and during it, every survivor mentions that he or she was expecting not just a stiff wind, or a strong wind, but a "gale." These residents had not built "storm cellars" to protect themselves against a fresh breeze, and they certainly did not build them as protection from a forest fire. They had built them from experience, from having already survived a Wisconsin tornado by hiding out underground until it passed.

Increase Lapham had already explained at length and in'great detail the treacherous wind patterns of Wisconsin, Illinois, and Kansas, which collectively might be called the tornado trio. In October 1871, if a tornado were brewing—it was the right season and Brookes's description of the clouds at least suggests the possibility—even if the Signal Service knew it, Lapham was forbidden to utter it. The reason for this panic over the word was that the press had created more problems than it was worth with their misuse of it. Reporters, aiming for drama, assigned the word to any gusty wind that blew. For these reasons, General Myer and Joseph Henry made it clear that the word was never to be used publicly. The Palmer Drought Severity Index (PDSI), which properly records the gradations of drought showing the "supply and demand concept of the regional water balance equation," did not exist yet. If it had, the PDSI would have indicated only dry conditions but not a full-scale drought.

The question then becomes: If not lack of rain then what had dried the land? It was wind, both the cold dry winds of the preceding winter, which had passed with less than average snowfall, and the dry sirocco-like winds of late summer. Both of these prevailing winds, combined with many days of solar radiation on a landscape that was being denuded rapidly had done more to alter the atmospheric conditions, change the soil moisture content, and dry the marshes than lack of rainfall alone. Presently, the winds and drying smoke blowing off the Minnesota plains were the fire's true accomplices.

＊

ABRAM PLACE WAS not going to ruminate long. He decided to move on instinct and good advice. He wondered why the Catholic

Menominee had not advised their priest the way the Chippewa had been advising him to prepare for a violent conflagration.

Other than Walter Newberry, a farmer, Abram Place owned more land in Peshtigo than anyone, a total of eight hundred acres. The fierce-looking bearded Vermonter had come to Peshtigo in 1838 and he married John Lawe's widow. John Lawe, along with John Jacobs and William Farnsworth, had been among the first settlers along the Menominee in its fur-trading days. At that time marriages between a white man and an Indian woman were rarely marriages of the heart. These were marriages of barter: fur in exchange for land, corn in exchange for fur. When either the Indian or the white settler had gotten what they wanted, the marriage was dissolved. Dissolution was simple; it involved walking to the magistrate's office and asking him to rip up the paper that stated a marriage had taken place. Sometimes the ending was even simpler than that, a decision made when two men decided to board a canoe or sit by the fire and "share a pipe of high wine."

Lawe had married a Chippewa native and after his death, Abram Place, who had always kept friendly relations with his Indian neighbors, married Therese Lawe. Unlike many of the white settlers, though, his marriage to Therese was as solid as their two-story frame house with its many windows and covered porch. Theirs was a graceful house, more elaborate than most, with a brick chimney rising off the back wall and two one-story extensions on either side of the main bay. There was even a small plain-columned portico over its front door. The house sat back from the road. Tall spruce and pine, stately as sentinels, rose along its frontage. The Place homestead was fenced in all around in white pine zigzag.

Although Place was a wealthy landowner, he also worked as a jobber for the Peshtigo Company. He welcomed any and all of the Indian tribes into his home, but the people of Peshtigo had mixed feelings toward Place. They disapproved of his real marriage to an

Indian woman, and when they saw Place and his sons raking up leaves and debris or plowing three-foot-deep trenches around his house and barns, their curiosity was not aroused but their disapproval hardened. They found it difficult to embrace Place's willingness to take the word of his Chippewa in-laws. Then they decided that Place had gathered secrets from them he was not prepared to share.

Place was merely creating a firebreak. The cleared trenches were designed to stop an approaching fire. By removing the dried leaves and twigs, Place was also removing fuel. Digging the trenches deep enough removed the chalky soil and exposed the moist layers beneath it. The moist soil, devoid of fuel, would stop the fire at the perimeter of the trench.

Place made no apologies. Yes, his Indian in-laws had told him to wet down blankets and cover the house and outbuildings with them, but Place could not help it if people observing his precautions were too stubborn and too judgmental to follow suit.

━

AS TWILIGHT DESCENDED over the city of Chicago on Friday evening, its fire department, which consisted of 185 men working seventeen steam pumper fire engines, had just extinguished its twenty-ninth fire of the week. History and myth often tell it differently: that all was well until suddenly, on October 8, a poor thirty-five-year-old Irish woman, a cow, a barn, and a kerosene lantern collided on De Koven Street, turning a city of overwrought buildings, rivers, mansions, shanties, and parks that housed 334,000 residents into an inferno.

Nothing so horrible happens so simply.

Superintendent Bliss was no longer sending messages north from his Chicago office or receiving any from Escanaba, Marinette, or

Peshtigo. However, between Chicago and Peshtigo, Green Bay was rimmed in glaring orange. Just south of that city, residents of Kewaunee and Brown Counties were beating back fires. On the western shore, fires insistently swiped at the houses and barns; on the eastern shores, Williamsonville and New Franken were being charred from the spot fires erupting on the stump-filled fields and in the trees.

Franklin Tilton stood outside the *Advocate* offices in Green Bay and looked around him at the night sky. "It was as if there were not one—but two sunsets," he'd written. All horizons, including Chicago's, were a vast neon sky scape. Tilton's language changed from lyrical to blunt: "The sky was brass; the earth was ashes."

The weather map published by the United States Department of Agriculture shows quite plainly the cyclonic storm swirling about the country, with a clearly defined low-pressure system out of the southwest from Galveston and a catalytic cold front veering down from Canada.

                    ➤

WILLIAM OGDEN'S GREAT city was simmering, but he was far removed from it and his public life there. The people of Chicago had not forgiven him for leaving this place where he and two other members of the Board of Sewers had enlisted engineer Ellis Sylvester Chesborough in 1855 and found a way to alleviate the city's drainage problem by reversing the flow of the Chicago River. Ogden had left the city where his barges and tugs transported lumber and woodenware from Peshtigo to the yards at Peshtigo Court.

Tonight the Ogden mansion on Ontario Street was dark, its long glass windows blind. In cool weather the four acres of trees surrounding the house were buffers against the winds. The leaves had fallen; the grounds and the gutters along the street were clogged with dried twigs. For years the groundskeeper, Thomas Kelly, had tended to the vast array of ornamental shrubs. He kept the graveled drive smooth and white, and when the "tours" came through on horse-drawn carriages, Kelly was proud to show off the conservatory of hothouse fruits and flowers. Few people saw Ogden in private moments, but Kelly had caught glimpses of his employer from time to time. He had seen Ogden fawning over his cultivated grapes. Ogden handled the Miller's Cluster, fine, small grapes with the tenderest vines, as he might have handled a delicate child.

In seasons past, the house had swelled with guests of great distinction, Daniel Webster among them. It had been a gathering place for great conversation and no excess. Good wine, but not too much, was served at dinner.

Ogden had married at last, a New York woman. He had turned over the management of his business dealings to others. Ogden was confident that on October 12, when Ike Stephenson was scheduled to travel to Green Bay, this time the meeting over the Sturgeon Bay Canal project would fare better than it had in the past.

From his windows at Boscobel, Ogden could see Washington Heights in the distance. He was dreaming up a new vision, one that made people raise an eyebrow. What about a *different* kind of train, he'd suggested to his niece, Anna Ogden West, one that ran beneath the ground through a network of dark tunnels? His mind raced with the idea. The New York subway system, that's what he was conjuring in 1871.

Whenever Ogden did return to his home, Ogden Grove, Chicagoans were in the habit of setting huge bonfires to greet him. That night, if Ogden had suddenly appeared in Chicago, lighting a bonfire for him would have been more dangerous than lighting matches in a house of wax.

NEW
DRUGSTORE

—— o ——

J. J. SHERMAN

Keeps constantly on hand a good supply of

Drugs and Medicines

Hair Oils, Perfumery, and Fancy Articles, Combs, Brushes, Pocket Cut-
lery, School Books and Stationery, Wire Gauze for
Doors and Windows

Also a general Assortment of

PATENT MEDICINES,

And all other articles generally found in a first class
Drug Store. Prescriptions carefully compounded
and medicines warranted.

Agent for Howe's Sewing Machine, Chap-
man's Soda Fount, and General Insu-
rance Agent.

9

The winds turned at 7:00 A.M. on Saturday, October 7. They were coming from the southwest and would continue flowing in from that direction, arrows simultaneously shot from a bow, sailing over the landscape, striking Chicago, New Franken, Williamsonville, the Sugar Bushes, Peshtigo, Marinette, and Menekaune.

Increase Lapham was not subtle when he called the southwest wind "the scourge of God" because of the damage it could do once it gathered momentum. There is no record of the wind speed or direction in Milwaukee that morning, only a record of the falling barometer, but on the weather map the isobars were tightly packed and curved, which meant a gale was forming with a strengthening speed and rotation.

In Chicago Sam Brookes went to the roof of his observation site on Clark Street. There the wind hit the anemometer cups and spun them; it was moving at 2 miles per hour or "a very light breeze," just enough to rustle the leaves in the gutters, to lift the hem of a lace curtain at an open window, or catch the hot embers from a man's cigar or a spark from the coal yards. The light breeze floated embers to the parched branches of the trees in Lincoln Park.

The same southwest breeze traveled northeasterly and wafted into Peshtigo. David Maxon shivered. He was at home with his family in their house next to the Peshtigo Company store where he was employed. Maxon and his wife had had high fevers all week. Maxon was dehydrated, but his wife was in worse shape, unable to get out of bed. Nothing seemed to break her fever and he wondered if the single case of typhoid Noyes had mentioned and stuffed in a small corner of the *Eagle* was spreading through the town. When he felt the breeze through the boards and windows of his house he was aware of its direction and he shivered again, but this time it was not from fever as much as it was from dread; he could not think of how he'd summon the energy for an escape if that breeze became a gale.

While the Maxons were too ill to talk or come up with a plan, C. R. Towsley and his wife, who owned a farm in the Lower Bush, had suddenly become philosophical that Saturday. Towsley was certain fire was on its way and he wanted a plan of action. The Towsleys had four children. That morning, the youngest was cuddled against his mother's breast, nursing. Mrs. Towsley's rocking chair thumped against the rough floorboards. She had a Bible open in her lap while she rocked.

"Do you think God would have brought us here to abandon us?" she asked.

He was as religious a man as any of the faithful in Peshtigo, but he was not stupid, "What if it's not up to God?"

God had brought a lot of people to this "wilderness," as his wife had put it. C. R. Towsley was certain that escape from a fire was man's burden, not God's.

A god would have been the only power that could stop the fire. Man could not reverse the counterclockwise rotation of the cyclonic storm as it grew stronger throughout the day; he could not have erected a barrier to the wind; he could not push back the cold front that was bearing down from the north.

In 1871, people used the terms *forest fire*, *prairie fire*, and *hearth fire*. They did not have specific words for the variety of phenomena such as "gustnadoes," crown fire, fire devil, controlled fire, backburn, fire whirl, ten o'clock fire, and blowup.

The Peshtigo fire was the ultimate mixed metaphor: a flamethrower, a monster, a giant, a fiend, a tempest arriving on waves, wings, columns, and plumes and always more beautiful than, faster than, fiercer than, hotter than the mind can fathom. A firestorm. Nothing compares to the extreme violence of a firestorm, and no other fire exhibits more unpredictable and outrageous behavior during which superheated flames of at least 2,000 degrees Fahrenheit (the temperature of a crematorium) advance on winds of 110 miles per hour or stronger. The diameter of such a fire ranges from one thousand to ten thousand feet—three to thirty-three football fields wide. When a firestorm erupts in a forest, it is a blowup, nature's nuclear explosion, generating the same heat and devastating power as an atomic bomb. The only precedent for a fire of such magnitude, the only frame of reference for a firestorm, was the Great Fire of London in 1666.

Most fires are containable, controllable; few ever reach dangerous proportions. In a firestorm, size is not as important as intensity, unpredictability, and the kaleidoscopic effects produced from such extremes of heat and movement. A firestorm's operatic voice displays incredible range, from the barely audible soft crackle to the roar. Its choreography is multipatterned; it slinks, streams, shoots, vibrates, marches, pitches, bursts, stalks, and rolls forward, upward, backward, and in circles. Because it is blind and deaf, it cannot be trusted to make distinctions, will not see or hear the pain of children, the cries of women, the shouts of men. A firestorm knows no empathy, only hunger—and never thirst. Wind is the invisible bully at its back, whipping flames into a frenzy of lusty gorging. It must eat and cannot get enough and the more food it consumes the hotter and more passionate it becomes. It cannot contain itself and blows its volatile, noxious breath sky-high in whirring convection columns as the cold air rushes in at its feet, pumping its overheated, bloated belly full of hot air upward. Sand will feed it, bark, kerosene, hay, sawdust, clothes, coal, leaves, wooden buildings, trees, flesh. Anything combustible will do. Staying alive is all that matters for a firestorm.

AT FOUR O'CLOCK on Saturday afternoon, Captain Hawley's steamer was making its regularly scheduled return trip from Green Bay. Hawley was carrying fifty to one hundred Scandinavian immigrants on board. Hawley docked at Peshtigo Harbor with difficulty because by late afternoon the winds were blowing more strongly, and no one could see more than a rod, or just over sixteen feet, in front of him. The newcomers stepped off the steamer onto the tramway, struggling for breath. Their eyes smarted. All around them flakes of ashes sifted down through the scrim of smoke. The atmosphere had been the same in Green Bay when they boarded the *Union*. Some were met by relatives who'd convinced them to come here and who greeted them at the dock to help haul their trunks and bags home.

When these foreigners looked around they saw life pulsing. Children were playing. Businesses were open as usual. That night at the Peshtigo House the railroad gangs would drink to John Mulligan, who'd won in a boxing match at the railroad site the night before. The loggers would make their way into town as usual, their mackinaws flapping open, their boots sounding out a staccato beat against the boards.

The people of Peshtigo could not see the vast area of burning, the sleeping giant stirring, stretching itself from Chicago to Michigan.

On that Saturday afternoon in Peshtigo, no one could see his next-door neighbor's face, let alone the landscape south and north of him. They saw embers dropping at a fantastic rate. Grit that looked like black snow. An *Advocate* correspondent would write: "If you suppose the worst snow storm you ever witnessed, and each snow-flake a coal or spark driven before a fierce wind you have some idea of the state of the atmosphere at the time the fire struck the town."

Still, as loggers, railroad men, shopkeepers, and farmers, they stayed.

~

LORENZO AND HARLEY Race tried to convince their father, Martin, that they should leave their home in Middle Bush. Lorenzo was twenty-two years old and had just bought himself the Elton Francour farm as an investment. His seventeen-year-old brother, Harley, worked at the Peshtigo sawmill. They had two younger siblings: Charley, who had just turned thirteen, and their sister Ida, nine years old. Neither Martin Race nor his wife, Almira, wanted to hear any talk of leaving. Almira Race did not alter one of her daily chores or habits that Saturday. People in the Bushes depended on her. She was ten years younger than her husband, a woman of many talents who acted as midwife, nurse to the sick, and preparer of the dead for burial. When she was not caring for her own or her neighbor's children and family members, Almira found time to teach reading to the children who were not able to attend one of the three Red schools. With the threat of catastrophe so present, she may have thought staying put to be of service to her neighbors was the best recourse. She had no reason to believe that the fire or a tornado, if they came, would be any worse than the other forest fires or tornadoes she'd seen in her life.

Almira Race felt safe enough. Martin had allowed Lorenzo and Harley to fill the troughs with water and put ladders into the well, even though Martin remained adamant about staying on the farm. Martin Race told his sons that if God wanted him then so be it; if it was his time to die, he would not fight it.

By late afternoon the railroad gang at Mulligan's camp near the McGregor farm had quit work for the day and were heading off into town for drinks. Earlier in the week John McGregor had plowed the "whole triangle from the railroad grade to his south and east lines." On Saturday he had stocked barrels of water from their dug well and had made certain that ladders were leaning against each of the cedar-shingled buildings. Mary had stocked the storm cellar with bedding, water, and food should a storm kick up, forcing them to spend the night there. Late in the day, John went out to the storm cellar to throw soil up around the ventilator flue, but he was discouraged. The soil was so dry it simply rolled off.

As the new immigrants found their way through the streets of Peshtigo, Father Pernin was preparing to leave the town and head up to Cedar River where he'd promised the Catholics he would say Mass on Saturday night. Pernin rode his horse out of Peshtigo following Old Peshtigo Road and made it as far as the wharf at Menominee, where he planned to board the *Dunlap* and travel by boat to Cedar River. Pernin waited for hours on the wharf as the afternoon faded away. He had never known the steamer to be off schedule. The *Dunlap* never arrived. The thick blanket of smoke obscured the glow from the lighthouse on Green Island four miles off the shore of Marinette.

Samuel Peter Drew was the lighthouse keeper on Green Island. During the navigation season members of the Drew family could be spotted traveling to the mainland in a small sailboat. Sometimes they came for a weekend visit. At other times, especially when lighthouse duties and the school year collided, Samuel Drew made extra trips so his children could attend school.

While Peter Pernin waited by the wharf, the Drews were in their two-room house next to the large lighthouse station. That day Samuel Drew kept the lighthouse lit even in daylight, but the fourth-order lens could not cut through the smoke. The *Dunlap* was out in the waters of Green Bay, searching for the lighted beacon.

Finally, Pernin gave up hope of making it to Cedar River and rode back into Peshtigo. He decided that he could offer Mass in his own home next to the church if he composed a makeshift altar in one of his rooms. After that was accomplished, Pernin thought he could make his way back to Marinette to chant vespers there and then say high Mass in Peshtigo on Sunday morning.

For the second time that week Pernin's plans changed. He wrote that several of his parishioners "strongly opposed" his leaving Peshtigo. "I deemed it best to yield to the representations made me and remain where I was." Pernin ended up staying where he normally would not have been but he said, "God willed that I should be at the post of danger."

GEORGE W. WATSON, a resident of Green Bay, was not staying put on Saturday. Accompanied by his friend G. A. Lawson, a banker, he set out from Green Bay on a thirty-six-mile drive to Kewaunee. Rather than driving a wagon, they traveled by buckboard with a pair of horses. Watson planned to visit with his sister and brother-in-law, Willard Lamb, in New Franken, which was on the way to Kewaunee on the Kewaunee–Door County Peninsula. Watson's brother-in-

law Lamb owned most of the property in the town that had been
settled by Bavarians in 1845. Now the settlement had a boardinghouse, a mill, a company store, a post office, a blacksmith shop, and
even a schoolhouse. Watson's sister was well provided for. Her husband had built her a two-story house and Watson was looking forward to the midday meal of roast goose he and Lawson would enjoy
once they arrived in New Franken.

Watson's sister did prepare a satisfying meal, but she seemed
especially jumpy as they ate. Her husband was not at home and her
father was "exhausted by being up nearly all the time, night and day,
for nearly two weeks previous." The elder Watson was being kept
awake by fire watches, Watson's sister explained. She was worried
there would be more. Watson assured her that after the meal he and
Lawson would go have a look-see at these "fires" to be sure they
were not threatening Willard Lamb's mill.

Lamb's mill produced both lumber and shingles. Watson was
proud of the fact that his brother-in-law had been a pioneer lumberman, turning the thickly wooded area into a fine thriving village.
Willard Lamb's men obviously respected him and felt compelled to
protect their source of income. They had been guarding the mill
area for weeks. When Watson and Lawson arrived there to chat,
they were told that the fires had often sprouted up "alarmingly" but
they now had everything under control. Watson was satisfied. He
and Lawson climbed onto their buckboard and continued on their
way to Kewaunee.

Watson's drive was filled with the unexpected. Several times
flames darted across his path. On either side of the road Watson was
stunned to see ruins instead of houses, shells of smoky and abandoned dwellings, fences destroyed. In Kewaunee a man named
Drecker explained that the small hamlets Watson had passed
through had been burning off and on for weeks. Now, Drecker said,
he had just got word that the town of Casco and a mill there had

been demolished by flame. There was another fourteen miles to travel before they would reach Casco, so Watson and Lawson spent the night of October 7 with Drecker, hoping that the destruction of Casco was merely a rumor. In the morning they planned to ride into Casco with Drecker and see for themselves.

—→

BY NINE P.M. on October 7, except for the rowdy drinkers at the Peshtigo House, at John McLennan's billiard hall in Marinette, at P. Jordan's tavern Briney's, the towns of Peshtigo and Marinette fell into a restive sleep. Denial and foreboding were the townspeople's contradictory bedfellows that night. Caught between the desire to stay and the impulse to leave, they slept.

They slept unaware that as their night passed safely in Peshtigo, south of them in Chicago the call boxes were ringing for the thirtieth time. On Chicago's west side another fire broke out, this time at the Lull & Holmes Planing Mill. The fire raged for six hours and wiped out four square blocks, reducing the mill to a heap of smoldering ash. It also required the full force of the Chicago Fire Department to control the blaze so that by three-thirty in the morning the men were depleted, many horses were blistered and badly burned, and the water supply was ebbing even lower.

After the fire was extinguished the exhausted firefighters were faced with hours of work cleaning out their bays, cleaning their engines, feeding the hungry horses, and trimming their horses' singed manes. The men, some with ragged oozing burns that had seared the flesh to the bone after eating through their fire coats, and each one feeling the effects of having inhaled so much smoke—light-headed, nauseated, dehydrated—forced themselves to carry out the tasks at hand. They could not permit themselves to think about lying down to rest or closing their eyes to sleep.

10

The survivors would never forget the sound. The sound "of judgment," some said. The sound of an angel heralding the end of the world, blasting gusts of fire from his horn. "Like a thousand locomotives rushing at full speed," some wrote. Like the devil had opened his mouth with a "deafening, persistent roar that never stopped but kept growing louder," or "a pounding waterfall," or a "hurricane." Phineas Eames wrote to his brother that the sound was a "sullen roar, like an earthquake . . . more than deafening it was grand; it was like the thunder and the roar of the sea all combined. It was fearfully sublime."

Luther Noyes noted that John Belanger, proprietor of the Dunlap House, had returned to Marinette by Sunday, October 8; his weeklong absence went unexplained, but a new advertisement for the hotel appeared in the *Eagle:*

> This house fitted specially to meet the needs of the Traveling Public! Good rooms, clean beds. Table as well supplied as is possible in this market. Stabling. Try us and see.

The Dunlap House had just opened its vast third floor for dancing and exhibitions, a space large enough for people to dance ten quadrilles simultaneously.

LUKE HOWARD'S GIFT to meteorology was the Latin cloud classification that Sam Brookes and Increase Lapham and all the observers of the Signal Service were using that day. Howard was a British apothecary whose classification first appeared in his book *Climate of London* in 1820, a system of description combined with that of the more famous thinker of the time, Carolus Linnaeus. Like Emerson, Howard revered the atmosphere and the messages written in the sky. "The ocean of air in which we live and move," he wrote, "in which the bolt of heaven is forged, and the fructifying rain condensed, can never be to the zealous Naturalist a subject of tame and unfeeling contemplation."

Franklin Tilton and Luther Noyes had devoted weeks to contemplating the sky. Noyes's description of the moon in the October 7 issue of the *Eagle* was a harbinger after all. He had been straining to see the moon through the cloud he could not name: the *stratus opacus*. Had those clouds thinned out and transformed into *translucidus* clouds to reveal the moon's face, it would have meant the cloud was about to disperse, that no storm was on the way. But from the moment Noyes first noted it, the stubborn *opacus* obscured the moon and would again that night.

Survivors described "streaks of bloody mist like meteors falling." Some would even insist that these streaks were a meteor shower. But the streaks, known as fall streaks or virga, are the graceful shafts of dry lightning preceding a storm. Rain never falls because the dry subcloud evaporates the moisture before it can be released. Dry lightning strikes were making a spectacular showing.

ELBRIDGE MERRILL MADE his way back to his village. The night before, sensing danger, he had walked five miles into town. "The hot gusts from the woods that swept across the road" had filled him with "a nameless horror." He believed the time had come to remove the women and children from his village and get them to a place of safety. What he received from his partners in town was a "promise of prompt assistance on Monday." By the time he made it back to the mill in his village late Sunday it was already dark, and after he informed everyone that help was on its way, he turned to the men. They knew that expression on his face by now, the barely masked lines of worry around his mouth, so they also knew what was coming next: the ritual cutting of the cards, then drawing lots for the fire watch they'd been keeping for three weeks.

That night the watch fell to Merrill and Charles Clark. Merrill told everyone else they'd best be off to sleep. He and Clark lit lanterns, which they set out on the porch where they sat together talking, alert and waiting.

MARTIN RACE WAS waiting, too, and while he waited he had cooked supper for his four children and had set aside food for his wife, Almira. She had left the house earlier in the day when "someone arrived around noon," asking if she would come to deliver a baby about three miles away near the Abram Place homestead. The air smelled "like hell itself, the smoke from the clearing fires were so strong," but Almira gathered the necessary items, wrapped her shawl around her shoulders, and went off to perform her task.

Mr. Peck lived across the road from the Martin Race family. Late in the afternoon he walked to Martin's house and told him that his family had "decided to go to the middle of a winter wheat field and dig themselves into the soil." Peck wanted Martin and his children to join them, but Martin declined the offer. He was going to stay put, he said, and wait for Almira to come home.

It was already dark by the time Almira Race delivered the baby and was able to begin making her way back to her husband and children. She set out on the road, the wind blowing hot, sand-spiked puffs around her.

➤

THE LAMP FAMILY had gone to church that Sunday morning. They followed their regular morning worship with a meal of the last round of ham, which Karl had cut down from the smokehouse. A very pregnant and overdue Fredricke fried the meat and served it with apples and the onions and carrots from her well-cared-for garden. Afterward, on this day of rest, the three youngest girls went down for a nap while the oldest, Caroline, helped her mother wash the dishes.

Karl glanced at his wife who was gathering birthing cloths and blankets. He wondered briefly if their next child would be a son before he told Fredricke he was going out to harness the work horses and feed them. Outside he watered the oats. Karl had worked long and hard to own these fine animals, and he wanted to be sure he kept their kidneys in good working condition. As he drenched the oats, it was the wind that distracted him. It blew a gust strong enough to rattle the windows on the west side of his house. He wondered whether he should prepare a shelter under the highest bank or make a shelter near the stone well or simply leave altogether: hitch up the wagon, gather his family into it, and head out to Sophie and Gus's place. But then the wind seemed to die out again, so Karl did what his neighbors had done. He placed ladders against the eaves and a ladder into the well.

It was not until much later, during supper, that Fredricke felt the sharp pains in her back and announced that the baby was coming.

"Do you want to go to Sophie's?" Karl asked.

Fredricke said she wasn't sure yet, she just wanted to lie down and would he draw more water from the well? They would need it if the baby was on its way. Karl did as she asked. By the time he'd filled more barrels of water there was only a trickle left in the well.

At the McGregor farm along the railroad right-of-way, John McGregor had fed his animals at noon. Shortly after he and Mary ate supper, he returned to his barns and set all of his animals loose and "then hung his new harness in the well."

A population of over six thousand people was now moving in slow motion. As the day wore on, the temperature began to climb and the sky pressed down on them. The smell was pervasive and unnameable. One survivor reduced the description of the air to a stark memorable phrase: "Inhalation was annihilation." The dried marshes lying six miles south of Peshtigo had been emitting gases for weeks. Now waves of gas mixed into the smoke to cast an eerie radiation glow over the roads. Sometime in the later part of the afternoon a pack of cats herded together and scrambled along Oconto Avenue as if being prodded by ghosts. A deer, perhaps the same startled deer who'd been living at Levi Hale's place, stumbled out into the road, then stood unharmed and unblinking. Loose dogs who would have normally attacked the deer crouched near its feet without so much as whimper. Father Pernin recalled that his bird began beating its wings, rattling the bars of its cage.

Superintendent Bliss had his hands full in Chicago at the telegraph office. After the demanding blaze that had used them up the night before, the enervated firefighters and their resources were flagging. Weather observer Sam Brookes clocked the afternoon wind at 45 miles per hour, a 5 on his chart, designating "high wind" from the southwest. The temperature was 85 degrees; the day before at the same hour it was 68 degrees and the day before that only 54 degrees. No telegrams came from the north but plenty of telegrams were crackling through the wires from Chicago calling for help. In what firefighters termed the call for mutual aid, extra teams were immediately sent from Milwaukee and Green Bay: a cavalry of pumpers and extra hose speeding toward Chicago at precisely the same time the temperature spiked in Peshtigo where people were preparing for a calamity with only buckets of water and wet blankets. In Milwaukee, the barometer reading took a nosedive between seven A.M. and two that afternoon, dipping from 29. 395 to 29. 280; the relative humidity was 55 percent. Chicago was only one edge of the immense storm.

Survivors in Chicago, Peshtigo, Menekaune, and Williamsonville described the "great round balls," "black balls," that "hurtled down" as if shot from a cannon. These round spheres suggested the presence of crispy, ominous, and darkly colored protruding *mammatus* clouds, which form just before a tornado makes contact with the ground. The *mammatus* are even more reliable as indicators of a thunderstorm with very strong updrafts. In either case, the pouches are startling during a setting sun, which lights them from beneath as they descend from the dark parent anvil cloud. From minute to minute the shapes change; sometimes they even begin to blur, taking on the appearance of streaming virga.

Around eight P.M. Sunday, as the storm closed in for its touchdown onto a superheated landscape, the isobars were tightening their curve, accelerating the rotation, a movement best compared to the "way figure skaters accelerate their spin when they pull their arms in close to the body." The wind, which had increased to a speed of 60 miles per hour, classified as a strong gale, was prepared to make itself heard and felt like never before.

"It was just as if the wind were a breath of fire," Father Pernin wrote. He was with Mrs. Dress at the time standing in the middle of a field on her property when he saw the trunks of the trees "blaze out," although no spark had struck them. Pernin and Mrs. Dress extinguished the flames and the wind fell still. Pernin decided to make his way back to his house next to the church; he hurried along, glancing west where he noticed a "dense cloud of smoke overhanging the earth, a vivid red reflection of immense extent." The wall cloud was settling down farther and Pernin was so taken with its size and color at first he did not hear the distant roaring; the sound was still muffled at that point, but even the mumble from above announced to him "that the elements were in commotion somewhere." That "commotion" was still in the south and west, in Chicago, Williamsonville, and New Franken.

The first macroburst of the gale hit Chicago just as Pernin apprehended this "commotion." The Chicago courthouse tower watchman, Mathias Schaffer, looked through his spyglass to the flames on the west side of the city and immediately sent a message through the voice box to William J. Brown at the central fire alarm office. "Strike box 342!" he shouted. Brown followed orders and struck the alarm, rousing the city and the firefighters. Within seconds engines and fireman were scrambling to the call. Schaffer looked out at the flames. He was instantly confused. He had mislocated the fire by about a mile or so. Either that or—and this did not seem possible—the fire was coming from two directions at once. Schaffer sent out another order from the voice box, telling Brown to strike box 319 instead, but Brown did not do it, thinking it would confuse everyone more.

Out in the Sugar Bush, John McGregor could not see south of

him either. He only felt the gust and saw the sudden shower of sparks flying onto his house. The wind bit him, flash fire burned his face. His voice was not audible above the inrushing gale. He and Mary thrashed their way to the root cellar with their dog and cat.

Pernin set his horse free into the street and began digging a trench, working with an odd vigor that was not energy so much as "fear growing more strongly . . . into certainty." The reflection in the sky was widening, dropping closer. With the growth of the wall cloud, nearly a mile wide by now, the "sound of this strange and unknown voice of nature constantly augmenting in terrible majesty" grew louder, more dissonant.

Next door to his house, Mrs. Tyler had been entertaining eight guests at evening tea. Pernin heard trills of laughter from the open window next door. He dug deeper wondering how they could laugh, how they remained deaf to the thunderous rumble approaching. It was just a little before nine P.M. when Mrs. Tyler and her company, having seen Pernin digging from her dining room window, came outside to talk to him. She wanted to know if she should be concerned. "If a fire breaks out, what are we to do?" she asked.

"Seek the river at once," Pernin told her. He'd spent too much time and labor digging his trench, so that when he uttered those words to Mrs. Tyler, it suddenly dawned on them both that they must get to the river now. But as she and her guests scurried away, he hesitated. He could not leave the Blessed Sacrament behind, so he took the time to run back into the house to retrieve it, thinking he'd slip it out of the tabernacle where it was housed. Whether it was from perspiration or just nervousness he dropped the key to the tabernacle, and knowing there wasn't time to go searching for it, Pernin lifted the wooden tabernacle, an awkward square pine box he could not quite manage alone with any ease, and carried it to his wagon outside. Pernin was aware of the commotion now stirring in the streets: The rising tide of voices calling out to run, to get to the river. The sound of the whistle from the company store. Tommy Hay shouted that a "fireball" flung itself into a tree with the speed of a meteor and had sent a flurry of fire to the surrounding houses.

Pernin should move, move fast—he knew it—but he'd forgotten the chalice, and could not bear to go on without it. He ran back into the house once again. Inside sparks were blazing and flying from room to room, making a "sharp detonating sound," convincing Pernin the air was saturated with gas. "I could not help thinking if this gas lighted up from mere contact with the breath of hot wind, what would it be when fire would come in contact with it?"

At a distance of almost eleven miles north of Peshtigo, Phineas Eames was wondering the same thing. His house was in a clearing of twelve acres but he had been "out in all directions looking for fire," off and on throughout the day. He did not find fire but he could not rest that evening "on account of the dense smoke and a peculiar smell accompanying it." Eames sent his wife and four children to bed that night, but he stayed awake, waiting.

Back in Peshtigo, about eight-forty-five P.M., Pernin finally found the chalice and he made it to the front gate, thinking he could move his wagon out to the street. One hand was on the front gate and at that instant he realized he had waited too long. *Faster than it takes to write these words* is the phrase every survivor used. They used it to describe the speed of a fireball hitting a house and setting it into instant flames; they used it to describe the speed with which one house was lifted from its foundation, then thrown through the air "a hundred feet" before it detonated midflight and sent strips of flaming wood flying like shrapnel. They used the phrase to explain the unforgettable sight of sixteen-year-old Peshtigo resident Helga Rockstead running along the boardwalk. Her long, waist-length hair was streaming out behind her and she was running from the flames, but she could not run fast enough from the fiery predator.

Fire caught her by the hair and several onlookers watched as "her head burst into flame." The next thing they knew she was wrapped in a sheet of fire. They used it to describe the sight of a small boy, separated from his family, and how he knelt on the ground, crouching in prayer as fire lit his body. *Faster than it takes to write these words.* That quickly Pernin's gate, fence, and loose planks were blown away "into space."

Within five minutes no one in Peshtigo could distinguish the main fire from the tornado or the main fire from the secondary fires or the firebrands. The fires throughout Oconto County had "crowned" in the trees and when a fire crowns in the forest even trained firefighters get out of its way. At this point the fire was reaching maximum temperatures. It was creating huge convection updrafts, which in turn intensified the fire's wind. The gorging fire, hungry for oxygen and determined to maintain its life, belched flamethrowers or firebrands in advance of itself. These long darts of flame projected from the crown fire are capable of leaping to trees hundreds of yards ahead of the advancing fire. When these angry flames hit a target, they created more wind, while behind them the whirling advancing fire—already a mammoth churning mountain—swept these multiple vortices of wind and flame into its greedy arms, in turn gaining even more heat and strength.

~

THERE WAS NO refuge for miles. Farther south on the eastern shore of Green Bay, the town of Williamsonville had been hit. There in the small mill-town named after its founders Tom and John Williamson, their mother, Maggie, and her young cousin, little Maggie, looked out of their living-room window. Panic soured in their throats; fire was raging from all directions.

"Take wet blankets and run," Tom Williamson told his mother.

Maggie did not want to be separated from her son, but he shouted at her, "Mother, there's nothing I can do. Save yourself."

Maggie was wrapped in a wet blanket but once she got outside she saw that everything—from the sapwood fence protecting the potato field to the buildings and barns—was ablaze. Something was raining down from above and at first she thought it was hail or the rain they so desperately needed. No. Chunks of burning coals were pelting people and houses alike, setting them on fire instantly when they struck.

Maggie struggled on through the wind and fire and stopped when she came to a clearing. She recognized her neighbor Mrs. Demerau sitting in the clearing. Thinking they were safe, Maggie sat down next to her, but within seconds Mrs. Demerau was shrieking loudly to her husband, "Nelson! I'm on fire." No sooner did she shout the words than she burst into flame from head to toe. Maggie struggled away from the burning woman. In the distance, through the pall of smoke she saw another woman lying on the ground, instructing her child to lie on her back; then, like a snake slithering along the hot ground, the mother bearing the child on her back struggled toward the water.

Maggie's only desire was escape and for the second time she believed she found a safe place among the rocks protruding up from the ground. By then she could barely see. She kept her head hidden in the blanket, but nothing could blot out the crying or the hiss of sap from the burning trees. Someone stumbled against her, crying out loudly, and when Maggie parted the blanket to peer out she saw a woman, her body on fire, stretched out beside her. Maggie did not know which of her relatives it was, only that the roasting body was wearing earrings and her young niece had just received earrings as an engagement gift that day. The flames from the burning woman blew directly at Maggie as she tried to push the incinerated head away from her. She could hear flesh crackle.

THE ROADS AND settlements on the way into Peshtigo were nothing but swaths of flame and wind. All were trying to get to town and the river. But the Peshtigo River was a nightmare of struggling men, women, and children fighting for water and breath, floating among the frightened animals. Even in the water the fire relentlessly attacked, setting the floating logs on fire. The searing logs pulsed toward the people, smashing into them. Logs had become sparkling missiles. Those trying to run to safety across the bridge from the west side of town crashed into those struggling to cross over into the east; under the weight of the load the bridge collapsed, tossing more helpless people into the water, which was no less hellish than the sky or the hot ground.

The Maxon family floated to safety on a wet featherbed, but C. R. Towsley and his wife and three children were encircled in the fire's path outside their home with no means of escape. Towsley had grabbed a kitchen knife, not knowing what he intended to do with it, or what possible protection it could afford him against a five-mile-high wall of flame and a vortex of wind. Standing paralyzed and awestruck before the fire, he tightened his grip on the knife. He watched as his wife and one child were hit with a firebrand.

The women and young girls were particularly vulnerable to the fire. When their clothes caught, the clothing acted as a covering wrapped around a lighted candle would, securing the wax drippings inside the candle, thereby intensifying the heat. Because females have higher fat contents in their bodies and wore so many layers of clothing, once they were set to flame, the fat naturally acted as extra fuel. Like the superheated resin inside the trees that made the trunks explode, the intensely hot human "fat drippings" caused Mrs. Towsley's body to combust.

Helpless to rescue his other children as the flames advanced, Towsley took the knife and slit their throats, then killed himself.

—

OUT ON GREEN Island the Drew family huddled together around the kitchen table, praying. The sky was on fire. Embers and burning shards of wood from the mainland, whipped up by the wind, pounded the island like thunderbolts. Samuel Drew could do nothing to prevent the three-masted schooner *George L. Newman* from a shipwreck. The captain could not distinguish the beacon through the flying streaks of fire.

The tornado, which was indistinguishable from the massive fire, tore along Old Peshtigo Road with frightening speed, approaching Marinette and Menominee where it split in two, creating more microbursts of violent fire and wind. Half of the fire jumped Green Bay while the other burst sped along the northwestern shore of the bay.

Near the Menominee River, Elbridge Merrill and his men tried desperately to put out the fires with buckets of water, but it was no use. They knew their only chance for survival was the riverbank and they immediately struggled to get to the water. The pain was unbearable, coming in waves, usually on inhalation. There's less than a thirty-second window in which to take a breath during a firestorm without searing the lungs. If they missed that window, the lungs burned and spontaneous pneumothorax, or the collapse of the lungs and thoracic cavity, occurs. "We little knew our enemy," Merrill wrote. A "literal wave of fire" rolled toward them, "reared its crest," and then "swept like lightning" through the woods.

There was only one escape from death: to duck under the water and stay there until compelled to come up for a breath. Sheltered by the ten-foot bank, the main body of the flame passed over Merrill and his friends' heads, but for at least an hour "an almost solid ceiling of flame" threatened them. Merrill had spotted Clark's baby laying on the ground in his path to the riverbank and he picked up the infant instinctively. Merrill was holding an old "Scotch cap," which he held between himself and the baby. He covered the baby's face with the cap and pressed his own face onto it, breathing back and forth between them, in order to save both their lives. He realized that "the baby thought I was trying to murder it," and fought back, twisting and kicking. As the baby jammed its feet against Merrill and fought to push the cap away, Merrill saw that the baby's light hair was on fire "time and time again." In the water Merrill ducked himself and the struggling child. "Once or twice it seemed to know when we were going down and would hold its breath like an adult," but above the water the child screeched continually. Merrill expected the baby would die first and he would follow right after. He'd been separated from his friends by a twist in the river. At first he could hear their plaintive voices but as time passed the sounds grew dimmer and then the child's crying "turned to moans; its little limbs had grown cold and were swollen, its hair had been scorched off to its skull."

─────

KARL HEARD FREDRICKE scream. His legs felt like paste as he struggled against the wind trying to get to her, to get inside the house. He found her on the floor huddled in a corner with their five girls gathered around her. The six of them were wearing shawls, scarves; Fredricke held her small bag of birthing cloths. If not for the firebrands hitting the barns, and the swirl of smoke and fire sprouting up, they looked ready for a trip.

Fredricke told him to get the horses, they could all make it out, they could get into the farm wagon and flee. Karl hitched the mares. He cursed himself for not moving the woodpile that was so close to the house; showers of firebrands were striking it, setting it aflame. Somehow he'd managed to get them all on board and he gave the reins to Fredricke who always had been the better and more fearless driver, while he hooked a harness to a tree.

The horses jumped and knocked Karl down, taking off with the wagon, Fredricke, and his children. Karl did not know if she had control of the reins. All he could make out as the fire burned his face and arms were the horses galloping off. To his left the zigzag rail fence was on fire. He ran, pumping his legs until he could grab the rim of the wagon box, but he could not climb aboard. "It was then that he saw in his horror that the wagon box was bouncing." The wagon was about to fly off the gears. As far as he knew, Fredricke still had the reins. Karl did not feel the fire boring a hole into his side. The back of his shirt caught fire but he did not stop running. He ripped off the shirt, then stretched his hands out like claws desperate to catch the wagon box. Fredricke was still in control of the reins when the wagon approached the creek where the wind had sucked away the crossing boards. Karl kept leaping, running, a frightful stitch in his side as he tried to get to the front wheel of the wagon, shouting at Fredricke that the boards would be gone. In the deafening roar of the firestorm she could not hear him. A flying, blazing rail from a burning fence hit the mare in the hindquarter. Her leg buckled and she was down. At last the wagon had stopped. "Cover yourself and the children!" he screamed, then he circled to the front of the wagon to help the mare up. The horse stood still, but before Karl knew what was happening, she shucked the harness and galloped ahead, her mane and tail streaming plumes of fire. Karl raced after her. No one knows if he caught her, only that just as he turned around again, he saw his other mare and the wagon and his family engulfed in fire.

———

IN CHICAGO, BUILDINGS were collapsing. "Horses maddened by heat and noise and falling sparks bit each other." William Ogden's lumberyards at Peshtigo Court were reduced to ash. Sam Brookes had no idea how fast the wind was traveling in the center of the inferno. The gale had knocked out the anemometers.

———

THE CLOCK STRUCK eleven. Phineas Eames saw lights approaching his home. He woke his wife and children; he told them to dress while he went outside to see who was coming. The visitors were Mr. and Mrs. Baurett and their family, who wanted to gather at the Eames home, to be with their neighbors as they too were "feeling the approach of some unseen foe."

The men hurried their wives and children into the house, but only seconds after they closed the front door, "all at once" they saw "a bright light approaching, in size as large as a half-bushel measure." It approached like a "ball of fire," passed over the house and cleared it, and seemed to disappear into the darkness. Next they heard the "great explosion" and the ground beneath their feet shook. Suddenly the atmosphere changed, growing warmer and warmer by the second. Hot puffs of wind swirled around them and at once the Eames house was on fire. When Eames looked left, he saw the barn was on fire as well, that the flame was "crawling along on top of the barn, on top of the house, in the tops of the trees, in the air and yet no fire on the ground."

Eames and Mr. Baurett ushered their families out of the house. Eames looked toward the ridge west of his house and decided that going up to the top of the hill was their only chance for safety. But the ridge had presented exactly the sharp change in topography that creates a wind shear, meaning the advancing fire would meet with another furious whirl of wind as soon as the flames reached the ridge.

As Eames and Baurett struggled ahead, the darkness suddenly shifted to blinding light and "the whole heavens seemed one vast wave of fire." Eames took the baby from his wife and as they got about sixty feet away from the house on their way to the ridge, Mrs. Eames shouted that their only son, Lincoln, was still in the house. Eames placed their baby girl in his wife's arms and told her to "follow the rest to the hill, while I run back and see, and if he is there, I will bring him to you, dead or alive."

Eames entered his burning house with fire falling down around him from every direction, but his son was nowhere in sight. Eames was shocked to find his wife in the exact spot where he'd left her. "He's not in the house!" Eames shouted. "He must have gone ahead with the rest. Give me the baby!"

Just as Eames took the baby from his wife he saw his son running toward them screaming, "Papa. I'll be burned up. What shall I do?"

Eames told the boy to give him his hand and not to let go. "See? Papa's got the baby and mother. Let's go together."

So, Eames, holding the baby in one arm and his son's hand in his own, told his wife to "take hold of my vest collar." His wife was struck dumb by the fire above and never said another word as they hurried on toward the ridge. By now the wind had increased to hurricane force, at least 100 miles per hour. Eames and his family were being tossed toward the ridge. Just as they met up with the Baurett family, Eames's boy let go of his hand and "bounded away like a deer" toward his sisters when a "wave of living fire" surrounded them, throwing them to the ground.

Eames was struck in the face. His long beard and hair caught fire and blinded him as he fell forward with the baby still in his arms. Eames, his son, the baby, and his wife were all burning. His wife fell across his feet; the baby was dead. Eames rolled his wife's burning body from his feet and he gently lay the baby on the ground next to him. In the "midst of this fearful ruin," Eames said, "I had no desire to live . . . and, in agony of spirit, I prayed to go too. But was not allowed to die." Eames said he heard a voice, "distinct and clear," saying to him: "Get up; get up, and look for your children." He struggled to his feet, moved forward several paces, and there, lying at his feet, he saw "a little form, roasted to a crisp." Eames supposed it was his son and he cried out, "Oh, my boy," before losing all sense of reality. Caught in the increasing deafening wind, on fire himself, Eames said, "I knew nothing."

Within the space of two hours on October 8, 1871, the cyclonic storm front served to make the main fire a veritable monster. The persistent surging and whirring rendered each obstacle in its path yet another opportunity to create more violent wind, which in turn created another vortex, which in turn strengthened the wind, which in turn fed the atmospheric turbulence—until the sky and the ground and everything in between was ablaze. Chicago was in flames, and Oconto County, Wisconsin, situated at 88 degrees west longitude and 45 degrees north latitude, had become a roaring ocean of fire.

Part Three

REVELATIONS

11

Between the hours of three in the morning and midnight on Monday, October 9, there was only one fact: fires were still raging in Chicago. The nation's—and the world's—attention was focused on that city alone. Early reports stated that Lake, Randolph, Clark, Washington, Madison, Dearborn, South Water, Kinzie, and Market Streets had already been destroyed. The massive wooden Water Works Building was gone and "no water was to be had," which left the exhausted firefighters with one option, to drink from the dirty Chicago River.

The Western Telegraph office where Superintendent Bliss worked was in ashes. Messages to adjacent villages and settlements calling for extra fire engines were being wired from the only telegraph lines working northward: the Engine House of the Chicago & Northwestern Railway office and the train dispatcher's office. The business portion of the city was in ruins, as were the depots for the Pittsburgh & Wayne, Chicago & Alton, and the Northwest passenger train depots.

Blue flames, the color of gas jets, emanated from the basements of the jail and homes alike. Until people heard the official reports later in the day confirming that the prisoners were alive, the residents believed that the 185 people who had been incarcerated in the City Hall basement had baked inside the burning building. Coal yards smouldered. People stood in the streets "dumb with horror and despair." The *Advocate* reported that the blaze was "so unutterably fierce" when it struck the court house, with its "walls of solid rock and ribs of iron," that the building "seemed to explode like a rocket." Under a violent canopy of flame and ash the sick were being carried out of hospitals and loaded onto express wagons; many wore nothing but their bedclothes. The city groaned and sizzled.

"Many who were yesterday millionaires are today beggars," the *Advocate* reported. "The prairies and farms for twenty miles are covered with fugitives . . . the description of this terrific yet gorgeous scene is graphic. The sparks fell from the heavens like the flakes of a driving snow storm when they fall so quickly as to blind the sight, and they drifted in the streets like snow drifts when it falls to a great depth in a gale of wind."

To the north and west of Chicago, the Minnesota conflagration was still burning. And a world away in England Queen Victoria, still mourning the loss of her beloved husband, Prince Albert, "bellowed" that his soul was with her, that she could hold communication with him. The *Advocate* reported that the mourning queen had ordered the prince's boots cleaned and that a fork and knife be placed on the table for his meal. Grief was the note of the day, and it resounded from the fiery waste of Chicago to England and back again. As trains and wagons raced out of Chicago, bearing the burned and the destitute eastward or to outlying villages, refugees from the previous days' fires on the peninsula and surrounding areas brought word of the Chicago disaster to the people of Green Bay. Even as people anxiously tried to find out about friends and family who lived in the burned areas, the unbelievable message arrived, "Chicago is burning!"

For Franklin Tilton and the citizens of Green Bay, this news was overwhelming. For the people of the surrounding counties, their own recent losses from fire only made them "feel more deeply the sufferings of our Chicago neighbors." In Green Bay, "all business was forgotten" in the wake of the news. Those who'd survived the maelstrom of fire in Chicago could not imagine a greater hell.

But there was a greater hell—in Peshtigo.

❦

JUST BEFORE DAWN that same Monday morning, Isaac Stephenson, looking a little worse for wear, had wandered out into the dusty streets of Marinette to survey the damage from the previous night. He saw a man on horseback coming toward him through the gray haze wearing only a shirt and pants, riding bareback and using only a piece of rope for a halter. Stephenson saw it was John Mulligan, the ex-boxer who worked for him as a boss at one of his lumber camps in Peshtigo. Usually at this hour Mulligan would have been supervising the camp near the McGregors' farm, not riding into Marinette. As Mulligan drew closer, his face blackened from smoke, Stephenson sensed something was wrong.

"Johnny, what is the matter?"

"Peshtigo is burned up," Mulligan said.

At first Stephenson was not sure what to make of the news. His own town of Marinette had been struck; he and the residents had fought the blazes rolling toward them from Peshtigo the night before, but this morning—by some miracle or trick of nature—most of Marinette, including Stephenson's mansion, stood unharmed. Marinette had lost only fourteen buildings to the fire. It did not seem possible then that in Peshtigo, as Mulligan was saying, "50 to 60 bodies" lay roasted in its streets.

Mulligan tried as best he could to explain the terrible scene six miles south, but hearing his voice grow ragged, he finally gave up and told Stephenson he could not understand unless he went into Peshtigo to see for himself. Mulligan did not even bother to tell Stephenson about John and Mary McGregor, who'd descended into their root cellar. They might as well have entered a furnace. The cellar burned up from "within and without."

"Just get help quickly," he told Stephenson.

They needed to organize the residents of Marinette, then transport food, water, doctors—any help they could spare—into Peshtigo.

Stephenson put out the word that Peshtigo had "suffered far more greatly" than Marinette. It was still only a little past six in the morning when Luther Noyes heard about Peshtigo and he agreed to accompany Stephenson. Meanwhile Stephenson, knowing he could count on his brothers Robert and Samuel to help, sent John Mulligan across the bridge to Menominee to tell them that extra wagons and supplies might be needed. Finally, before riding out of Marinette with Noyes, Stephenson asked John Belanger of the Dunlap House to prepare its third floor for the fire victims if need be, and to make sure Drs. J. J. Sherman and J. C. Hall would be on call at the Dunlap to receive them.

As yet, neither Noyes nor Stephenson had any inkling that Chicago was burning, and nothing could have prepared them for what they discovered in Peshtigo.

———

FIFTY OR SIXTY bodies would have been tragic, but the true devastation Stephenson and Noyes found as they rode into Peshtigo was unspeakable, a landscape neither one had ever seen before or could have imagined. Stephenson had not fought in the Civil War, but Noyes, who believed he'd seen the worst of human carnage at Cold Harbor, was rendered speechless at the sight of calcined body parts and clumps of ash, "barely enough to fill a thimble," that had been a human being. Wails of newborn babies drifted up from the riverbanks. Four births occurred during the night, yet Noyes could not even begin to count the number of dead infants and children scattered among the uprooted smoldering trees, some lying next to their mothers, others flung several feet away. "No pen dipped in liquid fire can begin to describe, can paint the scene—language 'in thoughts that breathe and words that burn,' gives but the faintest impression of its horrors," Noyes would write over and over, trying to give expression to the inexpressible.

At seven A.M. that morning, Noyes could not fathom what had hit the mill town, only that the fire had been like no other fire, so successfully had it wiped out every house, except for parts of one; leveled every building including the boardinghouse; devoured the company store, the mill, the churches. Stephenson's and Noyes's minds were reeling. What fire had split boulders in two, melted church bells and the wheels on railroad cars? What wind had hurled train cars loaded with logs into the air and ravaged trees so thoroughly they were now twisted, torn from the ground by their roots? These were unanswerable questions. For now, the exact nature of a fire that demolished an entire town and most of its population was secondary to rescuing those who had survived it.

Stephenson was worried and so was Noyes. The resources of Marinette were limited; they knew that the survivors would need more help than Marinette could offer. Upon their return to Marinette, Stephenson went first to the Dunlap House and wrote pleas for help, addressing them to Governor Lucius Fairchild and the mayors of Milwaukee, Green Bay, Oshkosh, and Fond du Lac. His message to Governor Fairchild was blunt: "We are burning up. Send help."

With no telegraph line operating and all the roads blocked by fallen trees, dead horses, cattle, bodies, and debris, the only way out of the burned area was by water, so Stephenson took his messages to Captain Hawley. The *Union* was in port and by the time Stephenson arrived at the Merryman dock, hundreds of people who had sought refuge on the steamer the night before were walking onto the tramway. The tumult of the night before had passed into a deathly silence by morning. The refugees were too numb to speak.

Stephenson told Hawley to make for Green Bay and send the pleas for help as soon as he could find a telegraph line that was open. Hawley agreed, but he said it would be some time before he would be ready to set sail. Stephenson urged all speed.

By the time Stephenson left Hawley, the sun was rising and more stories of disaster began filtering into Marinette. One of the first stories came from Anton Place and his helper who had arrived at the Dunlap House riding on the one horse of his team that had survived. The men standing outside the hotel listened, convinced at first that the losses in Peshtigo were no worse than their own. Then, just as they were considering Place's news, John Mulligan and Isaac Stephenson arrived and confirmed that the seemingly unbelievable stories of bodies exploding into flame and buildings lashed by the wind were true.

Even though Menominee was separated from Marinette by the one-thousand-foot-wide Menominee River, the fire had easily leaped this expanse. One branch of the flames had attacked the Spafford & Gimore mill reducing it and all the buildings and houses around it to ashes in a few minutes. Then, instead of turning to devour the rest of Menominee, the flames swept out onto the waters of the bay where they threatened the ships and those on them who thought themselves safe from the inferno on the mainland.

It seemed impossible, but the schooner *C. I. Hutchinson* had her decks covered with cinders and her rigging set on fire by burning coals falling from the sky even though she floated at anchor two miles from land. The fire had threatened several other ships; the wind driving the flames had shot partially burned pieces of roof shingles, some as big as five inches square, onto the decks of the schooner *Atlanta* seven miles out in the bay.

Menekaune, however, had not been as lucky as Menominee. Except for a few scattered buildings on the outskirts of the town, the new Spaulding, Houghtaling & Johnson sawmill, and two other sawmills, thirty-five houses, two hotels, a flour mill, three stores, a dock, shipyard, warehouse, and almost 1 million feet of lumber had been incinerated. Miraculously, not one life had been lost.

As the people of Marinette prepared to take provisions into Peshtigo, Captain Hawley, bearing Stephenson's plea for help, made his way south. Hawley had no way of knowing that during those early morning hours, Chicago was still burning. The fire there was now coming from two directions, north and south. The northern pincer of fire raced toward Lincoln Park while its southern pincer tore toward the lakefront mansions along South Michigan Avenue. On that northern end, in an area known as the Sands, William Ogden's vast lumberyard erupted into flame as the "sun disappeared, the winds increased . . . and people were on fire."

Governor Lucius Fairchild and all the state officers of Wisconsin had gotten news of Chicago and had left Madison immediately to render what aid they could. They took trainloads of supplies with them for the victims of Chicago.

Back in Marinette, Isaac Stephenson conferred with William A. Ellis, aware that they also needed to get word to Ogden that

Peshtigo had been destroyed. Even if the telegraph lines had been operating, it would not have relieved the general confusion during the first half of that day. As Stephenson later lamented, the fire and its aftermath had altered everyone's sense of time, had unmoored them from reality and reduced them to the "helpless state of children."

Helplessness was what Sandy Mac, a farmer from the middle Bush, felt when he lifted his head from the riverbank. His mind worked in fragments and from that morning on, every time he tried to explain, the words ushered from his lips in choppy phrases, a bereaved man's mantra: "Bridge on fire. Wind, people, horses, screamin'. Horses fightin' loose, runnin' back. Had only one driven' line left, used it to pull Star onto a wagon layin' on its side. My shirt was on fire, ripped it off. Jumped out and turned to get Rose and the little ones down to the water. Wagon, wagon, was empty. Nothin' in the box. Empty."

His horse Star stood close by. Sandy Mac's clothes, what was left of them, were soaked. He scraped his way along the bank, digging his fingers into the dirt, feeling for water to splash on his eyes. At first he believed he was blind, until he felt his face, discovering that his eyelids were pasted shut and his face was swollen to three times its normal size. He would not have known it, but his facial burns were as severe as radiation burns in which the top layers of skin are so thoroughly seared that the skin bloats and stretches tautly over the bones of the face, often searing the retinas and sealing the eyelids closed. He rinsed his eyes. The water was soothing but he had to pull his eyelids open and then he did the same for Star.

It was not until then that he realized he was surrounded by people dragging themselves from the northern bend of the Peshtigo River. Babies and children were crying, but the men and women were silent. Star's burnt leather line still stuck to Sandy's blistered hand. He did not yet feel the blisters that covered his back and head, but he saw that Star's mane and foretop had been burned off, leaving only raw, bloody patches. Her tail had burned down to just a stub, and the skin was peeling off her tongue. Sandy Mac pulled the leather line, leading the horse up the riverbank. With only one thought he began to pick his way south. He had to find his wife, Rose, and his children.

A man, his wife, and their little boy joined Sandy and Star as they moved away from the river. No one spoke, but everyone had the same purpose: to go home and see whether any of those lost in the chaos of last night were alive.

It was difficult walking. Their shoes had been burned off and in many places the ground was still too hot to walk on. They had to pick their way, avoiding the hot spots. There was no road, at least no recognizable road. Everything had been burned flat. No matter where he looked—left or right, behind him or ahead—Sandy saw that the houses had disappeared, leaving only the stone foundations where fires still smoldered and the foul-smelling smoke streamed upward. Now that there were not any recognizable markers to guide them, Sandy looked for the mounds of ashes from the rail fences that had lined the roads. Sometimes he could recognize the ruins of a farm he knew. The fields were strewn with burned carcasses, but he could not tell whether the remains were human or animal.

Sandy could not even tell there had been a road where he found the iron wheel rims, axles, and wagon irons mixed with the mound of ashes. He stood and stared at all that was left of his wagon and flashes from the night flickered in his mind. *Wagon . . . wagon was empty. Nothin' in the box. Empty.* Rose and the little ones, he had put them in the wagon. Now he started to walk to it but stopped. He could not bear to look. Instead, he bent down and picked up the three-legged iron kettle that was lying close to the ashes of his family. He tucked it in the crook of his arm where there was unburned skin. Then he turned and walked away.

The air was getting colder. Everyone in the small group was thirsty, hungry, and exhausted. In the distance Sandy saw what looked to be a small building still standing. Picking their way across the smoldering field, they passed a well. Even though he did not have a rope, Sandy looked down to see if anyone had tried to escape the fire by hiding in the well. He peered over its rim, so sickened by the smell that he had to turn away. He did not need a rope. They had all smothered.

Up past the well, the small house that remained was charred from the roof to the foundation. It looked like a crude child's drawing with its roof twisted and the windows blown out. But they went inside, grateful for what little shelter they had. They needed a fire to warm them, but the chimney had collapsed. Everyone was desperately thirsty, so Sandy looked for water and he needed water for Star, knowing it would not be long before the burned animal's kidneys started to fail. The little boy in their party was crying. Sandy could not find any water, but he did find some cornmeal in a clap jar, which he put in his iron kettle. Then he gave the rest to the man for his family who had decided to stay in the house and rest. Sandy had to go on. He had to find his farm. He left, never having learned their names.

As he headed off carrying the kettle that was the only part of Rose he had left, it started to rain, just a little, and he lifted his head toward the sky. He opened his mouth, felt his skin tearing with the effort, felt the rain falling on his cracked lips and his eyelids. He stayed that way, head arched back feeling the rain; it seemed impossible to keep his eyes open unless he could continue to wet them.

Again, he tried to figure out where his farm was. But there were no more ashes from the fences to follow. He decided to strike out across country. His farm had to be close now, maybe only a mile or so away. Slowly he and Star made their way across the ruins.

After an hour or so he saw three rock piles, and he knew he was almost home. He looked for the familiar buildings but saw nothing. As he got closer he saw just the stone foundations of his home. Star whinnied. Despite the smoke and destruction, she knew she was home. Sandy stood by the stone culvert where the farm gate once stood. There was no use going any farther.

He was not sure if he was hallucinating or whether the whimpering he heard was real. The roads and farms had been so transformed into stretches of silvered, hot ash, it could have been a nightmare. He looked in the culvert, amazed to see his dog, Brownie, whose tail and ears had been burned off.

When he saw Brownie's burns he knew both the animals and he needed water desperately if they were to survive. Sandy picked his way through the rubble of his farm, across the yard strewn with dead chickens, to the well he had dug years ago. The fire had burned the well rope so he had no way to raise the bucket. But he remembered that he had filled his big iron kettle with water just before the fire and left it on the stone hearth. He searched through the ruins, trying to figure out where the kettle would be. Finally he found it. Although it had a big crack from the fire, there were still about five quarts of water left in it. The water was filled with bits of burned wood, but it was drinkable.

Sandy took the little bit of cornmeal he had, mixed it with some water, and fed it to Star. The horse was all he had and he needed to take care of her. He found one of the burned chickens and tore the liver from it and fed it to Brownie. Then he washed his eyes and the eyes of both the dog and the horse with the remains of the water. It was time to leave.

Sandy climbed on Star and held Brownie. The horse needed no

guidance to find her way to town, a trip she had made many times on the road.

He was about two miles from town, believing that the fire had struck only the Sugar Bushes and that in Peshtigo he would find food, water, and treatment for his burns when he saw a man, his wife, and two small children. They were dazed and wandering. "Do you know the way to Peshtigo?" the man asked. The children were horribly burned and barely alive. Sandy got off Star, and he and the man put the woman and children on the horse. The man stood alongside the horse, holding the woman and children in place. Sandy carried Brownie and Rose's iron kettle. The smallest child, a girl, was coughing constantly. After a while, when she had stopped coughing, the father carried the body the rest of the way.

When they came to the rise in the road that overlooked Peshtigo, there was no town.

Frank Tilton (center with white beard) with his assembled family in a picture taken in the late 1800s (*Original courtesy Peshtigo Fire Museum; photograph by Katie Harpt*)

Luther B. Noyes, founder and editor of the *Marinette and Peshtigo Eagle* (*Courtesy* Marinette-Menominee Eagle Herald)

William B. Ogden, first mayor of Chicago and owner of the Peshtigo Company (*Courtesy Chicago Historical Society*)

Isaac Stephenson, lumber baron, business partner of William Ogden, and the most important businessman in Marinette (*Courtesy Marinette County Historical Society*)

William Ellis, superintendent of the Peshtigo Company sawmill and woodenware factory (*Courtesy* Peshtigo Times)

Many "pevees," the loggers who pried apart a logjam, were crushed between the logs. (*Courtesy Wisconsin Historical Society*)

In 1871, the Peshtigo Woodenware Factory was the largest of its kind in the world. (*Courtesy* Peshtigo Times)

Queen Marinette welcomed both Menominee Indians and white settlers to her home, reputedly the first frame house on the Menominee River. (*Courtesy Marinette County Historical Society*)

BELOW LEFT: This woodcut is the only known picture of Father Peter Pernin, the French missionary priest who wrote the most popular account of the firestorm in an effort to focus the world's attention on it and raise money for the survivors. (*Courtesy Wisconsin Historical Society*)

BELOW RIGHT: Geologist, engineer, canal builder, meteorologist, conservationist, and weather observer, Increase Lapham was one of America's great scientists and the only person who sensed the impending disaster. (*Courtesy Wisconsin Historical Society*)

The Albin Butler home, located near the woodenware factory, was destroyed in the fire, but the family survived. (*Courtesy* Peshtigo Times)

ABOVE: This photo of the Peshtigo House of Learning was taken in 1870. (*Courtesy Wisconsin Historical Society*)

BELOW: The first church rebuilt after the fire, the Congregationalist church was sold to the Catholic Church in 1927 and moved from the east side of the river to its present location on the west side. In 1963 the church became the Peshtigo Fire Museum. (*Courtesy* Peshtigo Times)

Abram Place, whose farm served as a hospital for many fire victims (*Courtesy* Peshtigo Times)

BELOW: The descendants of Karl Lamp (Lemke) still live on the farm he built after the fire. (*Courtesy* Peshtigo Times)

LEFT: Lorenzo Race with his bride Ellen Wright Race on their wedding day. Note his left hand, which shows the effects of his injuries in the fire. (*Courtesy Joseph Race*)

This drawing of Peshtigo was made shortly before the fire. (*Courtesy Wisconsin Historical Society*)

The fire did not strike Peshtigo harbor, which prospered for many years after the fire before the decline in available trees led to its demise. (*Courtesy* Peshtigo Times)

The actual fire was much greater than depicted here, and the trees were far bigger and the forest much denser. (*Courtesy Wisconsin Historical Society*)

This imaginative drawing of people fleeing to safety in the river appeared in the November 25, 1871, issue of *Harper's Weekly*. (*Courtesy Wisconsin Historical Society*)

Many families sought safety in clearings, but the fire was so intense most of them died where they stood. (*Courtesy Wisconsin Historical Society*)

A lithograph presenting a dramatic and popular view of the Chicago fire (*Courtesy Cigna Museum and Art Collection*)

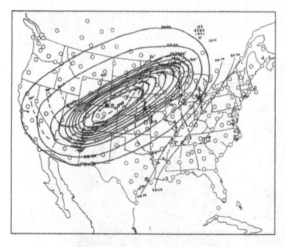

The Weather Bureau of the U.S. Department of Agriculture prepared this map using the reports made by U.S. Army Signal Corps observers at 5:35 P.M. Central Standard Time, October 8, 1871. (*Courtesy Wisconsin Historical Society*)

ABOVE: In 1902, this brick building replaced the wooden Dunlap House on Dunlap Square. (*Courtesy of the authors*)

LEFT: Dr. Jonathan Cory Hall, a pioneer physician in Marinette, treated many of those injured in the fire. (*Courtesy Marinette County Historical Society*)

ABOVE LEFT: Governor Lucius Fairchild, the Civil War hero, who organized a massive relief effort for the fire survivors (*Courtesy Wisconsin Historical Society*)

ABOVE RIGHT: Frances "Frank" Fairchild, Governor Fairchild's wife, who became the unofficial governor of Wisconsin as she directed emergency supplies to fire survivors (*Courtesy Wisconsin Historical Society*)

BELOW: The front page of the Madison, Wisconsin, newspaper with first reports of the fire (*Courtesy Wisconsin Historical Society*)

The fire stripped the land of all trees, as revealed in this picture of the devastation around the Peshtigo River. (*Courtesy Wisconsin Historical Society*)

After the firestorm, these wheels were all that remained of a train loaded with logs. (*Courtesy Wisconsin Historical Society*)

The fire had a devastating effect on wildlife, killing thousands of deer and other animals. (*Courtesy Wisconsin Historical Society*)

A street in Peshtigo after the fire shows the total destruction left by the firestorm. (*Courtesy Wisconsin Historical Society*)

In 1951 these four survivors of the fire attended the ceremonies dedicating the historical marker at the Peshtigo Fire Cemetery. From left: Mrs. John (Hansen) Anderson, Mrs. A. M. Aagot (Hansen) Farm, John Albrecht, and William Dolan (*Courtesy* Peshtigo Times)

Mrs. Amelia (Stoney) Desrochers, the last fire survivor to place a wreath on the mass grave in the Peshtigo Fire Cemetery, was five years old at the time of the fire. She died on August 27, 1966, at the age of one hundred. (*Courtesy* Peshtigo Times)

ABOVE LEFT: A modest sign in the Harmony Cemetery marks the grave site of an unknown number of victims of the fire. (*Photograph by Katie Harpt*)

ABOVE RIGHT: This four-sided obelisk in the May's Corners Cemetery marks the graves of the twelve members of the Newberry family who died in the fire. (*Photograph by Katie Harpt*)

BELOW LEFT: The marker for the graves of Fredricke Lamp (Lemke) and her children (*Photograph by Katie Harpt*)

BELOW RIGHT: Frank Noyes, the son of Luther, erected this memorial to those who died in the fire. (*Courtesy of the authors*)

The lamb that marks the grave of one of the many children who died in the fire (*Courtesy of the authors*)

This tree stump in the Harmony Cemetery reveals the size of the 1 billion trees destroyed in the fire. (*Courtesy of the authors*)

12

Late Monday morning, the telegrams arrived in New York one after the other, an incessant recital repeating the same message: "All Chicago is on fire."

When Ogden received word of the disaster, true to his nature, he sent telegrams to his agents in Chicago asking for complete information on the extent of the destruction to the city generally and to his holdings specifically. He was informed that the section where his house was located was completely destroyed save for his house, Ogden Grove, which remained untouched. Until he saw the damage for himself, Ogden could only speculate about his losses. He boarded a train at once for Chicago.

Meanwhile, Captain Hawley's steamer was making slow progress toward Green Bay. Usually, he could count on docking in Green Bay by one in the afternoon, but today he knew it would be impossible; the atmosphere was soupy with smoke and flying ashes.

In Peshtigo, Father Peter Pernin began committing each lurid scene to memory. Supplies were coming in from Marinette, but for

Pernin the horror of the previous night and the impressions of the grim reality before him were forming a narrative in his mind.

"Danger is a successful teacher," he wrote. Pernin found it ironic that at the very moment he believed the danger had passed, the morning after the whirlwind of fire proved no less painful or dangerous.

He had struggled to get to the dam on the east side of the river the night before, a high stretch of earth that would have acted as a shelter against the sheet of flames rolling over the town. He never made it that far, but he did submerge himself in the river, and it was three-thirty in the morning when he finally was able to drag himself onto land. That's when he saw that the boardinghouse had been reduced to one long, single burning beam while the remainder of the five-story-high building was rubble. He could not remember whether people were in the boardinghouse at the time of the fire. He shivered and crawled toward the heat from a pile of burning fragments, where he took off his shoes and socks and buried his feet in the warm sand.

The first thing he noticed were the smoking ruins of the woodenware factory. Piles of iron hoops from the pails and other items made at the factory were scattered on the ground and a number of men were lying prostrate over the hot metal. Pernin did not know whether they were alive or dead, whether they'd been blown that way by the fingers of the fire or were so cold and shocked they had flung themselves across the hot metal rims, not caring if they burned even more.

People stumbled about, disfigured chimeras making their way to the ruins, seeking warmth. In silence each person removed his clothes and dried them on stumps or chunks of metal, oblivious of their naked bodies so that the task of drying their clothes "was easy even to the most scrupulous and delicate" among them.

As the sun rose Father Pernin heard his name called. He turned to the sound of the voice. However, someone took him by the arm and led him to where a small group had found refuge from the fire. It was the very place he had hoped to reach the night before, only to be kept from it by the force of the wind.

The little valley dipped downward near the river's edge, sheltered by sand hills; the fire had blown over the heads of those who lay on the bottom. These fortunate few had suffered little of what the others had. Nearby, however, an old woman whose fear of drowning was greater than her fear of burning had been too terrified to plunge into the river. Instead she had clung to the bank with only her lower extremities submerged. Pernin saw that her torso was burned to a crisp but she was still alive. Her moaning sounded like the baleful howl of a wounded and wretched dog, but there was nothing anyone could do for her. Pernin said he was in such a "depressed state" himself he seemed to have forgotten how to give consolation at this moment of the old woman's slow death. He could not keep his eyes open without holding them open with his fingers and he found it impossible to speak.

Those who could left the safety of the small valley, trying to find those they had lost and to see what remained of their town. Parents and children had been separated from each other in the mad rush to the river. A man who had dragged a woman through the torrent of fire trying to get to the banks wailed when he made it only to realize he had not saved his wife at all, but a stranger. Eight days after their marriage, J. G. Clements, who had vowed to his mother-in-law, Mrs. Trudell, that he would "die for his new wife," was now dead. He had run through the fire behind the buckboard carrying his wife, his shirt and hair blazing after he had jumped off, knowing the lighter load would add fleetness to his wife's escape. She screamed and climbed to the outermost edge of buckboard, reaching for him, but her outstretched hands failed to link with his in the furious race to the river. He fell to the ground and she saw her new husband consumed by fire before passing out herself.

One by one they returned to the group in the valley. One man told Father Pernin how he found all the houses and the new church in ashes, and the entire area covered with bodies burned so badly that he could not recognize any of them.

Pernin said they could try to get to Marinette, to his other church with its new presbytery and to the schoolhouse, which could lodge the survivors.

And it was just as Pernin was planning this trek to Marinette that a large tent sent by Stephenson was erected. Seeking some refuge, the priest was lying in a corner when the man in charge promptly ordered him out, "accompanying the rude command with a perfect torrent of insulting words and blasphemies. Taking his orders quite literally, he would allow no one in the tent save women and children, and those so injured they could not walk." Without protest the priest simply rolled under the canvas to the outside.

People were beginning to grow hungry. No one had eaten since dinner the previous night. Some enterprising men found a few cabbages in a nearby field. After removing the burned outer leaves, they cut the remaining portion into slices and distributed a few pieces to those who could eat. It was not until one o'clock that afternoon that the supply wagons from Marinette arrived.

The drivers had been instructed to empty their wagons, then bring back as many survivors as they could carry. Recognizing a driver as one of his parishioners, Father Pernin asked him what had happened at Marinette, what condition it was in.

"Thank God, Father, no one perished. . . . All the mills and houses from our church down to the bay have gone."

"And the church?" asked the priest.

"Burned."

"The presbytery?"

"Burned."

"The new schoolhouse?"

"Burned also."

Pernin realized then that he had lost two churches, two presbyteries, and a schoolhouse, along with all his personal property. He was left with only the clothes he wore, and now the shelter he had offered to the people no longer existed. Not only could he not offer any assistance to others; he too had become dependent on the aid of others.

❧

In Birch Creek the fire was subsiding, and no one there had yet heard about Peshtigo. Elbridge West Merrill floated in the chilly water, drawing painful breaths and continuing to wet his and the Clark baby's head. He managed to pull himself and the baby from the water. The child was still alive, no longer kicking and struggling as it had the night before, its heart beating dully. Merrill dragged himself and the baby to drier land, convinced now that of his small group only he and the burned child he held had survived. Suddenly, he heard the companions he thought dead calling to him. He struggled to his feet and, still clutching the baby, he answered them as he made his way to join them.

When they met up with one another, everyone in the group was badly blistered and blind. They gathered together, huddling on the riverbank as they tried to determine what to do, where to go, how to get there. Fire still burned in the distance, and what remained of the forest around them was filled with smoke, hot ashes, and burning stumps. There was no refuge at the mill, which no longer existed, nor did they have any way to reach it if it were still standing. They decided to wait a while for the smoke to clear.

Later in the day, they were overjoyed when they heard a voice calling to them. It was the son-in-law of Eleazar Ingalls, the mill's owner, come to see what had happened to the mill and its occupants. He had walked to the mill from Frenchtown, where he left the wagon because the road was blocked by fallen trees and covered in many places with hot ashes. He was surprised to find anyone alive in the blackened wilderness.

They would have to walk to Frenchtown; from there he could take them in the wagon. Since they were all blinded they did not know how they could possibly make it to Frenchtown. Ingalls's son-in-law took a long coil of rope and tied each member of the group to one another in a line. "Walk straight ahead," he told them. "I'll lead you." Then he took the baby and started to walk, leading the group to safety.

They moved slowly, stumbling along, searing their feet in the hot ashes, often falling over debris only to be helped by the others. Their progress was slow and painful, but they moved steadily until they reached Frenchtown, grateful that they did not have to walk anymore; now they could ride in the wagon to Menominee. Upon arrival in Menominee, the survivors discovered that the hospital was full; the Dunlap House in Marinette was overflowing with victims, so Eleazar Ingalls did what many people who had not lost everything did: he took the victims into his home.

IN THE SUGAR Bush, as each hour passed, burned men, women, and children arose from the ground or the creek beds and the potato fields where they'd sought refuge.

After more than six hours in the water, William Newberry, the only other farmer with as much land as Abram Place, and two women crawled up on the creek bank. A baby was still asleep. They sat on the bank, huddled together, waiting. During the minutes or hours that passed (neither Newberry nor the women would ever be certain of the precise amount of time they sat on the dirt of the creek bank) they had no idea what they should do. They had entered the soupy, muddled dimension of grief-time and bewilderment in which the normal world of rituals, chores, and expectations had collapsed. In this post-fire landscape even sound had been altered: moaning and weeping replaced laughter and talk, crackling and spitting from the distant fires still simmering replaced birdsong. There was no way to assess the extinction of life and nature facing them. They could only wait, in their drenched clothes, for deliverance from their own bodies' need for warmth, for food, and for painless inhalation of air.

When they heard a human male voice calling out, it was William Newberry who managed to stand and press out parched "halloos" to guide the man to the creek bank. It wasn't until Karl Lamp stumbled into their group that they realized he was blind and was clutching the place where the fire had torn a gaping hole in his side. They could do little for him, but they had him lie down and they bathed his eyes and face with water from the stream.

With daylight, William Newberry set off to find others who had survived the fire. He had gone only a short distance down the creek when he saw the two charred lumps on the ground. He was sure at first they were logs, but the calcined lumps were human. He stumbled on through the smoking debris. Several times, he had to stop and breathe into the crook of his arm to keep himself from vomiting. The burned carcasses of hogs and cattle were scattered all over. Newberry began coughing; his eyes burned and he squinted even more as he tried to see. When it became impossible to see his way through the debris and smoking ruins, he turned back. On his way, he stooped down, pulled his short knife from his pocket, and cut off a chunk of meat from one of the burned cows. It did not take much time to finish cooking the meat over some burning logs when he got back to the others.

Later in the day they saw a wagon coming their way. They shouted and waved to the two men driving the wagon, Henry Bakeman and Henry Bartels. Bakeman and Bartels told Newberry and his group to board the wagon so they could take them to Marinette. Bartels wanted to get Karl Lamp to the Dunlap House. He said they'd hand Lamp over to the nurses, then continue to Menominee and leave William Newberry, the two women, and the baby with William's mother who had been visiting his sister at the time of the fire.

Bartels and Bakeman's rescue mission was only beginning. Afterward, they returned to the Sugar Bush, not knowing how many survivors they would find. As they rocked over the decimated roads their hopes diminished rapidly. They called out "halloos," but no sounds echoed back to them. They found only bodies, or pieces of them.

——◆——

AFTER THE FIRE had passed, Lorenzo Race pulled himself from the mud. His hands, especially his left hand and left arm, the one he had left exposed so he could splash water on himself, were badly burned. Even the wet blanket had not protected his lungs from the hot air and smoke. He staggered out of the creek bed looking for Harley, but he did not see him anywhere. His father, Martin, his younger sister, and his brother had burned in the furnace heat of their root cellar. His mother, Almira, had never returned home.

Later, as he wandered dazed through the flattened countryside, he saw a wagon coming down the road. Henry Bakeman and Henry Bartels quickly gathered up the injured young man and took him to a tent field hospital that had been erected on the Abram Place farm not far away. After he had rested for a day, he was taken to the hospital at the Dunlap House, where Dr. Jacob May duly entered the young man on his list of patients:

> Lorenzo Race, English, burned both hands, with acute bronchitis. Lost father, mother, brother, and sister.

Harley Race had survived the fire without injury and made his way to Marinette. There he decided to help in the hospital and began work as a nurse on Friday, the day after his brother had been brought to the hospital. Neither knew the other was alive until Harley came upon his brother, a bittersweet reunion as they realized the rest of the family was dead.

———

IT WAS UNFATHOMABLE that the fire of October 8 had swept so much away, but on the peninsula, Thomas Williamson thought he was the only person in Williamsonville still alive. He was aware of only two things: he could breathe again, and he was desperately thirsty. "I would have given all I ever had for water; I cannot tell you how I suffered for it," he wrote later. He wanted to find water, so he tried to stand up, but found he was too weak and collapsed back onto the ground. He rested, tried again, but still could not stand. He heard someone calling, and he answered as best he could, but he heard the call no more. After resting for some time, he struggled to his feet and called out again. This time he received an answer.

Coming toward him through the smoke and haze was an old man

by the name of "Cap" Richmond. Thomas asked the old man to get him some water. The old man said nothing, looked at him and nodded, then moved off through the burned field. Feeling better that some help was coming, Thomas lay back down and rested. It was only after some time that he realized the old man was not coming back to help him. He would have to help himself. He was feeling a little stronger after his long rest, so he got to his feet again. But in which direction should he walk? Everywhere he looked he saw nothing, nothing but black desolation. Finally he decided to head in the direction of the voice he had heard earlier. It was as good as any.

He "staggered like a drunken man" from exhaustion and from his burns. In addition to having little strength left, he was, like most of the survivors of the fire, almost blind. Still he struggled on, hoping to find whoever it was that had called out. Every building, every landmark had been burned away, so he had no sense of where he was. He yelled, hoping to find others alive. This time he received an answer, and the voice was not far away.

He moved toward the voice and found a small party of survivors, most of whom he did not know. But lying on the ground, covered with the burned blankets they had carried through the fire, were Tom Bush, Con McCusker, James Donlon, and his own mother. The blankets afforded little protection against the cold October night air. Even the sight of his mother still alive did not avert Thomas from his thirst. Before he even said anything to her, he asked the others for water. They pointed to a half-filled bucket.

"Tom Bush took that from the well," the man said. "But Thomas Cryin and a little French girl are in there. They're both dead."

Thomas Williamson grabbed the bucket and drank as much as he could, gulping it down. While it satiated his thirst, it did not taste like water. Only after he had drunk his fill did he turn to his mother.

When she asked him if he had seen any others of the family, he could only say no. Neither of them said anything after that. They were too exhausted, so they just lay there, trembling, trying to keep warm, until the sun came up.

As sunlight spread over the burned area, Thomas could see bodies lying close by, some not even six feet away. Everyone struggled to get up. They would have to move, to find someone who could help them. They had no idea if there was anyone left who could even come looking for them. If they were to survive, they would have to head in the direction of Little Sturgeon Bay. Surely they would find help at one of the farmhouses along the way.

Before they left, Thomas walked around the burned area, looking at the bodies, trying to find anyone he knew. He looked for his father, brother, and his cousin Maggie. He went from body to body until he came to the potato patch. There he found the thirty-five bodies all huddled together in an area no more than fifteen square feet.

None of the bodies was recognizable. Later, searchers would identify the bodies through pieces of clothing and other artifacts. The bodies of the men were on the outside of the circle, in an attempt to protect the women. The body of the blacksmith lay next to the huddled group, a little way from it. He was holding a piece of burnt shawl over the face of his little girl. Next to him lay his wife with their other two children nestled close to her as she tried to protect them. Maggie Williamson was part of the burned group, holding a handful of her curly black hair, which she had torn from her head. Only the pieces of jewelry in her hand identified the body of Maggie O'Neil.

Thomas asked Cyril Jarvis to call out for anyone alive. When someone answered, Thomas asked if he were John Williamson. No, came the answer. So he continued to look for his brother, wandering through the potato patch, examining each body he found. There were many scattered about. Finally, he found his brother's body.

Although both his shirts had been burned off, his pants were untouched. He looked natural, Thomas thought. He turned, and walked back to his mother, never looking back at the potato patch.

"John's dead," he told her simply.

She looked down, saying nothing. Then she looked at him and said, "Take me away from here. Take me to Little Sturgeon Bay or Big Sturgeon Bay, but just take me away from this place."

Thomas knew his mother was right. They had to leave because there was nothing they could do for all the friends and family that lay in the potato patch and scattered through the burned fields. There were no horses or other animals left alive, so they would have to walk. Byron J. Merrill, another survivor, came with them. The others remained in the ruins of the settlement to fend for themselves as best they could.

The small group set off. They had a difficult time making their way. They were all badly burned, exhausted from their ordeal of the night before, and weakened from lack of food and water. Thomas was just as thirsty as before and so were the other members of the group, but there was no water to be had. Not only had the fire erased all the landmarks, but the road was so covered with fallen and burned trees that it was nothing more than a winding vague track, so twisted and haunted they kept losing their way.

Tom knew the Murrays lived just three miles away and that they would find food and shelter there. Their thirst became greater as they walked. Finally, they came to the clearing where they expected to find rescue, only to find more devastation. All the buildings were gone, and there was no sign of life. They had not dreamed that the fire had been so large as to consume a farm this far away. At the farm they found a little muddy water, which they drank eagerly. Mrs. Williamson was gulping the water and finally Thomas realized he had to get his mother away from the puddle. He knew that unless he pulled her away she would continue to drink and then she would start to retch from swallowing too much of the dirty water.

They walked on, coming to the Langleys' house just half a mile away. Thomas hoped that Mr. Langley would hitch up his team and take them to Sturgeon Bay, but when they got to the farm their hopes were dashed again. The Langley house was razed; the barn was gone and there were no stirrings of life. Then he saw two horses standing in front of the remains of one of the burned buildings. They did not move as he approached them. He looked around and determined that the horses were standing in front of the remains of the barn. Langley must have freed the mares when he saw the fire coming and they had survived and returned to the barn. They were waiting patiently for their master to come and care for them.

Thomas led the two horses to where his mother was lying on the ground. Both she and Byron Merrill were depleted. He helped his mother onto one horse and Merrill onto the other. Then, leading the horses by their halters, he set off to find the next house. They came to the smoldering ruins of a house and mill. No one was there. Finally, at the next house they found the refuge they were seeking.

It had taken from dawn until three-thirty in the afternoon for the three of them to come the six miles to the Daily house. Although a half dozen families had already taken refuge in their house, the Dailys took them in and did what they could. The survivors were given water, hot food, and a place to sleep. The next day, Mr. Daily said he would take them to Sturgeon Bay where they could receive medical attention for their burns.

⤙

THE STEAMER *UNION* did not arrive in Green Bay until Monday evening. Captain Hawley's voyage had not been easy. He had navigated through smoke and haze so thick he feared for the safety of his ship. When he docked he saw that Green Bay itself was bedlam and he heard about Chicago for the first time. Hawley had brought with him some of those injured in the fire as well as a number of people who simply wanted to be as far from Peshtigo as they could get. He quickly dispatched a crewman to the local telegraph office to send Stephenson's plea for help to Governor Fairchild and to the mayors of Milwaukee, Oshkosh, and Fond du Lac.

There had been rumors that the fires to the north had caused great destruction, but Captain Hawley and those he brought with him provided the first eye-witness accounts, which acutely underestimated the extent of the tragedy. Hawley reported that Peshtigo had been destroyed. For an experienced newspaper man like Franklin Tilton, first reports of tragedies were never taken at face value. "The report seemed too horrible for credence . . . we could but hope that in the excitement of the moment the number of the dead had been overstated," he wrote. It would be some time before the unbelievable extent of the disaster would be known.

From Chicago to Peshtigo, Monday, October 9, ended as it began, in a sad chorus of destruction and desolation. There was only one difference between night and day: the rain the residents had been praying for had finally come.

BRING YOUR
JOB
PRINTING
TO THE
EAGLE OFFICE.

—

We have a

New Liberty Press,

Which enables us to do our work in very
quick time after being ordered.

—

We have also added to our stock, a quantity of

Beautiful New Type,

For the various branches of the art.

—

BILL HEADS,
LETTER HEADS,
BUSINESS CARDS,
VISITING CARDS,
BILLS of LADING,
SHIPPING TAGS,
PROGRAMMES,
HAND BILLS,
ENVELOPES,
RECEIPTS,
BLANKS,
LABELS,

In fact anything in the way of

PLAIN

And Ornamental

PRINTING,

Can be obtained

At the EAGLE Office,

BENTLEY'S BLOCK,

MARINETTE, - WISCONSIN.

13

Until now, Luther Noyes had remained persistently hopeful, looking to a better future even in the face of adversity. By Tuesday, October 10, the world as he knew it had turned inside out. On that cool autumn morning, John Belanger was not hauling crates of wine and whiskey through the Dunlap's front doors; instead he was helping the rescue teams carry victims from Peshtigo and the Sugar Bushes inside. In public Noyes would remain confident, but when he wrote a letter to his old friend Governor Fairchild, Noyes's fear and sorrow revealed themselves.

> *Office of the* Marinette and Peshtigo Eagle
> *Luther B. Noyes, Editor and Publisher.*
>
>
>
> *Marinette, Wis.*
> *Oct. 10th, 1871*
>
>
>
> *Hon. Lucius Fairchild:*
> Can you issue a proclamation to the people of Wisconsin asking for *aid*, money, provisions, clothing, medical supplies—in

short, anything that will relieve the suffering of the people of this section of the state? I enclose for you our extra, but I was not in possession of half the facts at the time it was issued excepting the destruction after tornado. Fully $2,000,000 of property and over 200 lives are lost by the tornado of fire last Sunday night, and over 1500 persons are now dependent on the community, (or what there is left of it) for support. I am writing you neither a phantasie nor a fancy sketch would to God it was it is a heartrending reality, and I am telling you the truth.

It is no ordinary calamity I assure you. Hour after hour, as the details come in they appear more sickening and horrible.

Yours truly

Luther B. Noyes

P.S. Hon. I. Stephenson asked me to write you in relation to this matter. We should have telegraphed you but the line between here and Green Bay is all down.

L. B. N.

Noyes knew that Lucius Fairchild was used to making quick decisions in stressful conditions, and Noyes banked on the hunch that Fairchild would be of help now. Like Isaac Stephenson, Noyes was unaware that the governor was not at the capital in Madison.

Lucius Fairchild had served with great distinction in the 2nd Wisconsin Infantry of the famous Iron Brigade during the Civil War. At Antietam he was so sick he had to be helped onto his horse, but he then led his regiment in "the bloodiest day America ever saw," in a battle where his regiment suffered casualties over 50 percent. At Gettysburg on July 1, 1863, Colonel Fairchild led his regiment as the Iron Brigade faced nine times their number in Herbst's Woods. When ordered to hold the woods "to the last extremity," they stood their ground. When they did receive the order to retire to Seminary Ridge, they fell back in good order, firing as they went.

With their fierce fighting, and their lives, they bought the time necessary for the rest of the Union army to fall back and prepare positions to meet the Rebel advance. One of the Rebel officers commented on the bravery of the men who refused to give ground in the face of overwhelming numbers, saying that "they lay in rows as if mustered on the parade ground." Only 69 men of the 2nd Wisconsin remained of the 302 who went into battle that day, and only 600 of the 1,883 men of the Iron Brigade were left. But they did not break and had stood fast to hold the Union line. In the midst of this carnage was Lucius Fairchild, leading each charge, organizing the line, calmly urging his regiment to stand fast and give even greater effort.

During the battle, Fairchild's left arm was completely severed just above the elbow by a cannonball, and for the rest of his life he proudly wore his empty left sleeve neatly folded and hanging at his side, reminding all who saw him of his service and his sacrifice. Now in the face of a state tragedy, Noyes was certain he could rely on Fairchild's willingness and ability to serve and lead in the worst circumstances.

Only clerks were left in the capitol offices when Isaac Stephenson's telegram arrived on the morning of Tuesday, October 10, and another day would pass before the governor received the letter Noyes had just written. An elderly clerk opened the telegram from Isaac Stephenson. When he read the urgent plea for help he did not know what to do. Everyone in any position of authority had gone to the aid of Chicago. With no one else to whom he could turn, he turned to the governor's wife.

He went quickly to the governor's house. Breathlessly he read the telegram to the governor's young wife, Frances "Frank" Fairchild. Even as he was reading it, the young woman grabbed her hat and cloak and ran out the door. The clerk ran after her, following her all the way to the capitol, where she, a mere twenty-four-year-old, quickly and firmly took charge. As she started to give orders, not a person there questioned her. Although she had no legal authority, they obeyed her instantly. Her daughter, Mary Fairchild Morris, recalled how "once there she took charge of everything and everybody, and they all obeyed her."

Frances Fairchild gave orders and dictated telegrams. When she discovered there was a freight car filled with relief supplies for Chicago waiting on a sidetrack, she simply commandeered it for the people of Peshtigo. She went to the railroad yard to inspect the contents for herself. She found the car filled with food and clothing. Knowing well the weather of northern Wisconsin at that time of year, she asked if the cargo included blankets. No, the railroad officials said. Besides, the car was full and had no room for any further cargo.

Frances Fairchild would not be denied. She sent clerks, servants, anyone she could to the homes of friends throughout Madison. "Bring all the blankets you can," she ordered them. And they did. As word spread through the town, people came to the railroad yard with their blankets and quilts, and the governor's wife supervised the packing of the train car. Railroad men who had declared the car full now watched as Frances Fairchild had dozens of blankets stuffed into the car. Only when there was no possible way to squeeze even one more blanket into the car did she order it sent north immediately, with precedence over all other traffic. Within hours of receiving the first plea for help, Frances Fairchild had supplies on the way to the end of the rail line at Fort Howard.

Even as the train was leaving, Frances Fairchild turned her efforts to gathering even more supplies. She called together the people of Madison, told them of the disaster in the north, and told them what was needed. Urgent telegrams were sent to Chicago to inform Governor Fairchild of the emergency in his own state.

FRANCES FAIRCHILD HAD acted on instinct regarding the number of blankets and supplies that were needed in Peshtigo. Her instinct proved correct. There were far more injured than could be handled in the hospital at the Dunlap House, so another was quickly established at the Kirby House in Menominee, and a third at A. C. Merryman's boardinghouse. Still, over three hundred injured were housed in homes and boardinghouses in Marinette and Menominee. And even hundreds more were taken to homes, hotels, boardinghouses, and hospitals in Green Bay and surrounding communities.

But it was to the Dunlap House that the first injured were taken. Here a father, mother, and six children including a baby all lay together, all terribly burned. An old man of seventy-six thrashed on his cot after losing his wife, daughter, son, and eight grandchildren, crying out, "*Meine Frau, meine Frau.*" Another family was snuffed to extinction as its members died one by one, the mother first, then one child, then another. Close by, an old woman writhed in pain, moaning loudly. A small boy rested on a cot without complaint even though his abdomen was so thoroughly burned his intestines bulged out.

Dr. Jacob May of Fond du Lac moved among the burned and dying, assisted by the young Dr. Ben Hall, fresh from medical school. Dr. May meticulously recorded in his notebooks the names and injuries of the sixty-four people he treated immediately after the fire. He also recorded the names of the eleven who died.

> Mr. Joseph Prestine, age 74, German, burned in both hands and face. Lost wife, daughter with husband and five children, another daughter with husband and five children.
> Mr. John Bush, Irish, burned both feet and arms and face, badly burned with bronchitis.

Mr. Joshua Creamer, Spaniard, burned both thighs and below knees, with acute bronchitis. Wife's father, mother and three brothers were lost.

Joshua Creamer, burned badly on breast, abdomen and side.

Mary Creamer, burned hand and arm.

Creamer child, (horribly burned on head and face) acute bronchitis.

Mr. Wm. Penerie, English, burned both hands and arms, lost wife, adopted child, wife's father and mother, brother-in-law, niece and nephew, and his own father, mother, and three brothers.

Joseph Helms, German, burned all over body and extremities, with acute bronchitis . . . Lost wife and child.

A German cook, burned both hands and feet, with acute bronchitis.

Many of the burn victims died of renal failure before they could ever reach help in Marinette or Menominee. Because burns cause serious electrolyte imbalances in the body and many survivors had to wait three or four days without food or water to correct fluid depletion, they died before help arrived. Many died as the jolting wagons carried them miles to the Dunlap House. Then, even if they were taken to one of the makeshift hospitals, they would find only a few trained doctors and nurses and untrained volunteers. In the worst burn cases, secondary infections were common, especially where the fire had eaten through all the layers of skin and muscle, leaving patches of exposed bone. These open wounds in unsterile surroundings led to gangrene and other septic infections, resistant to potions and ointments. Tinctures, salves, and clean dressings were the only remedies available for the care of burns. (In most cases, severe third-degree burns would require special baths and debridement procedures in a burn center today.) Those without serious burns were often suffering from critical respiratory problems:

collapsed lungs, seared lungs, bronchial swelling, and smoke inhalation. And still others died of cardiac arrest resulting from dehydration and hypovolemic shock.

———✦———

ON THE SECOND day after the fire, the passage of each hour brought another revelation. The fire had obliterated the settlement of Brussels on the Door County Peninsula; the Abram Place homestead was housing over fifty burn victims who had walked, half delirious, to his farm; Karl Lamp had been taken to the hospital but was so traumatized by the death of his family he could not speak; Almira Race's burned body had been found on a narrow trail, the shortcut that proved fatal when she tried to make her way home to her family; the Peshtigo River was littered with dead trout as well as the bodies of its townspeople; a man was found in Peshtigo looting one of the dead victims, and the men who discovered the thief decided on the spot to hang him; Lucius Fairchild had just discovered there was a greater disaster in his own state; and William Ogden, who'd asked to be kept informed by telegram along the rail line as he was heading westward, received the message that Peshtigo had been completely consumed.

Indeed, the ravages of the fire were vast and extraordinary. In both Chicago and Peshtigo, and all the other areas the fire "tornado" struck, the survivors' certainty that the world was coming to an end during the most intense moments of the firestorm appeared inarguable. Still, on October 10 no one could say precisely what had hit the states of Illinois, Wisconsin, and Michigan, nor could they explain the strange phenomena of that night except to recall its horrors. Even as they choked out their descriptions of fire from heaven or the earth shaking beneath their feet like an explosion or earthquake, they were still at a loss to capture the astonishing night in words.

Increase Lapham was in Milwaukee on that Tuesday morning, awaiting word from General Albert Myer, sensing he might be sent to Chicago to begin an investigation into the exact nature and causes of the blowup. The mean temperature that day in Milwaukee had dipped to 47 degrees Fahrenheit, quite a contrast to the 81 degrees and 82 degrees of the previous two days. The cloud cover was at a maximum of 10, and Lapham wrote in his notes: "Chicago and several towns burned. Great fires everywhere." The next day, as the magnitude of the fires became fact, he wrote: "Fires extending through Michigan and Canada."

In Chicago Sam Brookes's records indicated winds out of the west, recorded as a 2 and a 3, which designated a "gentle breeze" and a "fresh breeze" respectively. He made a one-word note: "Fires."

Lapham had already received a telegram from a Chicago friend who had heard wrongly that Lapham was dead. Lapham wired the friend that he was alive and well and said he would send money and provisions to his friend immediately.

Rumors of the dead who were not and misinformation about the extent of destruction were the order of the day. By the time William Ogden arrived in Chicago on the evening of the tenth, he, too, would be faced with a daunting error in communication despite dispatches he'd received during his express train ride from New York.

"When I reached the depot," he wrote, "it was quite dark, the burning district had no lamps, thousands of smoldering fires were all that could be seen, and they added to the mournful gloom."

Ogden hired a hack driver to transport him through the ruins, telling the driver to take the La Salle Street tunnel, which was still open, a bleak passageway through a bleaker, ash-silvered ruin. When Ogden emerged from the tunnel on the north side and tried to make his way on foot to Ontario Street, he was challenged by the wreckage of houses, the swamps of ash, and the flickering blue coal flames. At first he thought he must be walking in the wrong direction, until he was confronted with the fact that Ogden Grove with its hothouse and graveled drives, its protective and elegant shrubbery, and its magnificent Italianate mansion, were gone. The dispatches he'd received were incorrect: his brother Mahlon's house had been saved, not his.

Ogden was confronted with some harsh facts. All that he had built in Chicago was gone. He had returned in his old age to Chicago just as he had first arrived as a young man, if not penniless, then certainly not the prosperous millionaire who had retired to his private estate in New York, content to receive the profits from his investments. "Millions will not cover the loss of our family," he wrote to a friend in New York.

The next morning, Wednesday, October 11, as Ogden walked around the twisted tree trunks and shards of glass assaying his losses in Chicago, he received the second blow: confirmation that the preliminary report on Peshtigo was accurate. Ogden was informed that the sawmill, woodenware factory, boardinghouse, company store, and railroad equipment had been razed to the ground. Worse, as another day dawned, the death toll in the north had risen.

In Peshtigo, inspection committees and burial parties needed to be formed promptly. Chicago nearly boasted that their fire was "the greatest fire of the age." The city was perversely determined to outclass both the Great Fire of London in 1666 and the burning of Moscow in 1812 by Napoleon. In reality, the 250 deaths in Chicago were a mere fraction of the deaths in Wisconsin. Of Peshtigo's 2,000 known residents, over 1,800 of them were now dead. And there were many more dead in the Sugar Bushes and outlying districts, and on the Door County Peninsula.

Ogden remained in Chicago for several days, after which he boarded a steamer in Green Bay and set off for Peshtigo.

—◆—

TWO WEEKS LATER, a committee made up of reporters from Green Bay, businessmen, and Luther Noyes embarked on the inspection of Peshtigo and the outlying areas. They tried to follow the path they believed the fire and tornado, or the "fire tornado," took in an effort both to determine the nature of the phenomenon and to reconstruct its patterns. The more ground they covered on their walking tour, the more mysterious that hellish night seemed. The trees seemed to have been blown down, rather than burned down—yanked viciously from the ground by their roots. In one spot, the hot sand had been spun into a glass sheet around a tree trunk. It takes temperatures of more than 1,800 degrees to transform sand into glass.

Increase Lapham had received his orders to go to Chicago on October 12 in order to reconstruct the wind speeds of that night, then prepare a reasonable explanation for this conflagration. Until they received official scientific findings, both Noyes's *Eagle* and Tilton's *Advocate* reported the survivors' stories, then discounted them as "made from whole cloth."

The indisputable findings, however, were the people themselves. On the tour of the stricken countryside, one burial party encountered a boy, about twelve years old, who was digging graves on a small farm in the Upper Bush. The boy was working steadily, digging yet another grave next to a row of fresh graves. A row of small, plain coffins lay close to the graves. He was the sole survivor of his family. When the fire struck, he had crawled into a deep well and covered his head with a blanket that he kept wetting as the fire raged overhead, he explained. And when he emerged from the well he found everyone in his family dead, all nine of them.

The boy did not ask the burial party for anything. He simply said, "What am I to do alone in the world now?"

The bodies of the boy's family were not really bodies but lumps of charred flesh, some with a few remnants of burned clothing, others with bones sticking out. The burial party gathered what was left of the boy's family. There was so little left they did not need nine boxes. They just filled a few of them with the remains and buried them where they had found them. The men moved quickly and quietly.

After the burial party had moved on to the next farm, the boy dug up what was left of his family from their graves. He opened the boxes and distributed the remains among the nine coffins he had made. Then he nailed each coffin shut. The coffins were not very big. He picked up a coffin, placed it on his small shoulders, and walked the one mile from the farm to the cemetery. He buried each coffin in a grave.

The road to Peshtigo no longer cut through a forest so dense that men had a hard time walking through it. What peaty soil had not burned had been blown away by the tornado, which had also leveled the giant pine trees as if they were blades of grass. In many instances, the labyrinthian root systems of the fallen trees had been ripped from the ground. The smoking craters created from the torn root systems were as wide as the uppermost span of tree branches; therefore, fifty- to seventy-foot-wide holes pocked the landscape and posed great obstacles for those who needed to venture among them. The trees that had not been leveled had been reduced to stumps.

The group moved through the gray clouds as the horses and wagons plodded through the burned remains. Men wrapped their faces in handkerchiefs to keep from breathing the smoke and to block the smell of death. But the stench could not be stopped. Some men vom-ited. The fire may have passed, but its spirit remained, determined to extract the last full measure from those who had survived.

As they approached the town they came upon what was left of the wagons belonging to those who had tried to flee to what they thought would be the safety of Marinette. Only twisted, melted pieces of metal scattered among the ashes were left to mark where they fell in their doomed flight. Little was left of the occupants of those wagons.

———

IT SEEMED THAT even the neatly laid streets had been eroded away, and the composition of the soil had been transformed from dirt with some texture, deep color, and density to a fine, desertlike dust. Entering the ashes at the edge of the town, Noyes saw that nothing remained of the Congregationalist church but a few pieces of burned wood, a few bricks. A few yards away, where the finest houses in town once stood, including the summer home of William Ogden and other prominent citizens, not even foundations were left to mark where the houses had been. Farther on lay a shapeless lump of metal, all that remained of the several-hundred-pound fire bell that had hung in the cupola of the firehouse. An entire train loaded with lum-ber had simply disappeared, leaving only the partially melted wheels and the burned engine as markers of where it once stood.

However, it was what they saw lying amid all this devastation that left them numb. Bloated bodies floated in the river and lined the banks. The carcasses of fifty horses lay in regular rows where they had stood in their stalls in a livery stable. Nothing was left of the stable building. Sometimes they found bodies fully clothed and untouched by fire. More often they found naked bodies, most burned beyond recognition, only three-quarters their normal size. Survivors would point to a spot and tell how they had seen someone burst into flame and collapse there. Only some ashes and maybe a melted metal object marked where the person had fallen.

Dazed survivors moved through the town looking for family members or friends. Many were severely burned themselves, and still they asked, "Have you seen my children?" "Have you seen my wife?" "Have you seen my husband?" Few received any answer, let alone the answer they were seeking.

Some men vomited when they began to collect the bodies for burial, moving down the streets to the riverbank. Victims had died singly and in groups, almost seventy of them.

When the burial party picked up the body of one woman, they found she was lying on top of a baby. She had tried to protect her child with her body, but both had been completely burned. A small boy was kneeling, as if praying, his head bent down on his hands. He was completely roasted. Someone recognized him as the son of Mr. Tanner.

Some bodies were without arms or legs. When they tried to move a body with arms and legs, the limbs would break off. At first they used sticks and boards to pick up the bodies, but these tools only served to break the bodies apart. Even shovels only picked up an arm or leg. Someone gathered barrel staves from the smoldering ruins of the woodenware factory. They slid three or four staves under a body or body part, then slid a board through the row of staves, using it as a handle to pick up the hoops and the body part. Loggers, who had seen men crushed by falling tree limbs and rolling logs, who had seen men rip an opponent's eye out in a fight, fell to the ground and wept, unable to pick up one more child.

In many cases even the ashes were gone, blown away by the wind. Just before the fire struck the town, a group of Swedish workmen were seen digging a ditch as a firebreak. After the fire, burial parties found the ditch and the melted metal from their shovels and pick-axes, nothing else. A father cried that when he looked for the bodies of his three children he found nothing because the wind had blown even their ashes away. Silas McMinn identified his wife's body from the shawl pin that lay in the ashes.

Little remained of the people who had sought safety in the three-story Peshtigo Company boardinghouse, so no one knew how many people had died in the building. Fay Dooley's grandmother claimed there were two hundred people in the building when the fire struck it. Other reports put the number at no more than sixty. Among those who died in the building was the family of Donald Roy McDonald, superintendent of the woodenware factory. Since the building was on the east side of the Peshtigo River, McDonald thought his wife, Margaret, and their nine children would be safe since he did not believe the fire could cross the river. "Stay here, no matter what happens," he had told his wife, and she did. After the fire had passed, McDonald searched the ruins for some sign of his family, but like the burial parties searching with him, he found only "a heap of indistinguishable calcined bones and charred flesh . . . giving no clue to sex or number."

Perhaps the best evidence that both a tornado and a fire had rav-aged the town on October 8 was that the fire never touched the set-tlement at Peshtigo Harbor. True to a tornado's nature, the vortex stays on its terrifying course, creating the strange pattern of destruc-tion capable of leveling one city block while the opposite side remains intact. Peshtigo Harbor was six miles to the right of the tor-nado's path, but the self-sufficient settlement was safely not part of the storm's pattern.

Therefore, the sawmill at Peshtigo Harbor was working. Wagon loads of lumber were brought from this mill to Peshtigo where men made rough coffins. Whatever was left of a body was placed in a coffin and taken to the cemetery. A long line of wagons filled with coffins waited at the cemetery for graves to be dug, but there were not enough shovels. Burying the dead was going slowly. Those who were identified were given simple wooden markers with their name on it. The unidentified dead were gathered together in a mass grave.

Once the town had been cleared of bodies, the burial parties moved out into the Sugar Bushes. The steady stream of survivors seeking help in town had told them of the many who had died in the fields and of the many who had survived and needed help. Men piled wagons with lumber and nails, then struck off down a road looking for bodies. They did not have far to go.

In a cornfield just outside town, they found huddled together the bodies of sixty-eight people who had sought refuge in the open field. On the roads they found the remains of the wagons of those who had tried to flee from the fire. Burial parties found the dead in root cellars, wells, the smoldering foundations of houses and farm buildings, plowed fields, culverts, and gulleys.

Ben Phillips, who along with his family had found refuge in the mud of Place's Brook, found fifteen men, women, and children lying in a row facedown in a furrow. Even as he examined the bodies, he noticed a smoking heap across the road. When he investigated, he found "the remains of a dozen teams and wagons lined up in a row . . . they were the rigs of families racing for Peshtigo" when they were overtaken by fire. "One driver's horses, their manes and tails on fire, went berserk and rammed off the road into a stand of young maples. The first team was snared by its neck yoke, and the other horses followed like sheep. The people leaped from their wagons and ran toward Place's Brook, but they were struck down almost immediately."

A man from Marinette went to look for his sister and her family who had a farm in the Upper Bush. He placed the five rough coffins he had made in the back of the wagon and set out. Only the rows of ashes from the rail fences marked the Noquebay Road. Once this land had been filled with good farms and gardens, new houses, lots of livestock. Now it was completely burned. The burial parties had already passed this way.

He turned off the main road and rode along the rough side-road, passing a burnt heap with leg bones sticking out of it. The burial parties had not been down the side roads yet. He saw the ruins in the distance. The limestone doorstep, metal cook stove, and fallen chimney were all that was left of the farmhouse. In the yard he saw the remains of a wagon. He moved closer and saw there was something under the burned remnants of the axles and wheel rims. He took his shovel and put what was left of the man, woman, and three children on a piece of canvas. He wrapped the family in the canvas and placed them in one of the coffins he had brought. Then he took them home.

Throughout the Sugar Bush they found tragic scenes that would haunt some of them for the rest of their lives. Sam Woodward told his two children to "sit right by the yard fence." After the fire they found the two children still sitting there untouched by fire but dead from suffocation. They looked as if they were sleeping.

In the town of Brussels, "three or four children were found on their hands and knees, with their heads against a large stump, dead in this position . . . the victims had apparently died without a struggle, probably killed outright by the first hot breath they inhaled." John Bagnall found the body of a young girl with long, curly hair lying by a log as if sleeping. Bagnall was struck by how peaceful and lonely she looked. With no one to claim the body she would be buried in the mass grave. He leaned over and clipped a lock of her hair. He carried that lock of hair in his wallet for the rest of his life. He told his daughter that every time he looked at it, that unknown child was remembered.

Christ Diedrich found his brother's body lying with the bodies of his four children. All were burned beyond recognition. Nearby, leaning against the remains of a burned tree, stood the calcined body of his sister-in-law, standing silent watch over her dead family.

Those who died in wells died from suffocation or from the well curbs burning and falling in on them. A reporter wrote of the eight members of the Hill family dying when "the wooden house covering the well caught fire, fell in, and burned the entire party to death."

At the home of John Church, the town blacksmith, the burial party found the parents and their two younger sons dead, the burned bodies lying in the ruins of the house. Nearby lay the body of their twenty-two-year-old son, untouched by the fire. His throat had been slashed.

14

On Wednesday, October 11, Frances Fairchild quietly surrendered her position of unofficial acting chief executive of the state of Wisconsin and became once again the beautiful, charming wife and aide of her husband, the governor.

Governor Fairchild needed to know the extent and nature of the disaster before he could plan any relief efforts. In addition to the *Union*, the *St. Joseph* and the *George L. Newman* brought the injured and others to Green Bay. Their tales gave officials little information about the scope of the disaster and what kind of aid they needed to send. After reading the information telegraphed to him from Green Bay, Governor Fairchild decided he had to go immediately to Peshtigo to see for himself.

Based on his inspection trip and the reports of state agents he had sent to gather information about the outlying areas, Fairchild knew that the need for aid was greater than the resources at hand. In a day when people would never think of turning to the government for help, he saw it as his duty to solicit aid from the public, then see that the aid was delivered to those who needed it. Still, the need was so great that Fairchild wrote to Secretary of War William Belknap on the same day he issued his appeal for help. His plea was published not only in Wisconsin's newspapers but was carried by newspapers across the country and even in a number of foreign countries:

AN APPEAL

Green Bay
Oct. 13

To the People of Wisconsin:
The accounts of the appalling calamity which have fallen upon the east and west shores of Green Bay have not been exaggerated. The burned district comprises the counties of Oconto, Brown, Door and Kewaunee, and parts of Manitowoc and Outagamie. The great loss of life and property has resulted from the whirlwind of fire which swept over the country, making the roads and avenues of escape impassable with fallen timber and burned bridges. The previous long drouth [sic] had prepared everything for the flames. The loss of life has been very great. The first estimates were entirely inadequate, and even now it is feared that it is much greater than present accounts place it. It is known that at least one thousand persons have either burned, drowned or smothered. Of these deaths, six hundred or more at Peshtigo and adjacent places, and the others in Door, Kewaunee and Brown counties. Men are now penetrating that almost inaccessible region for the purpose of affording relief, and I fear that their reports will increase this estimate. From the most reliable sources of information I learn that not less than 3,000 men, women and children have been rendered entirely destitute. Mothers are left with fatherless children, fathers with motherless children, children are left homeless orphans. Distress and intense suffering are on every hand, where but a few days

ago were comfort and happiness. Scores of men, women and little children now lie helpless. They are burned and maimed, in temporary hospitals, cared for by more fortunate neighbors. These suffering people must be supplied with food, bedding, clothing, feed for cattle, and the means of providing shelter during the winter. The response by the good people of Wisconsin has already been prompt and generous. It is meeting the immediate need, and is being faithfully and energetically distributed through the relief organization at Green Bay, but provision must be made for months in the future. There are wanted flour, salt, and cured meat, NOT COOKED, blankets, bedding, stoves, building materials, lights, farming implements and tools, boots, shoes, clothing for men, women and children, log chains, axes with handles, nails, glass and house trimmings, and indeed, everything needed by a farming community that has lost everything.

To expedite the transfers at Green Bay all boxes should have cards attached to them, stating their contents, and all supplies should be sent to the Relief Committee at Green Bay. Money contributed should not be turned into supplies, but should be forwarded to the committee. Depots have been established at Green Bay, under management of public-spirited and energetic men who have the confidence of all, for the receiving and distributing of supplies. They have organized a system of regions, and steamboats and wagons are being sent out with supplies. Let us uphold their hands in the good work, and see that their depots be kept filled to overflowing. It is fortunate that we live in a wealthy and prosperous state, blessed with prosperity in business and overflowing harvests, and that thus we are, by a wise Providence, endowed with the means to help our less fortunate neighbors.

I am urged by the public-spirited citizens of the state to call an immediate extra session of the Legislature to provide for this calamity. I have given serious attention to this suggestion, and have concluded not to do so, for the reason that the

> expense of such session would be likely to equal the amount which the state would be asked to contribute. Believing, therefore, that the people and the Legislature will endorse my action in this emergency, I have, in conjunction with the State Treasurer, decided to advance such a moderate sum of money as seems to be appropriate in addition to that contributed.
>
> *Lucius Fairchild*
> *Governor of the State of Wisconsin*

Later, some members of the legislature charged that Fairchild had appropriated this money without proper legal authorization and had overstepped his authority. But the extent of the disaster would mute such voices to the point where Fairchild's successor, Cadwallader Washburn, would in his first speech to the legislature pointedly approve of Fairchild's actions. "I place before the Legislature, the very full and satisfactory report of my predecessor, detailing his actions in regard to the sufferers. The responsibility taken by him and the State Treasurer cannot fail to meet your approval. The urgency of the case fully justifies their action." As the relief effort expanded, Fairchild and the legislature decided that there was no need for additional state money and private aid was sufficient. The state needed only to coordinate and supervise the distribution of the aid.

Not until Fairchild left office in January 1872 did the legislature unanimously pass a resolution expressing its "special thanks" for his efforts. The resolution specifically thanked Fairchild for saving the state "the expense of calling an extra session of the Legislature," for assuming "the responsibility of drawing upon the State Treasurer for the relief of the sufferers," and for "organizing and executing effective plans for administering to the pressing necessities of so large a number of our inhabitants rendered helpless, homeless and destitute" by the recent disaster. The issue of Fairchild overstepping his authority was thus firmly and finally put to rest.

Spontaneously, relief committees had been formed in many

towns. These committees were busy raising funds and collecting and distributing supplies even as Fairchild issued his appeal. In Green Bay, the relief committee was formed at a public meeting on Tuesday afternoon, October 10, and set to work immediately. The Saturday issue of the *State Gazette* carried the committee's call for assistance.

"It is most appalling and frightful. Words are too weak, and language too tame to describe the great calamity. . . . Let us not weary in well-doing—let us not flag in our efforts to mitigate suffering— let us organize our forces not for temporary relief but for a continuance of effort during the dread winter which is coming on."

At its first meeting, the Green Bay relief committee heard the following letter read:

> *Menominee, Mich.*
> *10th Oct, 1871*
>
> *Mayor of Green Bay:*
> A terrible calamity fell upon these Towns on Sunday night and yesterday morning. Peshtigo Village, Mills, Factory and the Sugar Bush Settlement were entirely swept away by fire, and from one to three hundred lives lost, and a large number badly burned. The dead are lying in the streets, and it is horrible to look upon. We need all the medical aid that can be sent at once. Menekaune all burned and half of Marinette but Peshtigo is the greatest calamity of all, and needs aid at once. Pray send it and help us to save the people, who are destitute.
> *Isaac Stephenson*
> *Joseph Harris*

The Green Bay committee moved quickly to organize a systematic campaign to raise funds, collect supplies, and organize a distribution system even as aid was being sent to the affected areas on an ad hoc basis. "Loaded teams are constantly leaving for the country, containing supplies for the suffering people. Reports are constantly arriving of the pressing need of those along the East shore, and transportation cannot be obtained fast enough," Franklin Tilton reported in the *Advocate*.

Green Bay was located between the two areas that needed help, the Peshtigo area to the northwest and the peninsula to the east. Already over three hundred survivors from Peshtigo had arrived in Green Bay seeking shelter and medical care. "There were many with blistered faces and hands, some with their eyes almost put out, others with hair singed off, and maims and bruises upon their persons," according to one newspaper account. And more survivors from Williamsonville, New Franken, and other settlements streamed into town seeking aid and telling of people stranded in the burned areas without the means or ability to leave.

Every day brought new stories as survivors straggled into town. "Four badly burned persons were brought up on the *Ozakee* Thursday afternoon, from Williamsonville. They presented a horrid sight. It is feared that one them, whose face was burned to a crisp, cannot recover. They were immediately conveyed to the Turner Hall Hospital." Finally, the survivors were proof that "accounts have not been exaggerated. Indeed, the half has not been told," the *Gazette* reported. And the descriptions in the newspaper drove home this point again and again. "One member of a family, all blistered and disfigured, half starved and half naked, would state how the remaining members of the family had perished in the flames. Little children, whose parents had burned to death, were brought in by kind-hearted neighbors, themselves scarcely able to drag their own bodies over the weary miles."

KARL LAMP DID not remember when they removed him from the Dunlap House to the hospital in Green Bay. Once, when a nurse

in Green Bay was changing the dressings on his burns, he thought
he was in a boardinghouse in Peshtigo. When he was conscious
enough to speak, he could speak only German; he had lost the English words he had learned. A doctor who spoke German asked him
if he remembered how he had gotten to Green Bay, but Lamp could
only say in German, "Boat and wagon." While Lamp's body continued to heal, his mind refused.

He was healing slowly and did as he was told, saying nothing,
feeling nothing, moving as only a hollow man can move. As far as
Karl was concerned, now that he'd lost his wife and children, he was
lost, too. His soul disappeared into the flames with them, leaving
only the damaged husk of his body.

A doctor told Karl that the hole in his side would never completely close, that he would have to keep it covered with a clean
dressing and change it regularly. He began teaching Karl how to
take a piece of clean cloth, scorch it, and then cover the hole with it,
using a long strip of cloth to wrap around his body and hold the
dressing in place. Karl dutifully followed the doctor's instructions,
asking no questions.

◆

THE PEOPLE OF Green Bay rose to the task of supporting and
ministering to the victims, and the entire city directed all its efforts
to helping those who needed it. The *Gazette* reported: "In the city
there has been the most intense excitement . . . and the only activity noticeable has arisen from the efforts in behalf of the suffering
multitudes who have sought refuge here." Fortunately, relief supplies were flooding the city, providing ample supplies to meet the
demand.

Train cars had already arrived from Milwaukee, Madison, Fond
du Lac, Oshkosh, Appleton, Neenah, Baraboo, Oconomowoc, Rio,

Janesville, Edgerton, Ripon, Racine, and Berlin, and nine more cars were known to be on their way. The problem was how to get the supplies to the people who needed them most, and to get the right supplies to them. This would prove to be the most difficult task, and would lead later to some criticism of the relief efforts.

On October 18, Fairchild received a telegram from Lieutenant General P. H. Sheridan: "Can I be of any service to the sufferers from fire in the burnt district of your state if so what do you want? Please ask me only for what you know is necessary." And two days later, perhaps because President Grant and General Belknap remembered Fairchild's service during the war and wanted to return the service, the secretary of war notified Fairchild that he had ordered Sheridan to send not only the wagons, harnesses, coats, and pants, but also blankets, and 200,000 rations of hard bread, beans, bacon, dried beef, pork, sugar, rice, tea, and coffee.

Other offers of aid poured in. A committee of the chamber of commerce of the city of New York sent a telegram authorizing $15,000 in cash and Kidder Peabody of Boston sent $10,000. Dozens of other telegrams arrived offering amounts from $100 to $1,000. Even the Chicago Relief Committee sent $1,000 "to aid those who are suffering from the recent terrible fires in your State."

Fairchild moved quickly to organize the disparate relief efforts. He established two relief committees, one in Milwaukee and one in Green Bay, and assigned specific areas for them to cover. The Milwaukee committee supplied the eastern burned areas from the peninsula down to Manitowoc and Kewaunee Counties, while the Green Bay committee supplied the needs of Peshtigo, Marinette, Menominee, and the surrounding areas. Local committees were established in each village to distribute the supplies. In Peshtigo, F. J. Bartels, the owner of the general merchandise store whose loss of $30,000 of property in the fire was among the greatest, was placed in charge of local relief supplies.

While relief committees continued in many other towns, their efforts were coordinated with the two main relief committees.

On paper this looked to be a logical structure for organizing the flow of supplies to the burned district. But according to some accounts, this structure hampered rather than helped the relief effort. A newspaper correspondent from Chicago, who traveled throughout the burned district, criticized this committee structure. "I must say that, after a full investigation, I have come to the conclusion that there is too much committee entirely."

He was critical also of establishing a committee and a supply depot in Milwaukee. "For my part, I can not see any sense in directing any supplies for the Wisconsin sufferers to any point south of Green Bay."

Sending supplies to Milwaukee for distribution simply delayed the relief efforts while thousands suffered. Better, he wrote, to just send all supplies to Green Bay, "which is on the southern border of the burnt region, and whose citizens, with one will, are doing all they can to alleviate the misfortunes of the unfortunates. They are a whole-soul people, who without compensation, are doing a grand work. All they need is the goods, and they will see that only the deserving get anything."

Initially, most of the aid came from the people of Wisconsin because the rest of the country was transfixed by the Chicago fire. However, when the Chicago fire became old news in the New York tabloids, the newspapers and the public turned their attention to Peshtigo. None of the papers in New York or other states bothered to send a reporter to see the aftermath of the fire firsthand; instead, they simply ran rewritten accounts from local papers in Wisconsin. Many of these accounts were sensationalized, and they caught the public's attention. When the papers later published Governor Fairchild's appeal for help, the flood started.

Franklin Tilton was amazed when "food and clothing began to pour into Green Bay, first by the carload, and then by the trainload. There came cooked provisions and bread apparently enough to feed all the people of the State, until we were obliged to cry 'enough.'" In one day, fifteen carloads of clothing arrived in Green Bay. Large storage depots were established in Milwaukee and Green Bay to process all the supplies flooding in. Volunteers, most of them women, spent entire weeks sorting and repacking the supplies.

The perishable food was dispatched immediately. Other food, including canned goods, salted meat, and flour, was packed in barrels, crates, and boxes. As the flood of supplies grew, transportation became even more critical. There simply were not enough horses and wagons to move the aid to where it was needed most in the burned areas. Wagons and teams with drivers as well as steamboats were pressed into service. Men were sent deep into the burned areas in buckboards, on horseback, and even on foot, carrying supplies to the remotest farms. But the need was immediate and if help did not arrive quickly, tragedy could be piled on tragedy. On a remote farm, rescuers arrived with supplies only to find the young girl who was the only member of her family to survive the fire, dead of starvation.

Over nine thousand people were receiving some form of aid, from medical attention to food, clothing, shelter, and supplies, in order to start life anew. Still, not everyone was pleased with the relief efforts.

Captain A. J. Langworthy, chairman of the Peshtigo Relief Committee, who was assigned to report on the relief fund, noted that they had been forced to pay compensation to local committee workers because "the disagreeable duties of the office, and the clamorous demands of the people, who annoyed them at all hours of the day and night, occupying their entire time, made it necessary to give them some compensation, in order to have the work performed."

He called it "arduous and unpleasant work" that resulted in a constant turnover in both general and local committees. Perhaps the recipients of the aid resented that they had to prove their loss, that after all they had suffered they had to document the loss of all they had worked so hard to build. For their part, the aid administrators found recipients greedy. One aid administrator complained that people "lost a fence and wanted a farm."

Dr. B. T. Phillips, who had been placed in charge of the patients in A. C. Merryman's boardinghouse by Governor Fairchild, was also disturbed about the administration of relief efforts and the behavior of the relief administrators. He wrote a long letter to Governor Fairchild detailing his complaints. The Green Bay Relief Committee was questioning all medical attention given to survivors and doing all that it could to reduce what it saw as unnecessary expenses. Dr. Phillips had quite a different view of the situation, a view that he expressed strongly and in no uncertain terms to the governor.

Because Merryman insisted that he needed his boardinghouse for his own business, Dr. Phillips was forced to move his fifty-four patients into private homes and the company barracks. Thus, he had to travel widely to see his patients. Worse, conditions for most of them were more than "uncomfortable." He now had "10 bad cases of Typhoid fever, lying in quarters that would awaken the feelings of anyone and ought to arouse the indignation of every friend of humanity."

Such conditions were so bad that he felt "it is little better than murder to leave [patients] in such a place in their condition." Indeed, Dr. Phillips bluntly stated that treating the injured in the present facilities "cannot but prove disastrous and unsatisfactory and I am not willing to hazard my reputation, nor thus lightly play with human life, as one must to retain the responsibility under present circumstances."

He went on to charge that the relief committee was not doing its job. "I feel indignant at the manner in which I have been treated by persons purporting to be your agents." Captain Bourne of the Green Bay Relief Committee came to town and, without even visiting the hospital or consulting with Dr. Phillips about the condition of the patients, "began telling me that I must break up the Hospital and stop expenses." All the members of the local relief committee felt so badly treated by the Green Bay committee that they were discouraged from continuing their work.

The Green Bay committee became notorious for slow payment of any bills presented to it by another committee. Dr. Phillips wrote that A. C. Merryman would not allow the use of any more buildings because he had not yet been paid for any of his expenses and "he feared he might have to pay it himself." So slow was payment that he had ordered a second supply of medicine even while waiting for Green Bay to send payment for the first supply. This was typical of what everyone involved in the relief effort had to endure. "There has been altogether too much red tape in this matter," forcing him and others to wait "from one to three weeks for funds"—strong language in an age where decorous euphemisms were the order the day, especially in official correspondence.

Shortly after Captain Bourne insisted that Dr. Phillips reduce expenses, the new governor, Cadwallader Washburn, reported to the state legislature that the relief efforts were most successful, both in raising money and supplies and in delivering them to those who were in need. In his accounting, Washburn listed unexpended funds of $111,397.23, with donations arriving daily. Perhaps it was the disparity between the amount of aid donated and the amount delivered to the sufferers that prompted Dr. Phillips to write his letter.

Although he never saw the letter Dr. Phillips sent to the governor, one Chicago newspaper correspondent would certainly have agreed with its contents. He charged that the attitude of the aid administrators was hampering relief efforts and failing to meet the needs of those who needed help immediately. What was needed were administrators who would cut through the red tape "and when a poor wretch came pleading for clothing to keep him warm," the administrator should "at once give it to him."

Captain Langworthy paid passing attention to this disaffection, noting that "the general expression among" the survivors who received aid "is that 'they have *had nothing* compared with what their neighbors received,' and as long as there is any one to approach on the subject, will be seeking 'their share.'" But Langworthy maintained that the relief committee found people whose "earthly possessions had been completely swept away," and as a result of the committee's efforts "a great majority of them are now in as comfortable a position as they were before the fire." The multiple families sharing a one-room farmhouse with no water supply during the winter following the fire might have disagreed with the good captain.

—

FRANKLIN TILTON DID not share Captain Langworthy's optimistic view, for he saw losses that were not so easily made up with a flood of food and clothing. While there was serious loss of life of both humans and animals, Tilton noted that the loss was greater than that. "[H]ouses, barns and fences were all swept away, together with the crops, the grass roots were burned out, the timber entirely destroyed, and not a vestige of anything left upon which men or animals could subsist. So utter was the destruction, that the earth must remain for years a barren desert waste, unless seeded anew with grass. Much of the richest soil was alluvial deposit, and this particularly in swampy places, was destroyed, the earth burning in some instances to the depth of two or three feet, leaving nothing but sand and ashes where the best land had been."

In her reminiscence, Josephine Sawyer wrote how "the fire burned so deeply into the peat bogs . . . that it was still smoking a year later. At times, during the first winter after, smoke came up through the snow." In addition, the fire had dried up all the wells. The only water available was in the creeks and rivers. Some survivors had to travel five miles to find water, and there would be no hope for a closer supply until spring.

Tilton also noted that those who wanted to resume farming needed everything to get started again, from seeds to plows to work animals. Then, too, there was the entire infrastructure of the community that needed to be rebuilt. "The bridges and culverts on every road must be rebuilt," as well as the schoolhouses, churches, and other public buildings. How, Tilton asked, was this to be done "in a town in which every surviving inhabitant lost every dollar he possessed"?

➤

LUTHER NOYES HAD a simple answer to Tilton's question: William B. Ogden. Luther Noyes celebrated the coming of the town's savior in the October 14 issue of his newspaper.

> *Glorious News!*—Every cloud is said to have its silver lining. The dark cloud that has enveloped us here, has displayed its silver lining already. Mr. Thomas H. Beebe of Chicago is here, and brings the cheering intelligence, backed by the statement of the Hon. W. B. Ogden, that PESHTIGO IS TO BE RE-BUILT as fast as money and men can accomplish it! Mr. Ogden is expected at Peshtigo harbor today.

In the same issue Noyes confirmed the news that Ogden planned to rebuild with a report from Isaac Stephenson.

> *Hon. I. Stephenson* informs us that the Peshtigo Company are busy purchasing teams, oxen, horses, etc., to replace those that were consumed at the late fire: that he has already bought five teams, several wagons and sleds, five setts [sic] of harness and that fifty million feet of logs will be put in by the company this winter. Employment for all who want to work will be furnished, at liberal wages.

As soon as Ogden arrived at the end of October, he announced, "We will rebuild this village—the mills, the shops—and do a larger winter's logging than ever before." One observer said that as soon as Ogden set to work he seemed to throw off "at once 30 years of his age, becoming a young man of exhaustless energy, untiring industry, and contagious enthusiasm."

In Peshtigo, Ogden and his friend and business partner, engineer General Moses Strong, immediately met with Stephenson, William Ellis, Temple Emery, and Fred Burke who supervised the harbor mill. The group drew up the plans for rebuilding the sawmill and railroad and necessary attendant buildings. Ogden wanted to expand Peshtigo Harbor to handle the shipment of more lumber, and he stressed the need to restore the telegraph line. He was especially insistent on completing the railroad line to Menominee by the end of the year.

For over two months Ogden lived and worked in Peshtigo, inspiring others by his example.

"At daylight in the morning he was up, and worked with the men till dark constantly exposed to the rain and sleet and snow. When night came he would go on an open car drawn by mules eight miles to the harbor. All the evening until late in the night he was engaged with his clerks and assistants in drawing plans, writing letters and sending telegrams to his agents and the next morning break of day would find him again at the head of his men at Peshtigo. During all this period he was cheerful and pleasant and inspired everybody with courage and faith in the future. This terrible strain upon him, and overwork for a man of his years, probably shortened his life."

All the qualities that Ogden had exhibited throughout his life came to the fore during this moment of crisis. Just as he had as a young twenty-nine-year-old legislator in New York, Ogden stood out not just because of his vision but because of his dedication. As Moses Strong would later say, "Ogden possessed many of the qualities of a great and successful general, *viz* unflinching courage, coolness in times of danger, rare presence of mind in emergencies, decision, a constitution of iron, great physical strength, executive power of a high order, ability to master the details of anything he had on hand, firmness of purpose, faith in his own judgment and plans, and an unbending will." Ogden drew on all these qualities as he faced one of the most serious crises in his life.

Ogden now had to work even harder to save a significant part of his fortune. According to his own accounts, he lost $1 million in the Chicago fire and $1.5 million in Peshtigo. But for Ogden it was not simply a matter of money. The fire had snuffed out the railroad construction, and in his heart of hearts mass transit by rail was still Ogden's dream.

In order to speed the progress of the railroad, Ogden offered a $75,000 bonus to the builder if he completed laying the rails to Menominee by the end of the year. Despite the natural obstacles and the obstacles left by the fire, the crews managed to meet Ogden's deadline when the freshly laid rails reached Marinette on December 22, and Menominee on December 27, 1871. But this success was not without incident.

Many people blamed the source of the great fire on the railroad crews who slashed through a wide swath of forest, piled the logs on either side of the right-of-way, and then burned them. As the rails moved deeper into the forest, the number of piles of logs increased, and no one monitored them. The carelessness of the railroad crews was a major part of the cause of the firestorm, but no one wanted to be blamed. Ogden, who had pushed for the completion of the rail laying in dangerously dry conditions, certainly did not want to take the blame. He threatened to sue the builder he had hired for laying the tracks if further investigations proved these burning piles of slashings had caused the fire. But in a move scented with self-interest, Ogden dropped his threat when the builder agreed to forego payment in exchange for the railroad right-of-way, which meant Ogden had control of a significant path of land from Green Bay to Menominee. For Ogden it meant that he did not have to use any of his cash to pay for building his railroad, cash that he needed to rebuild his investments in Peshtigo and Chicago. His threat to sue over the source of the fire was by any account a shrewd maneuver.

＊

THE FARMERS, LOGGERS, lumbermen, shop keepers, and other people of Peshtigo would, over time and in the face of incredible hardship, begin rebuilding. This was the theme that Luther Noyes repeated in the pages of the *Eagle*, just as he had before the fire. Noyes made only an occasional or passing reference to the fire. Better instead, reasoned Noyes, to focus on the future, which would bring an even more prosperous Peshtigo.

＊

LUTHER NOYES SAT at his writing desk in the offices of the *Eagle* on a cold December morning. He had just finished writing the copy for the next issue. He put down his pen, rubbed his eyes, and read quickly through the items for the column he titled "Our Home

Budget," the collection of observations, notices, announcements, and, some would say, gossip that told his readers who was doing what in town and in the Sugar Bushes. He shivered and pulled his coat tighter. It was almost 20 degrees below zero, and he felt the cold despite his thick waistcoat and the fire he maintained in the potbellied stove. He thought fleetingly of the farmers who were now living in barely heated houses wherever they could find room.

In every issue of the *Eagle*, Noyes tried his best to restore the once vibrant energy of the three Edens. But as he leaned back in his chair and looked out the window, he saw a bleak Wisconsin winter. The first snow had arrived, bringing with it a relentless wind. Trees that once "gleamed like steel" now littered the ground—grim, ice-encrusted relics.

The mood among the remaining people of Peshtigo reflected the Gothic desolation of the denuded and decimated landscape. Snow could not mask the scars of the firestorm. Noyes knew that nothing would doom Peshtigo more than a lack of will and an unrelieved pessimism. He did not see hope in the faces of the people he passed on what little was left of the streets of Peshtigo. The bitter Wisconsin winter wind made everyone wrap their faces in thick woolen scarves, leaving only their watery eyes squinting at him from under the brim of a hat or head shawl. They muttered a brief muffled greeting at him as they moved quickly down the street.

Christmas in Peshtigo in 1871 gave little cause for celebration. The railroad line was completed, but on the long Wisconsin winter nights, the remains of three and four families struggled to survive in a one-room farmhouse with little heat, wearing ill-fitting clothes from the relief committee and eating tinned pork, dried apples, sauerkraut, and whatever other food they could get from the relief committee.

Two days before Christmas, Luther Noyes published a short essay in the *Eagle* that reveals more about the state of mind of the people of Peshtigo than any news item could ever reveal.

> Be Cheerful
>
> Look happy, if you do not feel so. Present a cheerful exterior, though your heart and mind be troubled. Never wear a face which, as Sidney Smith says, "is a breach of the peace." Dr. Johnson used to observe that the habit of looking at the best side of a thing was worth more to a man than a thousand pounds a year, and Samuel Smiles observes: "We possess the power, to a great extent, of so exercising the will as to direct the thoughts upon objects calculated to yield happiness and improvement rather than their opposites. In this way, the habit of happy thought may be made to spring up like any other habit. And to bring up men or women with a genuine nature of this sort, a good temper and a happy frame of mind is, perhaps, of even more importance in many cases, than to perfect them in much knowledge and many accomplishments."

Noyes had quoted Samuel Smiles, the author of the 1859 publication *Self-Help*, a compendium of sketches and biographies of the successful men of the industrial age, an earnest attempt to instruct readers in how they might model themselves on ideal citizens. Noyes's editorial, instructing people to "be cheerful," was cloying and yet, in its way, it was a perfect example of the American spirit determined to triumph in the face of tragedy.

Noyes's role as a civic booster was never more tested than it was as 1871 came to a close and the new year rang in. Optimistic prose and self-help prescriptions could not overpower the realities in the wake of the fire. In January, when Mayor Mason of Chicago was succeeded by the "fireproof candidate" Joseph Medill, Medill's inauguration speech—long, hard-hitting, and direct—revealed the illusions and sleight of hand behind which the burgeoning, newly industrialized west had been operating in its lust for expansion and mass transit by rail. What was true of Chicago was also true of Peshtigo; both places were tinderboxes and Medill made it abundantly clear it was a miracle that Chicago had not burned sooner or longer.

The reality of a city built upon marshes with an elevation that made it impossible to erect a water reservoir with enough capacity to pump sufficient water for even a small fire, much less a firestorm, was an awakening for its citizens, a fact that had been ignored by all except Increase Lapham. Lapham had repeatedly warned government officials about the relationship between soil content, topography, wind patterns, and their effects on fire. And now, after they did not listen, it was Lapham whom they called in, along with Captain Langworthy, to explain the mechanics of the fire of October 8.

FIVE DAYS INTO the new year, Noyes published the obituary that caused more sorrow among the residents of both Marinette and Peshtigo. Margaret Stephenson, the long-suffering wife of Isaac Stephenson, dead, at the age of forty-two, in her Marinette home. "The light of the household is quenched in the darkness of death," Noyes wrote, "and the footsteps that were ever ready to move to the call of love, friendship or duty, now tread the pearly sands of the Eternal Shore." Not long after his wife's death, despite the assurances that both Marinette and Peshtigo would return to their former glory, Isaac Stephenson's gaze was turning south, toward New Orleans and the Carolina pines.

NOYES WAS NOT alone in his effort to cheer and bolster the public spirit. In Green Bay, on January 18, Franklin Tilton published a rather remarkable editorial by a contributor named only "M."

AFTER THE FIRE

Significant and thrilling words! How much of sorrow and distress they ordinarily imply; but how doubly impressive now, when our very community has been literally baptized with fire, and the hearts of our great nation—it could almost be said the nations of the earth, have been sinned, overwhelmed with grief and dismay; and we have been doomed to gaze—with not a glass between, upon the most forbidding picture in the "Book of Time"—when we have seen, with our very eyes, a large portion of our beautiful and growing West in flames—ashes, when we have heard, with our very ears, the groans of the dying, and the "sighs of the bereaved"—when it has been our sad lot to gaze upon the vague and stone-like features of some solitary relic of a once large and happy family, who have been rushed into eternity with scarcely a moment's warning.

No wonder that the brain sometimes grows wild with unshed tears; no wonder that the features become vague and stone-like; no wonder that the stricken heart sickens and refuses to be comforted; no wonder that the words "after the fire" have such an electrifying import.

But while we so mournfully deplore this sad event, is there no bright side to this dark picture? Did the "destroying angel," who came on the wings of flaming fire and left nothing but blackness and desolation in his path, leave our hearts too, in the blackness of despair? For a time, yes! but when the sad news was transmitted, with lightning-speed, over our glorious country, and sympathizing hearts vibrated to hearts, and emotion responded to emotion, how loving and swiftly came the angels of sympathy and charity and spread their broad, downy wings, and encircled these sorrowing ones in their tender and loving embrace.

Everyone longed for that "loving embrace" and the grit to continue. Some searched for the relatives they would never find.

Franklin Tilton published the account of one man's search in the January 4 *Advocate:*

At Forestville, Door County, just before snow fell, Mr. John Gloveson of Detroit was searching for tidings of his missing brother-in-law, named Halvy, of Quebec, who is supposed to have perished in the burning woods while prospecting for a location. In his wanderings, he came across a bit of forest where the fires still smouldered and flickered in the ground, and where the flames had done great damage, and he sat down to rest. In a moment he became aware of a horrible stench, and looking around him, he made a terrible discovery. Fifteen or twenty feet away was a large log, or the remains of one, for the fire had burned up all but the end which had become heavy with water from resting in the neck of a small marsh, dry then, but fed by a creek at other times. Sticking out from the hollow of this log were the feet and legs of a skeleton, nothing but the bare bones left, and beyond the skeleton feet was the roasted body of a man, the flesh cooked and shriveled down, but emitting a smell which Gloveson could only stand for a moment at a time without retreating. At length he seized hold of the bones and drew the body out, when the sight and stench were still more horrible. At the shoulders the fire seemed to have stopped, leaving the flesh half cooked, and it was now ready to fall from the bones. The hair was gone from the head, the countenance so disfigured that there was no identifying it, and bones of one hand were as clean and white as chalk. Every particle of clothing was gone, and down in the ashes below Gloveson found a number of bootnails.

Doubtless the victim, whoever he was, had been caught in that vicinity by the fire, and having no other resort crawled into the log, hoping that the fire would sweep over it. The dry end caught fire, and he was roasted alive, enduring the most horible death imaginable. There was excavation *close* at hand made by the uprooting of a tree, and into this place the skeleton was dragged and the bank caved in on it as a covering.

> Returning to Forestville, Gloveson made such inquiries as
> led him to believe that the skeleton was not that of any resi-
> dent of that locality, and he then ended his search.

In the January 27 issue of the *Eagle*, Noyes was confident in his prediction that in the spring, "we will witness the liveliest re-building and re-juvenation of a town totally destroyed, on the old site of Peshtigo, that was ever known to modern history."

Noyes's doubt seeped through the lines just as the biting winter wind seeped through the tiny cracks in his office walls. The careful reader could see that many if not most of the people did not feel that old energy returning. The buyers of and investors in Peshtigo real estate were as scarce as the smiles of the survivors. Peshtigo was now a grim, hard, cold place to be. But Noyes would not give up, despite the reality that lay just outside his window.

In the same issue Noyes published the good news that William Ellis had completed construction of his new house, "the only struc-ture of any kind that escaped the great conflagration of last October. It was then in an unfinished state, but has since been completed and rendered comfortable." Here, thought Noyes, was the perfect sym-bol of hope for the future of Peshtigo. Ellis was the superintendent of the Peshtigo Company. Not only had he built a new house, but he had used the only structure to survive the fire. That one surviving house would be the seed from which the new Peshtigo would grow. Ellis's new residence indicated also the company's commitment to rebuilding the town.

It may seem odd that in every issue of his newspaper Noyes would run such items as "Peshtigo is continually improving. The company's store is now nearly complete," or "Life, energy, activity, perseverance, and pluck, are the watchwords in the rejuvenation of once annihilated Peshtigo." The people of Peshtigo could see for themselves whether there was any progress in building their town.

They walked the same streets as Noyes; they saw the same stretches of ashes and burned foundations. Noyes could tell his readers nothing they had not already seen for themselves.

But Noyes knew his audience resided far beyond Peshtigo, and even far beyond Wisconsin. The flow of immigrants that had been so important for the growth and development of Peshtigo and the Sugar Bushes had been completely dried up by the news of the fire and the destruction it had caused. No longer were the steamers unloading fifty to one hundred new immigrants each week. The immigrants were going elsewhere, some to the forests farther west or to work the iron mines in Escanaba. Noyes was determined to bring the immigrants back where he believed they rightfully belonged. Since the *Eagle* was widely circulated to other newspapers in the state and elsewhere, and it was highly respected by other editors, as was Noyes himself, he had decided to convince this audience that Peshtigo was still the place to start a new, prosperous life.

Throughout the new year Noyes published all the good economic news he could. He filled his newspaper with notices of progress on the construction of the Peshtigo Company's new store, boardinghouse, machine shop, and mill. He commented on the abundance of logs being cut and transported to the mills for sawing. Yet every so often he could not deny reality, as his short piece in the April 27, 1872, issue reveals.

> To the casual observer as he travels the line of the railroad, Peshtigo appears thoroughly resurrected from the ghastly demise it suffered last fall by the great conflagration. But now since the snow has gone, as one walks through the many deserted streets, and sees yet the terrible evidences of the fire, and the many vacant lots where once stood happy homes or thriving business establishments, a sense of drear loneliness and inexpressible sadness comes unbidden over the heart.
>
> Yet Peshtigo has shown, under the circumstances, a won-

derful recuperative energy and a perseverance and pluck that do honor to the occasion, reflects credit on its inhabitants, and challenges the admiration of the world. Nearly all of the business buildings of the Peshtigo company have been rebuilt in better shape than ever before, excepting the wooden ware factory. No movement has as yet been made toward the rebuilding of this great industrial establishment. Hopes are entertained that something will be done in this direction, but as yet, all is uncertainty.

Despite the good news Noyes could scare up—"Everybody is busy and idlers are scarce in Peshtigo"—there was plenty of uncertainty. The cleanup and rebuilding efforts were not enough to restore the town, neither its industry nor its residences. Large stretches of land lay exactly as the fire left them, with the burned ruins reminders of the Peshtigo that was and the work yet to be done, the work that was not being done. Even around the town the signs of the disaster were a mute testimony to what had happened, and might happen again, which prompted Noyes to chide local authorities that action needed to be taken.

The debris of fallen timber partially burned, in the immediate region of the town, to the south and west, forms plenty of food for another fire to feed on, whenever the weather gets sufficiently dry.

For at least one mile back from the village, this debris ought to be collected in heaps and burned at times when there is no danger of the fire spreading so as to do any damage. A little precaution, taken now, may save another horrid catastrophe.

Noyes knew the future of the town resided in the hands of one man, William B. Ogden, and without Ogden and his money, Peshtigo was doomed.

Noyes announced the news of Ogden's expected return in the

February 24, 1872, issue: "[T]he action of this gentleman since the great disaster, has been of more real advantage to the village of Peshtigo and her people, than all the ample and generous relief forwarded by a sympathizing and noble hearted public." Noyes had cast his lot with Ogden from the moment he first arrived in Marinette, and now more than ever he and the town they both had championed needed Ogden.

But Ogden never did return and the woodenware factory was not rebuilt. Without funding the people of Peshtigo would have to will the factory into existence.

> Rumors are rife of the building of the Wooden-ware Factory. We have not been able, as yet, to trace them to any definite source.

The source, of course, was Noyes, who repeatedly predicted the rise of the factory, knowing that his prediction was based only on his hope for its rebuilding.

> Many expected that when Mr. Wm. B. Ogden came, some conclusion would be reached in reference to the rebuilding of the Wooden Ware Factory. As yet, however, nothing definite has been ascertained, excepting that some of the parties interested are in favor of rebuilding; but very likely, under the circumstances, there will be nothing done in any event until another season.

Noyes's hopeful comment turned to bitter resentment.

> The dilapidated pile of bricks and all that was left of the wooden ware factory and dry houses, after the great fire of October, 1871, still haunts the town with its hideous deformity, a sad memento of one of the most horrible events in history. Will it ever be removed, and will another stately and magnificent building occupy the old site, vocal with the hum

of industry from busy hundreds of operatives of yore? are
questions of recurrence, which constantly agitate the anxious
minds of those who now inhabit resurrected Peshtigo.

Finally, it dawned on Noyes that Ogden had no plans to rebuild
the woodenware factory. In a short article, he argued that there was
a local demand for the products of the factory, obviously responding
to the fact that there was a glutted market for such products and the
factory would simply be uneconomical. But Noyes did not give up
easily. In an almost nostalgic comment that both looks back on the
Peshtigo that was and the Peshtigo he knew would never be again,
he laid bare his heart and his commitment to Peshtigo.

> We thought, several years ago, when we first passed through
> here, that we saw the elements of one of the first manufactur-
> ing cities on the Bay shore, and we have seen no reason to
> change that opinion. We have cast our lot here as a journalist,
> and shall continue to labor in every way possible to bring the
> peculiar merits and advantages of this locality, which is our
> chosen home, to the knowledge and comprehension of non-
> resident capitalists who are men of enterprise, nerve and
> pluck, to the end that the capital they possess may seek
> investment here in our midst.

Later that month, Noyes put his case more succinctly.

> If the Peshtigo Co. had grit enough to rebuild the Wooden-
> ware Factory, Peshtigo would soon be again on the high road
> to prosperity.

Ogden probably never intended to rebuild the factory. As Isaac
Stephenson wrote in his autobiography, the factory had not made a
profit and there was no reason to believe that it could. Ogden simply decided to cut his losses and concentrate instead where he knew
he could make money, the mill at Peshtigo Harbor. After the fire

Ogden expanded Peshtigo Harbor, increasing the size of the mill and the docking facilities. He left the woodenware business and focused on the lumber business. Noyes wanted to build a town; Ogden wanted to make money. Noyes had made the mistake of thinking his interests were the same as Ogden's.

While Peshtigo was building houses and stores, it had lost the momentum. Without the woodenware factory, the town had only its mills, but so did many other towns. Economic development moved north with the building of the railroad to Escanaba, Michigan, and its treasure trove of iron and blast furnaces.

Peshtigo was just another small town with no distinguishing economic characteristics.

PREPARE NOW

For Another

Great Conflagration!

The last vestige of Humbug is about to depart. Confidence games in Mercantile transactions are hereafter to be at a discount **TRIED BY FIRE!** Purged from dross, the pure gold is appearing.

We hang our banners on the outer walls and the cry is "Still they Come!" WHERE! WHERE!! WHERE!!! Everybody asks, in a breath; and echo with a joyous shout sends back the glad response, "WHY TO

Chas. JOHNSTON & Co.'s

OF COURSE."

The true haven of Mercantile bliss, the harbinger of "The Good Time Coming," where you will get just what you bargain and pay for, and your full money's worth every time; where you, and particularly your Ladies and families can get everything in the line of

DRY GOODS

GROCERIES, NOTIONS,

Ladies' and Gents' Furnishing Goods, Etc.,

—In short everything from a Peanut to a hogshead of Sugar; from a cambric needle to a full fledged and blooming Dolly Varden!

☞ CHEAP AS THE CHEAPEST ☜

FRIENDS, this is no fancy sketch, although it may be highly wrought and the coloring thrown in, as Joshin Billings says, "PERMISCUS."

But come and try us and we will surely do you good. Remember the location.

Cor. Main and Wells Sts.,
MARINETTE, • • WISCONSIN
April 25th, 1872.

15

And then, as if there had not been enough to contend with, in late spring of 1872, when Peshtigo was expecting relief, the town was invaded by army worms, a particularly loathsome, destructive, and tenacious worm.

Luther Noyes acknowledged the invasion of the worms, but he adopted his old reasoned voice and tried to downplay their destructive power. "Army worms are destroying much of the vegetation on the farms in this region and on the farms in the Peshtigo Sugar Bush. But we are told that the reports of their depredations have been greatly exaggerated," he wrote.

But the army worms would not go away simply because Noyes and others would not pay attention to them. In the Sugar Bush and surrounding areas they continued to destroy the hopes of all the farmers who had tried to plant a crop the first planting season after the fire.

So named because of their massive numbers and their habit of moving in only one direction, the one-and-a-half-inch army worms ·

erupted from the earth after having spent the winter burrowed deep in the soil of the burned district. Once they appeared, they began to move northerly through the Sugar Bush, a writhing mass devouring whatever lay in their path on the ground. Since the fire had killed or driven off the birds and beetles that would have naturally eaten the worms, their numbers grew unchecked. Some places were so thick with them that they could be shoveled up by the bucket. The worms did not deviate from their direction of travel. They clogged wells and streams, making the water undrinkable; they slithered across buildings in their blind drive toward more food. They ate through onions and infested the entire Sugar Bush. Only when one of their natural enemies, a parasitic fly, appeared did their numbers begin to decrease.

But it was a futile cycle of pestilence. The people of Peshtigo were delivered from one plague only to be afflicted by another. The fly invasion was worse than the army worm assault because, while the worm had infested the Sugar Bush and remained on the ground, the flies infested the burned land and flew into the houses, barns, stores, and mills, covering animals, buzzing within buildings and stables. At times it looked as if a black, moving blanket, as oppressive as the smoke had been, had descended on the town. For the fire survivors, it appeared that Nature itself, if not God, was determined to drive them from their land.

In the midst of all these afflictions, there were no crops. "The seeds fell on dead ground," one survivor said. "I looked for just one dandelion, but there were none on our place." Throughout the burned area nothing would grow, despite the most persistent efforts. "I kept watching our best clearing. Emil first planted it to oats, then when that turned yellow and died, he planted rye. When the rye fell over, he said the land should have been left fallow. . . . We did not have it so good that winter of '72–'73. . . . There was no one to help us."

FATHER PERNIN TRIED to bring some solace to the town. After his brief recuperation at Mr. Garon's home in Marinette, Peter Pernin went to St. Louis to raise funds to rebuild his churches in Marinette and Peshtigo. He returned with $2,000 and began an energetic campaign to raise the additional money he needed. The people of the area were generous. In one fund-raising trip to the lumber camps Father Pernin raised over $500.

In June 1872, Luther Noyes published his "Close of Volume 1" editorial in the *Eagle*, a summary of the events of his first year as editor. Noyes thanked his loyal patrons. He touted the success of the paper and its growth in just twelve months' time, but he also inadvertently coined a term that more than adequately described what Peshtigo and Marinette had lived through:

> The year has been an eventful one—one of the most remarkable in the annals of time. Accidents, catastrophes, famine, pestilence, and some of the most remarkable conflagrations the world ever knew, give it the unenviable title of the "Black Year." Peshtigo's annihilation, and its resume again from the ashes of that terrible fire, has made for it a history that will last among the ever recurring cycles of the ages.

Noyes could not have been more prophetic in stating the importance of the firestorm at Peshtigo. The Peshtigo Paradigm, as fire experts now refer to it, was then and remains the single deadliest fire in the United States and the third deadliest quasi-natural disaster in America.

Still, although Noyes recognized its magnitude, the anatomy of the firestorm would remain a mystery to the locals and a secret in the history of the nation. Over time, the incomplete, fragmented story took on the tone and winsome quality of myth, a Paul Bunyan tale. It became a bit of regional elementary-school history and the favorite topic of research papers and reports by high-school students in Peshtigo, Marinette, and Menominee.

It took Increase Lapham until August 1872 to file his report and theory on the causes and phenomena of the fire, which he then sent to Captain A. J. Langworthy.

> *Milwaukee*
> *August 19, 1872*
>
> *Dear Sir:*—The explanation already given of the "traveling sheets of flame" is the correct one. Burning gas (carburetted hydrogen) was produced by the excessive heat of the fire much faster than it could be consumed; hence it arose in great masses, taking the place of the atmospheric air; these masses were driven about by the wind, and would cause death by suffocation, precisely as when common gas is allowed to fill a sleeping apartment. Such masses of combustible gas could only be consumed at the surface where they come in contact with the oxygen of the air; hence they would present the appearance of great balls of fire. Whenever the air penetrated the gas, it at once became explosive . . . there is no evidence either from telegraph wires or otherwise, of any unusual electrical disturbances during the great fires; I think all the facts can be accounted for without calling in the aid of electricity.
>
> Samples of the Green Bay flies in their different stages of growth should be sent to some expert entomologist, who might give some additional light upon the subject. All facts known regarding them should also be communicated to him.
>
> *Yours truly,*
> *I. A. Lapham*

Captain Langworthy, who had explained the firestorm using a blowpipe to describe the formation of the convection columns, agreed with Lapham's explanation and wrote to C. F. Chandler of Columbia College expecting corroboration. What he received instead was the following:

School of Mines, Columbia College
Corner 49th Street and 4th Avenue
New York
September 24, 1872

My Dear Sir—I have read all that appeared in the New York papers on the subject of the western fires, and have carefully considered the observations which you record in your note to me, but I am compelled to say that I have never seen anything which will lead me to accept the theory of combustible gases in the atmosphere. I think that these terrible fires can be explained by referring them to the common, well-known phenomena of combustion, such as peculiarly dry combustible material and favorable winds. That the production of inflammable gases first would be necessary is totally beyond any thing that I have ever known to be observed, and the acceptation of this theory would require strong proof.

Respectfully yours,
C. F. Chandler, Secretary

Both Lapham and Chandler were correct, even though Chandler wanted to dismiss Lapham's gas theory. Indeed, there was enough gas in Chicago and enough gas in the atmosphere above the treetops in Peshtigo before the temperature spiked and the winds whipped to tornado force to make Lapham's theory logical. Chandler believed that mere dry conditions and a favorable wind without gas would sufficiently account for a large wildfire, but his theory does not begin to explain how the fire split into two whirling pincers traveling in opposite directions in both Chicago and Peshtigo. Nor does he explain the fire behavior—walls of flame lifting houses from their foundations and hurling them into the air and flinging locomotives hundreds of yards from their tracks.

Lapham and Chandler possessed only two-thirds of the solution to the mystery.

The missing piece of the mystery is hidden in Phineas Eames's long letter to his brother after the fire. Unwittingly, Eames's minute-to-minute detailed description of the fire's movement stands as proof that, if not a tornado and a fire, then a blowup—so widespread and violent it formed "gustnadoes," a fire resistant to even the most highly advanced modern firefighting techniques—occurred on that fateful night.

The "ridge west of his house" should have proved a safe shelter for Eames and his neighbors, as Eames instinctively believed it would in a normal forest fire. When Eames and his neighbors began running toward the ridge, they were correct in thinking they would be running toward safety.

However, the ridge—a sharp change in topography—created an obstacle as the fire raced on. When the fire met the ridge, a wind shear was created, bouncing off the promontory and creating two more whirls of fire: one behind the ridge and another unexpected whirl in front of the ridge. Until that moment, as Eames struggled toward the ridge, there had been no "fire on the ground" and then inexplicably, or so it seemed, there were fire whirls—"tornadoes"—blocking his path, knocking him off his feet.

By the time Phineas Eames's letter reached the public, readers were more captivated by its sorrowful tenor and gory details of death, and Eames's mesmerizing and eloquent retelling of his newfound spirituality following the fire, instead of this seemingly insignificant detail of how the fire changed on the ridge.

The Peshtigo Fire of 1871 was snuffed out under the winter snows, melted away in the spring muds, buried along with its dead and faded away, a partially solved mystery of catastrophe. Only Increase Lapham, who published his report on the tornadoes of Wisconsin in 1875, had understood from the start that fire and weather were inextricably linked, that the Law of Storms and the behavior of fire—wind, topography, and flame—in a specific area under unstable atmospheric conditions would create a hell on earth against which no one could hope to defend himself.

The Peshtigo Fire resurfaced as the model of a firestorm during the fires of 1910, which were named the Great Barbecue. It was only after this series of devastating fires that ravaged large tracts of land in the Western United States that the War Department, finally recognizing a "fire storm," formed the Department of Forestry and undertook studies to determine what produces it. These studies included those conducted by the U.S. Forest Service on the Peshtigo Fire in an attempt to understand its particular causes and nature. One of the many documents produced by these studies is the weather map of the conditions immediately before the fire struck Peshtigo, a map prepared by the U.S. Weather Bureau, using the reports by the Army Signal Service observers at 5:35 P.M. Central Standard Time on October 8, 1871.

Later, in 1941, Peshtigo would float up from its ghostly place again. As the clouds of war grew on the horizon, the U.S. military gathered all the information it could find to determine how to create the most devastating incendiary attacks on cities possible. Those responsible for planning the U.S. tactics in World War II would seek to understand how to create firestorm conditions using the information gathered from Peshtigo and other studies. Peshtigo was not only the first documented firestorm but it was the only firestorm to destroy seventeen towns, and when Chicago is included in the

Peshtigo Paradigm, the only firestorm to destroy towns, forests, and a major American city.

And in 1949, the mechanics of the Peshtigo fire's behavior would reappear in Mann Gulch, Montana, where the confusing wind patterns combined with fire on "the ridge" in a blowup that killed trained smoke jumpers.

The story of the Peshtigo Fire then has always been with us, the voices of its dead waiting to be heard and remembered.

———

THOSE WHO MANAGED to escape the "baptism by fire," like Thomas Williamson, did not talk about their experiences for the rest of their lives. Some found it difficult to put their experience into words; others did not want to remember, and, like Luther Noyes in the pages of the *Eagle*, simply buried the memory. As Alice Judy Behrend relates in her book, *Burning Bush*, survivors would, if pressed to talk, reply simply:

"My father saved his orphaned children in the mud of Bundy Creek, but our neighbors died in their root cellar."

"My oldest brother got us children to the river, but our mother fell behind with the baby in her arms. We found them in the potato field."

"Father had gone up north to work in the woods. Somehow, Mother harnessed the scared-wild team and got them to plow a deep furrow in the meadow. Two of my little sisters were on fire when Mother pulled the furrow over us. We were saved, though we had to stay in the field hospital at the Place farm till Father found us."

Most of the survivors wanted only to resume their lives. It is not surprising, then, that the number of first-person survivors' accounts is remarkably small. A few, like Thomas Williamson's, were written immediately after the fire in response to a request from a newspaper editor; some were written in later life by adults who were children at the time of the fire. Many others are secondhand, written by someone who had heard the story from a grandparent or other relative. In her book, Alice Behrend records many second- and thirdhand accounts of the fire, but few firsthand accounts.

Many survivors suffered mental and emotional problems after the fire. In his report to the legislature, Captain Langworthy noted that "many who escaped the fiery visitation . . . were paralyzed with fear, from the effects of which they will probably never recover." He goes on to state that "we found the people generally, immediately after the fire, in the depth of despair, with not a ray of hope in the future." All the survivors, injured and uninjured, were in shock, the injured from their wounds, the uninjured from losing friends and family, as well as everything they owned.

Alice Behrend recalls seeing "clearly the physical scars of those who lived to the automobile age, especially on their hands and faces and the pink patches of scar tissue in white hair. And there were psychological scars that had never healed. Some had lost their minds or retreated into themselves." She notes that there was a building behind the Presbyterian church in Marinette that was "home to 65 physically and emotionally traumatized Fire orphans."

A photograph taken on the 1951 commemorative weekend of the fire shows four survivors and the firestorm's lingering effects. The four elderly people sit stiffly, hands folded in their laps, staring straight ahead. Their eyes are wide and clear, yet they're as lifeless as the glass eyes of dolls; their mouths are clenched, resisting a smile. An indefinable weariness seeps outward from the photograph, the natural result of aging. But it's the other feeling, a palpable resentment that only here in Peshtigo for one weekend every October these survivors are thought of or called upon to remember.

They are the last remaining physical links to the night the rest of the nation remembers because of Chicago. Looking at their faces and those eyes, one knows immediately that they have seen what no one should ever see, and what no one can ever put into words.

❧

THERE ARE MANY different numbers given for the death toll from the fire. Generally, reference works say that fifteen hundred people died in the Sugar Bushes, Peshtigo, and on the Door County Peninsula that night. Yet there is strong evidence that this number is closer to twenty-five hundred. Although an accurate count is impossible, it is possible to get some sense of the magnitude of the loss.

In his report to the governor, Captain Langworthy says that the fire burned "not less than twenty-four-hundred square miles," in many instances sweeping away "whole neighborhoods" without "leaving any trace or record to tell the tale." The sheer size of the destroyed area suggests a higher number of dead than is usually ascribed to the fire. There was no systematic survey of the burned area, looking for and counting the dead. Instead, people simply looked for their friends and neighbors, in most instances going to their farms or homes to see whether anyone had survived. No one maintained any kind of master list or count of the dead. The official list of the dead published in the appendix to the *Wisconsin Assembly Journal, 1873* is simply a listing of the names of people who someone knew was dead. Even this list inexplicably omits the names of many people who were known to have died.

The official attempts to count the dead encountered many problems, the most obvious being the phenomenon that there was nothing left of many people, not even their ashes. Mrs. Carrie Hoppe (Carrie Jackson) recounts how her family sought refuge in the middle of an open, plowed field. Her uncle and brother were separated from the group. After the fire, "my father found one of my brother's shoes and some ashes. Most of the ashes had been blown away, but we know they were dead."

Pat Doyl farmed a 180-acre plot in the Upper Bush. He had a wife and eight children. After the fire, friends of the Doyl family searched repeatedly for their remains to give the family a decent burial. But they found nothing. The entire family had vanished completely in the fire. Again and again survivors tell of friends and family members simply disappearing in the fire, never to be seen again, leaving nothing to mark where they died.

Because no one knew just how many people were living in the Sugar Bushes, how many loggers were in the forest, how many transient workers were in the area, or even how many recently arrived immigrants were in the town, it is impossible to arrive at a reasonably accurate count of the dead. As Franklin Tilton points out, in Peshtigo "there were a large number of single men and persons continually going and coming. It is known that the village was unusually full of strangers on the night of the fire, and many are unaccounted for; and we had frequent inquiries from abroad for persons who were supposed to be in the vicinity."

Fay Dooley's grandmother told her of "fifty foreigners, mostly Italians, who arrived in town the day before the fire to work on the railroad. They were never heard of again." A newspaper reporter who toured the area in November was overwhelmed by the task of finding and counting the dead. "The half has not been told; the whole will never be known. The loss of life increases every hour. On Friday last, twenty-six dead bodies were found in the woods, and on Saturday, thirty-six. The woods and fields are literally full of dead bodies . . . we found some teeth, a jackknife and a slate pencil. It must have been all that remained of a promising boy."

For months and years after, people discovered the remains of someone who was killed in the fire. They found them not just in the woods and other isolated places but right in Peshtigo. The April 20, 1872, issue of the *Eagle* reported that "the remains of a woman and two children were found in the rear of the premises of Mr. McGillis at Peshtigo, a few days ago; they were burned beyond recognition. Thus, in groups, and one by one, the victims of the holocaust were still being found." In May, the body of "Ernest Kuncner, a tailor, in the employ of Harter & Horvath, was found in the mill pond between the site of the Wooden Ware Factory and the upper boom. He was recognized by a wooden leg."

The Sugar Bushes were dotted with simple wooden markers bearing inscriptions such as "Two Unknown Dead." In his 1873 report for the governor, Captain Langworthy refused to give an estimate of the number of dead. He was well aware that such an accounting was impossible. "Different intelligent people vary so much in their estimates of the number who perished, that it would be mere conjecture to attempt to give any figures on the subject."

The May 11, 1872, issue of the *Eagle* carried a plea from John Thompson of England. He was seeking information about his son, W. T. Thompson, and daughter-in-law, "who were lost in the great tornado of fire that swept Peshtigo out of existence on the night of October 8th 1871," and "no traces of either the young man or his wife have been seen since the fire." No one knows how many such cases there were.

The *Advocate* reported that "as the forests along the Menominee and Peshtigo rivers are explored, more burned persons are being found from time to time. On Friday last, the bodies of two men were found—burned so badly as to be unrecognizable. For a long time to come we shall hear of other cases of men, hunters, land explorers and others, who were caught in the woods on that fatal night."

Lovett Reed, a veteran of the Civil War, was caught in the forest when the fire struck. He ran for a clearing but saw that he could not make it. He took his pocketknife and stabbed himself in the chest several times, trying to hit his heart. After inflicting several severe but nonserious wounds, he accidentally dropped the knife. When he dropped to his knees looking for the knife, the fire passed over, leaving him untouched. He survived his wounds, although it took him some time to recover.

William Curtiss was more successful. He sought refuge in his well, but it was too shallow, so he looped the bucket chain around his neck and hung himself.

Sandy Mac never knew for sure where his family had been buried. Some years later he had a gravestone set in the cemetery behind the Methodist church in Harmony. Because he could not read, his boss wrote the inscription for him, but Sandy knew that inscription by heart: "My Darling Wife and Children. I'll See You in the Morning. Your loving Husband and Father." Sandy never went back to his farm. And he did not marry again. No one knows how old he was when he died in 1926. He was buried in the potter's field near Peshtigo.

At the Newberry farm, not far from the creek that had saved William Newberry and his small group, Henry Bartels and Henry Bakeman found a body near a barn wall, curled around a stake. Farther on, under a bridge that spanned the same creek, the rescuers found Walter Newberry, his wife, and their three children. A little distance farther they found the other members of the family and their hired workers lying in a group along the side of the road. The elder Walter Newberry's body would not be found until April 1872, the same time John McGregor's body was discovered.

In the May's Corners cemetery, in the southeast corner, there is a four-sided obelisk with its finial missing. Carved on the marker are the names of the members of the Newberry family who died in the fire: Henry Newberry, twenty-two; Selah F. Newberry, twenty; Walter B. Newberry, twelve; Louisa, wife of W. B. Newberry, twenty-eight; Nellie Newberry, four; Walter Newberry, two; infant Newberry; Edward S. Newberry, twenty-eight; Louisa A. Newberry, nineteen; Charles O. Newberry, thirty-two; Franklin A. Newberry, two; Jessie Newberry, five. All died on October 8, 1871. No explanation of the date was necessary. Those who erected the monument believed that date would be remembered ever after. Of the fifteen Newberrys, only five members of the family survived the fire.

Thomas Williamson returned to Williamsonville after recuperating for several days. He took stock of the losses, which were shocking. Of the seventy-six people in the settlement, fifty-nine had died. Only Thomas and his mother remained alive out of their family of eleven. Thomas had lost his father, two brothers, their wives, a child, a sister, and two cousins. Margaret Williamson would later say, "I cannot pretend to understand the providence of God which preserved me, an old woman, with my days fulfilled, and took my sons and daughters."

Thomas Williamson and his mother moved to Oshkosh where she died in 1894 at the age of seventy-six. Thomas married and moved to Negaunee, a town in Michigan's Upper Peninsula, where he ran a sawmill. Recently, an archaeologist at the University of Wisconsin–Milwaukee was conducting research on the Williamsonville site. When one of Thomas Williamson's great-granddaughters heard about the project, she contacted the researcher. Thomas, she said, never spoke of the fire, nor did he keep any written accounts of his experiences. The family knew only that he had been in the fire. Like so many of the survivors, Thomas did not want to remember that night.

THE DOCTORS WERE pleased as Karl's body continued to heal, nicely they thought. His hair, eyelashes, and eyebrows were all growing back as full as they had been, although now his once-black hair was pure white. The burned skin on his back had been completely replaced with new pink skin that remained tender under his coarse flannel shirt. Except for the scar on his head, he was almost as good as new, the doctors proclaimed, proud of their healing powers.

Karl simply blinked at them.

One day, as he sat in the sun doing the exercises he had been given to strengthen his hands, a nurse told him to go the hospital office. There a proud administrator told Karl that he was healed enough to leave the hospital and get back to his life, get back to work. The hospital would no longer support him. Of course; he would be provided with transportation back to Peshtigo.

Karl stared blankly ahead, shaking his head in confusion. "No place," was all he could say, and he said it in German, the only language he had spoken since the fire.

The administrator summoned a German-speaking worker at the hospital and tried explaining again to Karl that he was to leave the hospital and return home.

"You'll be given a train ticket to Marinette. There's a boardinghouse there that will provide you with room and board until you can get back to work. You'll be able to work with your hands in a few weeks."

The translator spoke to Karl, and as she spoke a flicker of light came to his eyes. Yes, it was time to leave the hospital. And if he stayed at the boardinghouse he would not have to go back to his farm until another winter scoured the land clean. Karl nodded, and stood up.

"*Danke*," he replied.

In Marinette, Karl Lamp stayed at a hotel for mill workers until the Dahls, a local German family, heard of him and invited him to live with them. He spoke little, but was considerate of the family that had taken him into their home. One day, his in-laws August and Sophie Prestin visited. They told him that Fredricke and the children had been given a proper burial next to the tombstone Karl had erected years ago for Luise, Karl, and Hanna.

Karl said nothing, refusing to think or speak of that night. August nodded his silent agreement and dropped the subject. As they were leaving, August turned to Karl and asked, "When will you return to your farm? We miss our neighbor. Herr Dahl will help you, I'm sure."

Karl looked out the window.

In August 1872, Herr Dahl did help Karl. He took him to the cemetery to find the graves of his family. At first Karl protested, but he was too polite to refuse his host. He climbed onto the wagon for the trip to Peshtigo.

Although the road had been cleared and rebuilt so that traffic could pass reasonably well, there were still many fallen trees and giant stumps. Most of the salvageable trees had been cleared. Only the useless ones remained, and there were many of those. Is this what my farm looks like, he thought? More than ever he was resolved not to return to it.

Peshtigo was filled with activity. Workmen were building a new sawmill for the Peshtigo Company, but Karl noticed that there was no work at the site where the woodenware factory had stood. Houses were under construction and a few new stores were already completed and open for business. For a brief moment Karl thought that if these people could rebuild so could he, but then he dismissed the thought. They had not lost what he had. Buildings can be replaced, but not people, Karl thought, as the wagon pulled up to the cemetery where he found an elderly man digging a grave.

Karl looked at all the graves. It was all so different. He could not remember where the tombstone for Luise, Karl, and Hanna was. He walked to the man digging the grave and asked, "Lembk?"

The man looked up out of the grave and studied him carefully. Karl noticed the red scar that ran from the back of the man's neck across his cheek. The man said nothing, but put his shovel down and climbed from the grave. He started walking down a long row of freshly dug graves. Karl and Herr Dahl followed him. He stopped before a simple wood cross made of two-by-fours that had been mortised and nailed together. Someone had painted LAMP in black paint on the cross. Nothing else. No names, no dates. Just one grave for all of them.

Not long after that, August Scheelke came to see Karl with an offer. August had been a good neighbor to Karl and Fredricke, and like Karl he was a member of the German Lutheran Church and the Odd Fellows. August explained how he had just bought another eighty acres and he needed someone to live on the land and work it for him; otherwise he would lose it. Karl knew that parcel of land because it touched the southwest corner of his farm.

"You and the Dahls can live in the house I've just built, and come spring you can begin to clear the land. We'll make a deal so you can make some money to get your farm started again."

Karl looked at him. "I'll help you, but I'm not a farmer. No more am I a farmer."

Karl and the Dahls moved into the house on August Scheelke's land just in time for winter to set in, a winter that was to change his life.

At the first signs of the winter thaw, the Dahls received a visit from Louisa Behnke, an attractive twenty-eight-year-old woman who was taken with the quiet forty-six-year-old Karl Lamp. The farmers in the Sugar Bush were slowly rebuilding. Rail fences started to appear, marking the roads and farms once again. Some farms had new buildings, and a few even had small patches where people tried to grow a few vegetables. Some farms had promising crops, while in other blackened fields sprigs of green were sprouting.

Meeting Louisa and seeing the fields starting to come back gave Karl some hope for life. His body had healed, and at last, in 1873, the land appeared to be healing. For the first time in nearly two years Karl Lamp faced not just his terrible loss but his fear of living without Fredricke and his children. Then he saw her face, his darling Fredricke, and heard her telling him to live as he had lived before.

The next day Karl Lamp went to his farm for the first time since that night of hell. Burned trees lay fallen every which way, and nothing was left of any of the buildings he had worked so hard to erect. But the brook was running free and clear. He looked at the field where he had carefully rotated his crops of grain, hay, peas, and potatoes.

"Where should we build our house?" he asked Louisa. He was ready to begin again.

Karl and Louisa built their farm into one of the most prosperous in the Sugar Bush. They had seven children. Karl died in 1904, and Louisa died thirty years later. They are buried in the May's Corners cemetery in the area once known as the Sugar Bush. Their descendants still farm the same land, but they go by the name of Lemke.

EPILOGUE

‿✦‿

William Butler Ogden died on August 3, 1877, at his residence Boscobel on the Harlem River. At the time of his death Ogden's wealth was calculated to be between five and ten million dollars. He was survived by his wife, Marian Arnot, the eldest daughter of the railroad and real estate owner, Mr. John Arnot of Elmira, New York. Ogden is buried in the Woodlawn Cemetery in the Bronx, New York City.

Isaac Stephenson died on March 15, 1918. In 1882 he was elected to Congress and served three terms. In 1901 he established the *Milwaukee Free Press*. In 1907 Stephenson was elected to the United States Senate and was re-elected by the legislature in 1909. His election was blocked twice by fraud investigations in both the state legislature and the United States Senate, but he was eventually vindicated and resumed his seat in the Senate, serving from May 1907 to March 1915. Stephenson retired to Marinette in 1915 and lived there until his death.

On September 14, 1875, Increase Allen Lapham published his

last scientific paper, a study of the small lakes of Wisconsin. By this time he had returned to his children's farm on the south shore of Lake Oconomowoc and resumed his inexhaustible but quiet study of the natural world. On the afternoon of September 14, he set out to the lake and climbed into his rowboat. He planned to do some fishing alone. At 6:30 P.M. Lapham's body was discovered lying in his boat, dead from a stroke. Wisconsin's premiere scientist had died on the lakes he loved. Asa Gray of Harvard said, "I have the idea that he had a happy, as well as a useful honored life. What more could be asked?"

Luther B. Noyes turned the *Eagle* over to his industrious son, Frank E. Noyes. It was Frank Noyes who entered into partnership with his father Luther Noyes in 1885, and who also erected the fire memorial marker in Peshtigo. In 1888 Luther Noyes and his son incorporated the business at the Eagle Printing Company with Frank Noyes acting as secretary and treasurer. Luther Noyes died in 1894, after which Frank Noyes became president of their company.

AFTERWORD

October 8, 2000

The temperature is below 30 degrees. Light snow swirls across Highway 41. The wind and cold on this fall day are premature, shocking to the outsider, but the natives of Peshtigo are unfazed by the weather. Once there was a forest, and now there are no breakers against the harsh wind, which cuts your skin, makes you want to walk backward against it, shielded. The tallest icon in Peshtigo is not the great *Pinus strobus*, it is the pale blue water tower along the highway. BOB'S HOMES is written across its belly in bright blue cursive, an advertisement for four-bedroom, three-bath mobile homes starting at $30 per square foot. Peshtigo has erected only one marker of that night 129 years ago. It's so small you can drive past it ten times a day and never notice it; you can drive past it for a lifetime and not see it.

But in the Harmony, Wisconsin, cemetery, close to the entrance, one tree stump—so large two people cannot touch hands reaching around it—takes its place among the tombstones.

The markers are so old and worn it's difficult to read the names at first, but among the scattered graves of Civil War veterans are some of the names from the endless roster of the victims of the Peshtigo firestorm. One marker, its edges softened by time and weather, is carved in the shape of a lamb no bigger than a human foot. It reads simply, EDDIE. The marker for a child. There are others: age twenty-one days, age three days, age eleven years.

The wind kicks the leaves, whistles across the flattened countryside with its modern houses and neatly trimmed lawns. An ordinary, peaceful place so remote and modest, it finally becomes clear why Oconto resident Edward Hall, who wrote a brief personal account of the fire, could not find language to describe what happened in Peshtigo except to write that the fire struck and destroyed a town and its people "as if by magic."

NOTES

Chapter 1

Our descriptions of life in a lumber camp are based on such works as Emmett Nelligan, *The Life of a Lumberman*, and Stewart Holbrook, *Holy Old Mackinaw*.

There is abundant literature on the history and composition of the forests of Wisconsin and the Midwest. See, for example, James I. Clark, *The Wisconsin Pineries*; Robert F. Fries, *Empire in Pine*; and John Riordan, *The Dark Peninsula*. Unless otherwise indicated in the notes, our descriptions of the trees around Peshtigo rely upon these and the other books on this subject listed in our bibliography.

At twenty-seven to thirty feet tall for a one-story building, the trees surrounding Peshtigo would have been four to six stories tall. With an average of approximately 640 trees in a square acre, the forest around Peshtigo was far denser than any forest in the United States today. Since there are 640 square acres in a square mile and, according to all reports, the fire covered over 2,400 square miles, the estimate of 1 billion trees destroyed in the fire is no exaggeration. The area destroyed by the fire is equivalent to 2.3 times the area of Rhode Island, 1.2 times the area of Delaware, or half the size of the area of Connecticut.

The "gaberal" horn is the angel Gabriel's horn, which Gabriel will blow to call the dead from their graves for the final judgment.

I Lived at Peshtigo Harbor, by Fred Burke, gives a detailed description of the Peshtigo River and its drainage basin.

Our descriptions of life in Peshtigo and the Sugar Bushes are drawn from both published and unpublished sources. Unless we specify a particular source, we have used information from the *Marinette and Peshtigo Eagle* and Alice Judy Behrend, *Burning Bush*. To describe the daily dress, habits, and rituals, as well as food and drink and the other elements of everyday life in the late nineteenth century, we consulted a number of sources, including Alan Brinkley, *The Unfinished Nation: A Concise History of the American People*, vol. 2, *From 1865*; Walter Licht, *Industrializing America: The Nineteenth Century*; and Daniel Sutherland, *The Expansion of Everyday Life, 1860–1876*.

Miss Delia and Hatty Baker were two of the better-known prostitutes ("doves") in the area. Robert Wells's *Embers of October* includes an amusing anecdote about the 225-pound, six-foot tobacco-chewing Miss Delia punching a logger and knocking him unconscious when he refused to remove his boots inside her establishment. The description of logger's pox is based on the description in Wells. The reference to the smallpox vaccination ("vaccinate") is from the *Marinette and Peshtigo Eagle*.

The $1.25 price for an acre of land in 1871 Peshtigo would be approximately $18 in today's money. However, according to many economists, calculating the value of 1871 money in terms of today's purchasing power is not as precise as the mathematical calculation would suggest. The standard of living in 1871 was far lower than today, because many items that are relatively inexpensive today cost more then as a percentage of income. For example, loggers were paid between $12 to $15 per month, yet they paid $4 for a pair of men's boots, or one-third of their monthly pay. In addition, the quality of goods today is much higher than in 1871. The boots you buy are far superior in materials and workmanship than any the loggers could buy in 1871. Adjusting the value of money to account for such differences is part art and part science.

For more information on calculating the value of money from one historic period to another, you can use the calculator on the Economic History Services website at: www.eh.net/ehresources/howmuch/dollarq.php. Professor John J. McCusker of Trinity University in San Antonio, Texas, cautions in his essay "How Much Is That Worth Today?" on this website that the result "while far from perfect—and increasingly less perfect the farther back in time we go—provides us with a reasonable approximation of the modern-day worth of a sum of money from some past time."

For more information on the history of Belgian settlers in Wisconsin, see John E. Cashman, "The Belgian Settlers of Northeast Wisconsin and Their Descendants," and Xavier Martin, "The Belgians of Northern Wisconsin."

For the history of Queen Marinette, the Menominee Indians, fur trading, and other topics in the settlement of the Menominee area, see Beverly Hayward Johnson, *Queen Marinette: Spirit of Survival on the Great Lakes Frontier.*

Chapter 2

Biographical information about Luther Noyes comes from *Commemorative Biographical Record of the West Shore of Green Bay, Wisconsin, Including the Counties of Brown, Oconto, Marinette and Florence, and History of Northern Wisconsin: Containing an Account of Settlement, Growth, Development and Resources.*

In his editorials, Noyes frequently referred to his favorite writers, including poet Robert Burns, essayist Ralph Waldo Emerson, and journalist Horace Greeley.

With the laying of the transatlantic cable immediately after the Civil War, news of the opportunities in the United States for immigrants was regularly communicated to Europe.

A model of the Washington press is on display at the Smithsonian Institution in Washington, D.C. A model printing office of that time is on display at the South Street Seaport Museum in New York City.

For the descriptions of the weather conditions in this chapter and throughout this book, we have drawn from the observations for the months of July through October 1871, as recorded by official observers in Chicago and Milwaukee. These records are located at the National Archives, College Park, Maryland. Noyes's weather reports were a regular feature in the *Marinette and Peshtigo Eagle.* Noyes's informal weather reports were based on the observations and anecdotal information passed on to him by farmers who lived in the outlying Sugar Bush areas.

Our account of the assault at Cold Harbor is based on Alan T. Nolan, *The Iron Brigade: A Military History*; James M. McPherson, *Battle Cry of Freedom*; Fletcher Pratt, *A Short History of the Civil War*; and David J. Eicher, *The Longest Night: A Military History of the Civil War.*

Records of weather observations and the original copies of the telegraphed bulletins are located at the National Archives Annex, College Park, Maryland.

The question, "Do you think they can tell anything about it?" appeared in an article on the possibility of predicting storms in *The Sentinel* (Milwaukee, Wisconsin), November 18, 1870. For Lincoln's remark, see Donald R. Whitnah, *A History of the United States Weather Bureau.*

We have drawn on a number of sources for information on the development of railroads in Wisconsin and the Midwest, including Robert J. Casey and W. A. S. Douglas, *Pioneer Railroad: The Story of the Chicago and North Western System.*

We have used a great variety of materials on the life of William B. Ogden, from personal reminiscences of those who knew him to his official obituary. Among these sources are George P. A. Healy, *Reminiscences of a Portrait Painter;* Anna Sheldon Ogden West, "Reminiscences Dealing Largely with the Great Fire of 1871 Chicago"; Donald L. Miller, *City of the Century: The Epic of Chicago and the Making of America.* One rare and especially moving account of William Ogden is given by his closest associate and friend, Isaac Arnold. In this account Arnold recalls a December evening in 1843 when he was living in Ogden's house on Ontario Street in Chicago. That night, Ogden showed Arnold a parcel of "preserved flowers, ribbons, a woman's glove, some notes and a poem," the relics of Ogden's fiancée who had died the night before their wedding. For all of his wealth and accomplishment, Ogden's memory of her "still lingered fondly and faithfully." Ogden remained a bachelor until very late in his life. In his last will and testament, he bequeathed a large portion of his wealth to his first love's family.

Isaac Stephenson, *Recollections of a Long Life: 1829–1915.* One of the difficulties in researching the lives of the major figures of Wisconsin in 1871 stems from their general reticence to divulge even the smallest personal details of their lives. For instance, throughout his memoirs Isaac Stephenson talks at length about his business dealings and political career, and he is quite forthcoming with his opinions regarding science, medicine, and government. However, he never mentions his marriage to Margaret, the births or deaths of two of his children, or his wife's death in January 1872. The autobiographies as well as the biographies are startling for their lack of personal information or meditation. In many cases, personal diaries, letters, and papers that might have shed light on the private person have been lost or destroyed.

The $50,000 Stephenson invested is equal to approximately $715,000 today.

Although William Ellis's salary of $525 every three months is equal to approximately $7,500 today, or a yearly salary of $30,000, he enjoyed far greater purchasing power. He could, for example, buy a complete breakfast for 75 cents, a pound of coffee beans for 28 cents, or stay in a first-class hotel room in Madison, Wisconsin, for $1 per day.

Ogden's suggestion that Jay Cooke should ease the way for the Northwest Pacific & Union Railroad with bribes is recorded in Todd D. Suavé, *Manifest Destiny and Western Canada.*

Chapter 3

Every city and community in the United States at that time was concerned about the condition of its roads. Even in the major cities, as Daniel E. Sutherland writes, "Paved streets—where they existed—remained primitive. Mining towns, cattle towns, farm towns, and small towns generally had no pavement at all, only dusty thoroughfares or muddy quagmires, depending on the weather." For the farmers in the Sugar Bushes, roads were critical both to transport their crops to town and to bring the supplies they needed from town. And as all those who lived in the Sugar Bush would soon discover, good roads were necessary for their safety. Most roads in the Sugar Bushes were nothing more than narrow dirt lanes wandering among the trees, following the old Indian trails. A few of the roads connecting the towns and the more important outlying lumber mills had been improved by laying logs transversely across them. The logs were laid tightly together, and over time they would settle into the dirt and mud, providing a better but much bumpier surface than the dirt roads. These were called corduroy roads and were built using techniques developed by the Union army during the Civil War. The streets in town were covered with sawdust or hay, or sometimes a combination of both. Even wood chips, pieces of logs, and scrap wood and lumber were scattered on a road in an attempt to make it more passable in bad weather. But even under the best of conditions, traveling by horse or wagon was difficult and slow.

The $500 spent on the Little River Road for the benefit of Ike Stephenson and his friends was over two and a half times the yearly pay of a lumberjack, not to mention more cash than a farmer would ever see at one time.

Elbridge West Merrill's handwritten account of his experiences in Birch Creek, "A Terrible Reminiscence. A Night of Horror and A Fight for Life," is in the collection at the State Historical Society of Wisconsin. Merrill's account is particularly significant because he unwittingly recorded accurate observations of the early development of the fire. Others have treated Merrill's account as just another personal reminiscence, but his observations on unusual fire behavior reveal the beginning stages of a potential blowup, making Merrill's account essential. In reconstructing the development of the fire into a firestorm, we have used Merrill's information with that provided by Stephen J. Pyne in a number of his works.

Among the sources on the life and work of the lumberjacks that we consulted are Emmett Nelligan, *The Life of a Lumberman*; Stewart Holbrook, *Holy Old Mackinaw*; and Robert F. Fries, *Empire in Pine*.

The monthly wage of $12 to $15 per month for a lumberjack is equivalent to approximately $170 to $215 today.

Our account of Karl and Fredricke Lamp is drawn from Alice Judy Behrend, *Burning Bush*.

Chapter 4

The $100,000 Noyes advocates for improving Peshtigo Harbor is equivalent to approximately $1.5 million today.

Information on the preparation Green Bay had made to fight fires is detailed in the *History of Northern Wisconsin: Containing an Account of Settlement, Growth, Development and Resources*. When the fire struck, the well-equipped Green Bay fire department answered the call for help from Chicago. No other city or town was as well prepared for fire as Green Bay. Chicago had a first-class fire department; however, because of Chicago's topography, the city did not have an elevated water reservoir with sufficient capacity and pressure to extinguish serious fires.

In the *Marinette and Peshtigo Eagle*, Luther Noyes records a number of instances of traveling preachers delivering sermons of doom for the sinful residents of the area. Alice Judy Behrend in *Burning Bush* also records the remarks of fire survivors who had vivid memories of such sermons. She also records the story of John and Mary McGregor.

Reverend Peter Pernin and Luther Noyes give extensive accounts of the fire of Saturday, September 23. The story of the fire in the woods is drawn from Peter Pernin's *The Great Peshtigo Fire: An Eyewitness Account*.

Frank Tilton describes the fires of September 23 and 24 in Oconto, Big and Little Suamico, Fort Howard, Manitowoc, and surrounding areas in his book, *Sketch of the Great Fires in Wisconsin*.

The scene of the frightened birds is recorded by Reverend Peter Pernin. The story of the widow Latour is recounted by Frank Tilton.

Chapter 5

Both Robert Wells in his book *Embers of October* and Luther Noyes in the *Marinette and Peshtigo Eagle* give detailed accounts of the September 24 fire.

The experience of Reverend Thomas Walker is recounted by Luther Noyes in the *Marinette and Peshtigo Eagle* and by John F. Boatman in volume one of his book, ". . . *And the River Flows On . . .*"

The potential for burned trees to ignite again is discussed in Kenneth P. Davis, *Forest Fire Control and Use*, and in Increase A. Lapham, "The Great Fires of 1871 in the Northwest."

Robert Wells tells the story of J. G. Clements in his book, *Embers of October*.

Chapter 6

Records of weather observations and the original copies of the tele-graphed bulletins and the telegrams between General Albert J. Myer, Increase A. Lapham, General Henry Howgate, Superintendent Bliss, Super-intendent Robinson, and others are located at the National Archives, Col-lege Park, Maryland.

The discussion of the Signal Service Corps and the beginnings of what was to become the Weather Bureau is based, among others, on Donald R. Whitnah, *A History of the United States Weather Bureau;* Mark Monmonier, *Air Apparent: How Meteorologists Learned to Map, Predict, and Dramatize Weather;* Increase A. Lapham, *Report of the Disastrous Effects of the Destruction of Forest Trees Now Going on Rapidly in the State of Wisconsin;* Eric R. Miller, "New Light on the Beginnings of the Weather Bureau from the Papers of Increase A. Lapham"; and James I. Clark, *Increase A. Lapham: Scientist and Scholar.*

The interest of Congressman Henry H. Paine in meteorology and his contributions to the formation of the Weather Bureau are discussed by Eric R. Miller in his article, "New Light on the Beginnings of the Weather Bureau from the Papers of Increase A. Lapham," and by Truman Abbe in his book, *Professor Abbe . . . and the Isobars. The Story of Cleveland Abbe, America's First Weatherman.*

The $237,000 General Howgate embezzled is the equivalent to approxi-mately $3.3 million in current money.

Chapter 7

The weather records, and their accompanying Casual Phenomena Sheets, as recorded by official observers in Chicago and Milwaukee, are located at the National Archives at College Park, Maryland. All references to these records in this chapter are from this source.

The discussion of wind, and wind and fire, in this chapter is based on David W. Goens, "Fire Whirls"; Norman Maclean, *Young Men and Fire;* Mark Monmonier, *Air Apparent: How Meteorologists Learned to Map, Predict, and Dramatize Weather;* Kenneth P. Davis, *Forest Fire Control and Use;* Eric R. Miller, "New Light on the Beginnings of the Weather Bureau from the Papers of Increase A. Lapham."

Chapter 8

The description of conditions in Minnesota is drawn from accounts in the St. Paul *Pioneer.*

Captain Hawley's schedule is listed in volume one of John F. Boatman, ". . . *And the River Flows On* . . ."

The Palmer Drought Severity Index (PDSI) is described in Donald A. Haines and R. W. Sando, "Climactic Conditions Preceding Historically Great Fires in the North Central Region"; and Jacqueline Smith, *The Facts on File Dictionary of Weather and Climate.*

The story of Abram Place, John Lawe, and the others is drawn from Beverly Hayward Johnson, *Queen Marinette: Spirit of Survival on the Great Lakes Frontier,* and Alice Judy Behrend, *Burning Bush.*

An overwhelming body of scholarship, as well as anecdotes, myths, folktales, and tall tales, exists on the Chicago fire. Among the sources we have consulted and used in this chapter are Robert Cromie, *The Great Chicago Fire;* Gerry and Janet Souter, *Fire Stations;* James W. Sheahan and George P. Upton, *The Great Conflagration. Chicago: Its Past, Present and Future;* and Donald L. Miller, *City of the Century: The Epic of Chicago and the Making of America.*

The pamphlet "William B. Ogden" by Isaac N. Arnold and J. Young Scammon describes Ogden's house and gardens in Chicago, as does the article "Private Gardens in Chicago" in the magazine *Prairie Farmer.*

At the time of the Chicago fire, Anna Sheldon Ogden West was visiting her uncle at his Harlem River home in New York. During a talk with her, he casually mentioned the possibility of a subway system in cities such as New York and Chicago. She recorded this conversation in "Reminiscences Dealing Largely with the Great Fire of 1871 Chicago," a letter in the collection of the Chicago Historical Society.

Chapter 9

Modern maps of the Wisconsin peninsula at the time of the fire place Williamsonville in the wrong location. Even Frank Tilton in his book *Sketch of the Great Fires in Wisconsin* placed the settlement too close to the Green Bay side of the peninsula. In his book *Embers of October,* Robert Wells places the settlement where the town of Little Sturgeon Bay was and is located. (The contemporary town of Sturgeon Bay was also known as Big Sturgeon Bay in 1871.) Subsequent maps seem to follow Wells, including the most recent map published in the second edition of Reverend Peter Pernin's account of the fire, *The Great Peshtigo Fire: An Eyewitness Account.*

This error is significant for at least two reasons. First, survivors' accounts appear to be confusing and in some cases contradictory. The survivors of Williamsonville recount how they sought aid in Sturgeon Bay, making it appear that, according to the incorrect map, they traveled twelve miles to Sturgeon Bay, instead of the five miles from Williamsonville to Little Sturgeon Bay. Second, and more important, the correct location of Williamsonville is essential to understanding the direction of the fire and to determining when the fire first struck the town. The incorrect placement of Williamsonville on the shore of Green Bay where Little Sturgeon Bay is located has led many to conclude incorrectly that the fire struck the peninsula after crossing over the fifty-mile-wide waters of Green Bay. However, knowing the correct location of Williamsonville, in conjunction with our current knowledge of fire, wind, and weather, allows us to reconstruct a more accurate account of the nature, development, and direction of the fire. It especially allows us to determine the timing of the fire.

Williamsonville was never rebuilt after the fire. However, another town, Tornado, was built in the same area, but it was abandoned before the end of the nineteenth century. In the 1930s a small county park called Tornado Memorial Park was constructed on the site of Williamsonville. The name and location of the park has led many writers to believe that the park marks the location of the town of Tornado and not Williamsonville. In fact, the park was named after the tornado of fire that had destroyed Williamsonville. Today, the site of Williamsonville is partially buried beneath State Highway 57, which passes through the middle of the settlement, and through the southeast portion of the park. The location of the graves of the fifty-nine people who died at Williamsonville is unknown today.

We are indebted to Professor Elizabeth D. Benchley of the University of West Florida for this crucial information on the correct location of Williamsonville, and we are grateful to her for sharing with us the results of her archaeological research on Williamsonville. For more detailed information on the location, history, and remains of Williamsonville, see Elizabeth D. Benchley, "'The Sky Was Brass, the Earth Was Ashes': The Williamsonville Site and the Peshtigo Fire of 1871," and Elizabeth D. Benchley, Gathel Weston, and Carrie A. Koster, "Preliminary Report of 1995 Archaeological Investigations State Highway 57 Improvement Project Brown, Kewaunee, and Door Counties Wisconsin."

Increase Lapham expresses his concern about the importance of the southwest wind in his *Report of the Disastrous Effects of the Destruction of Forest Trees Now Going on Rapidly in the State of Wisconsin.*

The Towsley story is told in a number of sources with great disagreement among them about the details. However, all the accounts agree on the murder-suicide. We have used the version recounted by Robert Wells in his book *Embers of October,* who also tells the story of David Maxon and his wife.

There is a growing body of scholarship on firestorms. Among other sources, we have used David W. Goens, "Fire Whirls"; Neil Hanson, *The Dreadful Judgement: The True Story of the Great London Fire*; and Dan Whipple, "Fire Storms."

The story of the Race family is told by Alice Judy Behrend in *Burning Bush*. Additional information on the Race family was provided by Joseph Race of Peshtigo, the grandson of Lorenzo Race.

Both Frank Tilton in *Sketch of the Great Fires in Wisconsin*, and Robert Wells in *Embers of October* tell the same stories of George W. Watson and G. A. Lawson, but disagree on important details. We've chosen the most complete and consistent account.

The burning of the Lull & Holmes Planing Mill is from Gerry and Janet Souter, *Fire Stations*, and Donald L. Miller, *City of the Century: The Epic of Chicago and the Making of America*.

Chapter 10

The descriptions of the sound of the fire are taken from accounts in Robert Wells, *Embers of October*; Peter Pernin, *The Great Peshtigo Fire: An Eyewitness Account*; Frank Tilton, *Sketch of the Great Fires in Wisconsin*; and Phineas Eames, "The Truths of Spiritualism. The Fire Test."

Luke Howard's contribution to meteorology and cloud classification specific to this storm front is related by Jacqueline Smith in *The Facts on File Dictionary of Weather and Climate*.

The accounts of Martin Race and Karl Lamp in this chapter are taken from Alice Judy Behrend's *Burning Bush*.

We do not have sufficient evidence to state categorically that a "true" tornado struck Peshtigo. However, the descriptions of the cloud formations associated with thunderheads and tornadoes, the direction of the winds, the cyclonic storm notation on the United States weather map for that date, and accounts of survivors who witnessed houses and loaded train cars hurled hundreds of feet through the air present evidence that the strongest-force tornado, an F5, struck Peshtigo at the time of the fire. An F5 tornado has wind speeds from 100 to 300 miles per hour, making it the only tornado capable of lifting buildings or very heavy objects into the air. Thomas Grazulis, a leading expert on tornadoes, discusses the complexities of tornadoes and tornado formation in his book, *Significant Tornadoes 1680–1991*. David Goens, in "Fire Whirls," makes further distinctions between fire tornadoes and true tornadoes.

Because of his severe injuries, Phineas Eames had to dictate his account to his sister-in-law. This account survives in manuscript and is also retold in both Frank Tilton, *Sketch of the Great Fires in Wisconsin*, and Robert Wells,

Embers of October. Both of these books also give the complete account of the fire in Williamsonville and the experiences of Maggie Williamson.

Chapter 11

Our account of the Chicago fire is drawn from the following sources: Robert Cromie, *The Great Chicago Fire;* Joseph Kirkland, *The Story of Chicago,* 2 vols.; Donald L. Miller, *City of the Century: The Epic of Chicago and the Making of America;* and James W. Sheahan and George P. Upton, *The Great Conflagration. Chicago: Its Past, Present and Future.*

Franklin Tilton expressed the shock felt by everyone when they heard the news of the Chicago fire. "Chicago was the pride of the West. It was typical of western enterprise and energy, and it was a sad day indeed when its magnificent marble buildings and its millions of wealth melted away as the frost-work on the window panes." Their own problems seemed to fade before the news of Chicago, "and no one cared to hear of aught but the news of the fires. The telegraph was monopolized by its recital, and the presses of the city were taxed to their utmost in printing extras containing the fearful news."

Stephenson records his meeting with Mulligan in his autobiography, *Recollections of a Long Life, 1829–1915.*

Stephenson records his telegram in *Recollections of a Long Life, 1829–1915.*

The account of Sandy Mac is based on information in Alice Judy Behrend's *Burning Bush.*

Chapter 12

Ogden's actions during this time are recounted by Jim Murphy in his book *The Great Fire.*

The story of J. G. Clements is drawn from the account in Robert Wells, *Embers of October.*

In 1874 a controversy erupted over the funds Father Pernin had raised in St. Louis for the new church. In an article in the *Eagle,* Father Pernin gave an accounting of the funds he had raised and used for the new church. It was his intention, he declared, to "give satisfaction to the good people at large who assisted most substantially and liberally." Father Pernin maintained that "the $2,000 was donated to me for me individually as is stated in a letter from St. Louis dated December 1872 which can be seen in the Eagle office." He was most upset that some people charged that "he had embezzled money from the church." He concluded his article with the question, "Whose slave or servant am I?"

The answer to that question, of course, is simple, as Father Pernin should have known: a priest is *servus servorum dei*, the servant of the servants of God. In short, he is the servant of his parishioners, something he seemed to have lost sight of. It is also curious that Father Pernin claimed the money was donated to him personally. Since he undoubtedly had taken the vow of poverty, he could own no property, and all that he had belonged to the Church. In any event, the scandal played out behind the scenes and no records reveal exactly what happened. Was Father Pernin an embezzler, or simply careless with church funds? The record, such as it is, raises many questions but offers no answers. However, we do know that in September 1875, after Father Pernin had rebuilt his church, the bishop saw fit to transfer him to Grand Rapids (later Wisconsin Rapids) where he served until 1878. From there he served in a number of parishes in Minnesota until his last assignment at St. Joseph's parish in Rushford, Minnesota. He died October 9, 1909, in Rochester, Minnesota.

When we contacted the diocese of Montreal for biographical information on Father Pernin we were told that there was no record of such a priest ever having served in the diocese. This is curious, because Pernin published his first account of the fire in a small pamphlet, the title page of which lists the "Rev. P. Pernin, United States Missionary," as the author, and states in large type that the pamphlet was "Published with the Approbation of His Lordship the Bishop of Montreal," and was "printed by John Lovell, St. Nicholas Street, Montreal."

Much of our account of William Newberry, Karl Lamp, and the rescue efforts of Henry Bakeman and Henry Bartels is drawn from James W. Sheahan and George P. Upton, *The Great Conflagration. Chicago: Its Past, Present and Future.*

Our account of Lorenzo and Harley Race is drawn from the accounts given by Alice Judy Behrend in *Burning Bush* and Robert Wells in *Embers of October.*

John Williamson wrote his account for Franklin Tilton and is published in Tilton's book, *Sketch of the Great Fires in Wisconsin.* Please see also the first note for chapter 9 in which we discuss the correct location of Williamsonville.

Chapter 13

Noyes's telegram to Fairchild is at the State Historical Society of Wisconsin.

We drew on a number of sources for our account of Governor Fairchild's military career, including Alan T. Nolan, *The Iron Brigade: A Military History,* as well as documents and papers at the State Historical Society of Wisconsin.

At five feet nine inches, Frances "Frank" Fairchild was taller than General Phil Sheridan and a number of other officers, but somehow they never noticed because of her warmth and genuine interest in each person she met. She was sixteen when she met the twenty-nine-year-old colonel Lucius Fairchild in 1861 at a ball in Washington, D.C. The good colonel had come to the ball specifically to meet Mrs. Willard, a well-known beauty, but when he was introduced to Frances and Mrs. Willard together, he had eyes only for Frank. "Frank, oh, Frank," he would say whenever he recounted their meeting. The man who had sworn he was "powder proof" had fallen instantly and hopelessly in love. From that moment until he died in 1896, Lucius Fairchild was as devoted to his Frank as she was to him.

Frances Fairchild was not quite eighteen when in 1864 she married Brigadier General Fairchild, the hero of Gettysburg. Shortly after their marriage, General Fairchild became secretary of state and then governor of Wisconsin, and Frances Fairchild plunged into political life as the young, charming wife of a rising political star. Since there was no governor's mansion, their small house served as the official residence. When the legislature was in session, she hosted a reception each week. Because the house was modest in size, she would receive a few of the members of the legislature each week until all had been the beneficiaries of her warmth and charm. She was an invaluable aid in supporting her husband's political career.

Both Robert Wells in *Embers of October* and Mary Fairchild Morris, in a letter that is part of the collection of the State Historical Society of Wisconsin, describe Frances Fairchild's activities at this time.

The notebook in which Dr. May recorded the dead and injured is preserved at the Marinette County Historical Society Museum.

The weather information in this chapter is based on the observations as recorded by official observers in Chicago and Milwaukee. These records are located at the National Archives, College Park, Maryland.

The account of Ogden's arrival and activities in Chicago at this time is based on information in Donald L. Miller's book, *City of the Century: The Epic of Chicago and the Making of America*.

Various sources give different estimates of Ogden's total losses in the fire at Chicago and Peshtigo. Some estimate his losses as low as $1.5 million while other estimates are as high as $3 million. Ogden himself claimed his losses totaled $2.5 million, but there is reason to believe his losses were higher. Robert Wells offers the higher number. Either way, Ogden's losses were considerable. In contemporary money, his losses were somewhere between $22 million and $43 million.

These numbers call into question the official figure for total losses from the fire, which was put at $2,883,800, or slightly over $41 million in today's money. Obviously this figure does not include Ogden's losses, nor does it include the value of the 1 billion trees that were destroyed. For example, the Peshtigo Company's sawmill produced 150,000 board feet of lumber each day. Since lumber sold for approximately $24 per thousand board feet, the destruction of these trees represented a loss of $86,400 per month (or over $1.25 million in contemporary money). The official estimates of total monetary losses and the number of dead appear, on closer inspection of the evidence, to be far too low, making this fire much more destructive to both life and property than has been recorded or recognized.

The account of the burial party's journey through the Sugar Bush, and finding the boy burying his family, is related in *The Great Conflagration. Chicago: Its Past, Present and Future* by James W. Sheahan and George P. Upton. Robert Wells in *Embers of October* and Franklin Tilton in *Sketch of the Great Fires in Wisconsin* also provide descriptions of the burial parties and their experiences.

Robert Wells in *Embers of October* and Franklin Tilton in *Sketch of the Great Fires in Wisconsin* tell the story of the Swedish workmen, the destruction of the boardinghouse, and Donald Roy McDonald's loss of his family. Fay Dooley recorded her grandmother's experiences in a manuscript now at the State Historical Society of Wisconsin.

Finding large numbers of bodies in open fields, as well in the ashes of their burned wagons, is described in *The Great Conflagration. Chicago: Its Past, Present and Future* by James W. Sheahan and George P. Upton; Robert Wells, *Embers of October*; and Franklin Tilton, *Sketch of the Great Fires in Wisconsin*.

Sheahan and Upton also note that the Davis family in Peshtigo met the same fate, and "I have heard of quite a number of such cases" (*The Great Conflagration. Chicago: Its Past, Present and Future*). One of the most persistent myths of the fire is that many people were boiled alive in rivers or wells. There are no accounts to document anyone dying this way. In fact, all the accounts specifically deny that anyone was boiled to death. Those who did die in wells died from suffocation or from the well curbs burning and falling in on them. One of the curiosities of the fire is that people who were saved by lying in creeks found dead fish floating in the water, even though the water was quite cold. No one has accounted for the dead fish, but survivors are unanimous that during the fire the water in all the creeks and rivers remained cold and did not heat up, let alone reach boiling.

Finding the body of John Church's son is related in *The Great Conflagration. Chicago: Its Past, Present and Future* by James W. Sheahan and George P. Upton; Robert Wells, *Embers of October*; Franklin Tilton, *Sketch of the Great Fires in Wisconsin*; and Alice Judy Behrend, *Burning Bush*.

Chapter 14

No one thought to turn first to the federal government for aid because no one expected such aid, nor did the government ever provide aid for disasters. Disaster assistance was not a function of the federal government, and President Grant would have been surprised to receive any request for aid. Still, Governor Fairchild wrote to Secretary of War William Belknap on the same day he issued his appeal for help. After noting that the farmers had lost their wagons and harness, he asked, "Has the United States any common harness and ordinary Army wagons to spare?" He asked for one hundred wagons and one hundred sets of harness, offering that "the State will account for them at their value if required to do so." He then went on to ask for one thousand army coats and pants, again offering to pay for them if necessary. Fairchild stressed that this "is no ordinary calamity and extraordinary measures must be taken to meet the demands of the occasion—hence I make this request confident that the President and yourself will assume any necessary responsibility." Governor Fairchild's letter is at the State Historical Society of Wisconsin.

Governor Cadwallader Washburn's comments on Governor Fairchild's actions and the legislature's resolution praising him are in the appendix to *Journal of Proceedings of the 26th Annual Session*, Wisconsin State Assembly, 1873.

The letter read to the Green Bay Relief Committee was published in the *Advocate*.

Kris Beisser Olson in her article, "The Great Fire of October 1871: A Nation Responds," describes some of the large number of telegrams that flooded the governor's office with offers of money and other aid. All of these telegrams are at the State Historical Society of Wisconsin.

It is impossible to know the total value of all the relief supplies that were donated and distributed in the burned districts. Each relief committee kept detailed records of its donations and expenditures, but a great deal of the supplies was goods for which the committees gave an estimated value. How accurate and how complete these estimates were, there is no way of knowing. What is known is how much in cash was collected and how it was spent.

In his accounting of December 31, 1872, to the governor, Captain A. J. Langworthy, head of the Green Bay Relief Committee, listed contributions of $141,612.36 and disbursements of $136,277.36. Frank Tilton reported that up to February 5, 1872, the Milwaukee Relief Committee disbursed $144,000 worth of supplies. He estimated total cash receipts for all the relief committees in the state at $350,000. This was in addition to all the supplies that had been donated. The $350,000 in cash donations is equivalent to a little over $5 million in contemporary money. For a detailed accounting of the receipts and expenditures of the relief committees, see A. J. Langworthy, "The Relief Fund. Reports of the Receipts and Disbursements," and Frank Tilton, *Sketch of the Great Fires in Wisconsin.*

The newspaper correspondent's comments are recorded in *The Great Conflagration. Chicago: Its Past, Present and Future,* by James W. Sheahan and George P. Upton.

Clothing especially had to be sorted. Some of it had to be mended, some of it badly needed washing, and some of it was simply not usable, such as dainty kid gloves, lace underwear, and silk gowns. There were several carloads of old summer clothing, worn-out shoes, and thousands of just one shoe of a pair. The women worked tirelessly through the mounds of clothing, sorting the good from the bad, the usable from the unusable, organizing it into categories appropriate for men, women, and children. Then they packed it into boxes and wrote the contents on each box.

Dr. Phillip's letter is at the State Historical Society of Wisconsin.

Ogden's offer of a $75,000 bonus would be worth over $1 million today.

Chapter 15

The account of the army worm invasion is taken from the appendix to *Journal of Proceedings of the 26th Annual Session,* Wisconsin State Assembly, 1873.

In the spring of 1873 the army worms returned, despite the assurances of Dr. William Le Baron, the state entomologist of Illinois, that "the army worm has rarely, if ever, been known to make its appearance in any considerable numbers in the same place two years in succession." "Army worms are marching through the farming district in the Sugar Bush, again this spring, destroying everything in their path," Luther Noyes noted in the May 31, 1872, issue of the *Eagle.*

Two planting seasons, the seasons that were to restore the farmers who had lost so much, produced little in the way of crops, certainly not the crops that the farmers needed to begin the long road back from the losses they had suffered in the fire. Yet even as the desperate survivors faced a second bleak winter, the relief committees were suspending their efforts because, as Captain Langworthy had reported, there had been "universally good crops over the entire burned district during the last season" and that "upon the whole, the 'relief' afforded those who were burned out, may be considered a success."

The comments on farming conditions can be found in Alice Judy Behrend, *Burning Bush.*

The letters of Lapham and C. F. Chandler to Captain Langworthy are in the appendix to *Journal of Proceedings of the 26th Annual Session*, Wisconsin State Assembly, 1873.

On the behavior of a fire when it encounters a ridge, see David W. Goens, "Fire Whirls."

The United States Geological Survey (www.usgs.gov) lists the top five deadliest disasters in U.S. history: (1) Galveston, Texas, hurricane of 1900, which killed between 6,000 to 8,000 people; (2) Johnstown, Pennsylvania, flood of 1889, which killed 2,200 people; (3) Peshtigo, Wisconsin, forest fire, which killed 1,200 people; (4) San Francisco earthquake of 1906, which killed 700 people; and (5) tristate hurricane of 1925 through Missouri, Illinois, and Indiana, which killed 695 people. We believe that the real death toll of over 2,500 people places the Peshtigo Fire second on the list of deadliest disasters in U.S. history, and it remains today the deadliest fire in U.S. history.

For a long time, politics dictated that little be written about the firebombings of World War II. When the cold war began, the Russian government used the bombing of Dresden, a city then under Soviet control in East Germany, as a propaganda tool. The U.S. Air Force responded with a "study" of the firebombings that was little more than a rebuttal of the Russian propaganda. However, there were some early studies that detailed the meticulous planning that went into these attacks.

Martin Caidin's *The Night Hamburg Died* (Ballantine, 1960) and David Irving's *The Destruction of Dresden* (Holt, 1963) caused something of a controversy when first published, with the British government vehemently denying that there had been any plan to destroy both these cities with incendiary attacks. Both books, however, present a solid argument that such planning did take place. Time has a way of changing viewpoints. Thus, Gordon Musgrove's book *Operation Gomorrah* (Jane's, 1981), using documents that had not been accessible earlier, presents in great detail the planning and execution of the firebombings of Hamburg. The code name for the operation clearly shows the intention of the raid. But Musgrove points out that the British and American forces were still learning just how to create a firestorm. The lessons learned at Hamburg would serve these forces well in planning the destruction of Dresden.

Alexander McKee's book *Dresden 1945: The Devil's Tinderbox* (Souvenir Press, 1982) details just how proficient the Allied bombing had become. Planners had learned the right combination of wind, fuel, and incendiary source, and they applied their new knowledge to Dresden with spectacular results. It is interesting to compare McKee's study, and the studies by Caidin, Irving, and Musgrove, with the official British report by Sir Charles Webster and Noble Frankland, *The Strategic Air Offensive Against Germany 1939–1945*, four volumes (H.M. Stationery Office, 1961), which like the American studies is decidedly slanted in favor of Allied policy and a justification for the firebombings.

Shortly after the end of World War II, the Korean war erupted and Japan became a crucial base for American operations in Korea. American authorities did everything they could to rally the support of the nation they had just defeated. Thus, the firebombings of Tokyo and sixty other Japanese cities were quickly forgotten as reconstruction continued apace. But even during World War II there was little criticism of the firebombing of Japan. The American public believed that the Japanese "had it coming to them." It's not a coincidence that the firebombing increased in intensity as the American public learned of the horrors of Japanese atrocities in such newly liberated places as the Philippines. Thus, it has been easier for historians to study this bombing campaign than the one in Europe.

E. Bartlett Kerr's book *Flames over Tokyo: The U.S. Army Air Force's Incendiary Campaign Against Japan 1944–1945* (Donald I. Fine, 1991) is a solid discussion of the origins, development, planning, and implementation of the bombing campaign against Japan. However, it does have some curious gaps. Fortunately, these gaps are filled in by Richard B. Frank's *Downfall: The End of the Imperial Japanese Empire* (Random House, 1999). Together these two books present the most detailed and documented study of the firebombings of Japan.

Other books discuss the firebombings to a limited extent but do contribute new information not found in other works. Both John Costello's *The Pacific War 1941–1945* (Quill, 1982) and John Dower's *War Without Mercy: Race and Power in the Pacific War* (Pantheon, 1986) offer significant information not found in other sources.

There is a series of U.S. Air Force reports (such as "Incendiary Attacks on Japanese Cities," U.S. Army Air Force Report, September 1, 1944) that offer insight on the planning and the implementation of the fire bombing of Japan. The *United States Strategic Bombing Report* (Office of the Chairman, U.S. Government Printing Office) is not quite as useful as one would hope because it is more concerned with advancing the cause of air power than with an objective analysis of the bombing campaigns of World War II.

On November 7, 1941, General George C. Marshall, U.S. Army Chief of Staff, instructed his aides to develop contingency plans for "general incendiary attacks to burn up the wood and paper structures of the densely populated Japanese cities." National Archives, RG 165, Army COS Project Decimal File, War Department, Chief of Staff of the Army, 1318-12-4-41.

BIBLIOGRAPHY

Official Publications and Reports

Chicago Common Council. "Inaugural Address of Mayor Joseph Medill, December 4, 1871." *Journal of Proceedings* (4 December 1871): 1–9.

——. "Inaugural Address of Mayor Roswell B. Mason, December 6, 1869." *Journal of Proceedings* (6 December 1869): 4–5.

Langworthy, A. J. "Phenomena of the Fire." Appendix to *Journal of Proceedings of the 26th Annual Session* (Wisconsin State Assembly) (1873): 216–18.

——. "The Relief Fund. Reports of the Receipts and Disbursements." Appendix to *Journal of Proceedings of the 26th Annual Session* (Wisconsin State Assembly) (1873): 157–73.

Lapham, Increase A. "The Great Fires of 1871 in the Northwest." *Wisconsin Academy Review* 12, no. 1 (1965): 6–9.

——. *Report of the Disastrous Effects of the Destruction of Forest Trees Now Going on Rapidly in the State of Wisconsin*. Atwood & Rublee, 1867.

LeBaron, William. "The Peshtigo Army Worm." Appendix to *Journal of Proceedings of the 26th Annual Session* (Wisconsin State Assembly) (1873): 219–22.

Noyes, Luther B. "Phenomenon of the Peshtigo Fire." Appendix to *Journal of Proceedings of the 26th Annual Session* (Wisconsin State Assembly) (1873): 222–24.

Register of Meteorological Observations, Under the Direction of the Smithsonian Institution, Adopted by the Commissioner of Agriculture for His Annual Report.

Milwaukee, Wisconsin, September 1871; Chicago, Illinois, July, September, October 1871. National Archives Annex, College Park, Maryland.

Report of the Chief Signal Officer. Executive Documents of the Third Session of the Forty-second U.S. Congress, vol. I. Printed by Order of the House of Representatives. Washington, D.C., 1873.

Robinson, C. D. "Account of the Great Peshtigo Fire of 1871." In *Report on Forestry to the Commissioner of Agriculture,* edited by F. B. Hough, vol. 3, pages 231–42. Washington, D.C., 1872.

Tilton, Frank. "The Burning of Williamsonville." Appendix to *Journal of Proceedings of the 26th Annual Session* (Wisconsin State Assembly) (1873): 225–31.

Manuscripts and Interviews

Benchley, Elizabeth D. "'The Sky Was Brass, the Earth Was Ashes': The Williamsonville Site and the Peshtigo Fire of 1871." University of West Florida Archaeology Institute. Paper presented at the Society for Historical Archaeology Annual Meetings, Corpus Christi, Tex., January 1997.

Benchley, Elizabeth D., Gathel Weston, and Carrie A. Koster. "Preliminary Report of 1995 Archaeological Investigations State Highway 57 Improvement Project Brown, Kewaunee, and Door Counties Wisconsin." Report prepared for the Wisconsin Department of Transportation, Project I.D. 1480-04/08-00. University of Wisconsin–Milwaukee Archaeological Research Laboratory, October 1995.

Berman, Dale. Mayor of Peshtigo. Interview. 6 October 2000.

Cashman, John E. "The Belgian Settlers of Northeast Wisconsin and Their Descendants." Nine pages. 1933. State Historical Society of Wisconsin.

Casson, John J. "Personal Reminiscence of the Peshtigo Fire, Oct. 8, 1871." Six pages. Undated. State Historical Society of Wisconsin.

Couvillion, Robert. Resident of Peshtigo and Local Historian. Interview. 9 October 2000.

Dooley, Fay S. "Peshtigo Fire Cemetery." Six pages. Undated. State Historical Society of Wisconsin.

———. Untitled Reminiscence. Five pages. October 1938. Marinette County Historical Society.

Eames, Phineas. "The Truths of Spiritualism. The Fire Test." Thirty-one pages. 8 November 1871. State Historical Society of Wisconsin, Green Bay Area Research Center, University of Wisconsin–Green Bay.

Ellis, Mrs. William A. Undated letter. *Peshtigo Times,* 7 October 1971.

Fairchild, Lucius. Letter to General Belknap. Two pages. 14 October 1871. State Historical Society of Wisconsin.

Gardon, Mary Ann. Employee of the *Peshtigo Times*. Interview. 9 October 2000.

Hall, Edward J. "Fearful Days." Two pages. Undated. Oconto County Wisconsin website: www.rootsweb.com/~wioconto/firehall.htm

Ingalls, Josephine Sawyer (Mrs. Alvah Littlefield Sawyer). "Reminiscence of the Peshtigo Fire of 1871." Seven pages. 1927. State Historical Society of Wisconsin.

Merrill, Elbridge West. "A Terrible Reminiscence. A Night of Horror and A Fight for Life." Nine pages. Undated. State Historical Society of Wisconsin.

Morris, Mary Fairchild. Letter. Two pages. 5 May 1927. State Historical Society of Wisconsin.

Kieth, Mary T. Letter. *Peshtigo Times*, 18 October 1952.

Lapham, Increase A. *Papers, 1825–1930*. State Historical Society of Wisconsin.

Peck, Neal. Letter. *Peshtigo Times*, 7 October 1971.

Phillips, Dr. B. J. Letter to Governor Lucius Fairchild. Four pages. 22 December 1871. State Historical Society of Wisconsin.

Race, Joseph R. "A Prominent Man from Peshtigo's Early History." Seven pages. May 1977. Courtesy of the author.

———. Resident of Peshtigo and Local Historian. Interview. 7 October 2000.

Sauer, Verra. Letter. Seven pages. 22 August 1967. State Historical Society of Wisconsin.

Shepherd, Fred S. "Yes, I Am a Survivor," *Asbury Park (NJ) Sunday Press*, 23 December 1934; reprinted in *Peshtigo Times*, 7 October 1998.

Sherman, Dr. J. J. "History of Marinette." Forty-nine pages. 1876. Spies Public Library, Menominee, Michigan.

West, Anna Sheldon Ogden. "Reminiscences Dealing Largely with the Great Fire of 1871 Chicago." Eight pages. Undated. Chicago Historical Society Collection.

Whitney, Eugene C. "The Great Fire of 1871, October 8." Thirteen pages. Undated. State Historical Society of Wisconsin, LaCrosse Area Research Center, University of Wisconsin–LaCrosse.

Local Histories and Biographical Materials

Abbe, Truman. *Professor Abbe . . . and the Isobars. The Story of Cleveland Abbe, America's First Weatherman*. Vantage Press, 1955.

Behrend, Alice Judy. *Burning Bush, Including Many Rivers to Cross*. Peshtigo Times, 1988.

Boatman, John F. "...And the River Flows On..." Memories from a Wisconsin-Michigan Border Town, The Marinette, Wisconsin Area. Vol. 1. From Ancient Times Until the Creation of Marinette County in 1879. University of Wisconsin–Milwaukee, 1998.

———. "...And the River Flows On..." Memories from a Wisconsin-Michigan Border Town, The Marinette, Wisconsin Area. Vol. 2. From the Creation of Marinette County Until Marinette Becomes a City in 1887. University of Wisconsin–Milwaukee, 1998.

Brown, Elton T. A History of the Great Minnesota Forest Fires. Brown Bros., 1894.

Burke, F. C. I Lived at Peshtigo Harbor. Peshtigo Times, 1998.

The Catholic Church in Wisconsin. A History of the Catholic Church in Wisconsin from the Earliest Time to the Present Day. Catholic Historical Publishing Company, 1895–1898.

Clark, James I. Increase A. Lapham: Scientist and Scholar. State Historical Society of Wisconsin, 1957.

Commemorative Biographical Record of the West Shore of Green Bay, Wisconsin, Including the Counties of Brown, Oconto, Marinette and Florence. J. H. Beers, 1896.

Dooley, Fay. "Busy Peshtigo Harbor Vanished After Boom," Marinette County Historian 14, no. 3 (1989): 1, 4.

Emich, Howard L. Menominee River Memories. Marinette County Historical Society, 2000.

Goodspeed, E. J. History of the Great Fires in Chicago and the West. H. S. Goodspeed, 1871.

Healy, George P. A. Reminiscences of a Portrait Painter. A. C. McClurg, 1894.

History of Northern Wisconsin: Containing an Account of Settlement, Growth, Development and Resources. Western Historical Co., 1881.

Holand, Hjalmar. "The Great Forest Fire of 1871." Peninsula Historical Review 3–4 (1931): 41–61.

Johnson, Beverly Hayward. Queen Marinette: Spirit of Survival on the Great Lakes Frontier. White Water Associates, 1995.

Lexington, Eleanor. "The Lapham Family. Authors, Statesmen, Men of Science and Antiquarians." Illustrated Weekly Magazine (27 May 1906): 19.

Martin, C. I. "The Great Fire of 1871." In History of Door County, Wisconsin. Expositor Job Printer, 1881, pages 101–05.

Martin, Deborah B. History of Brown County, Past and Present. S. J. Clarke, 1913.

Moran, Joseph, and Lee Somerville. "Tornadoes of Fire at Williamsonville, Wisconsin, Oct. 8, 1871." Transactions of the Wisconsin Academy of Sciences, Arts and Letters (1990).

Obituary. William B. Ogden. *Chicago Tribune*, 4 August 1877.

Pernin, Peter. *The Great Peshtigo Fire: An Eyewitness Account*, 2nd ed. State Historical Society of Wisconsin, 1999.

Sewell, Alfred L. *"The Great Calamity!" Scenes, Incidents and Lessons of the Great Chicago Fire of the 8th and 9th of October, 1871. Also Some Account of Other Great Conflagrations of Modern Times, and the Burning of Peshtigo, Wisconsin.* A. L. Sewell, 1871.

Stephenson, Isaac. *Recollections of a Long Life, 1829–1915.* Privately printed, 1915.

Tilton, Frank. *Sketch of the Great Fires in Wisconsin at Peshtigo, the Sugar Bush, Menekaune, Williamsonville, and Generally on the Shores of Green Bay; with Thrilling and Truthful Incidents by Eye Witnesses. Also, A Statement of Relief Funds Contributed.* Robinson & Kustermann, 1871.

Wells, Robert W. *Embers of October.* Prentice-Hall, 1968; reprinted by Peshtigo Historical Society, 1995.

"William Butler Ogden." In *The University of Chicago Biographical Sketches*, by Thomas Wakefield Goodspeed, vol. 1, University of Chicago Press, 1925.

Newspapers

Fond du Lac Daily
Green Bay Advocate
Green Bay Gazette
Green Bay Press-Gazette
Madison Democrat
Marinette and Peshtigo Eagle
Marinette Eagle-Star
Marinette-Menominee Eagle Herald
Menominee Herald
Milwaukee Journal
Milwaukee Sentinel
New York Herald
New York Times
New York Tribune
Oconto Lumberman
Oconto Pioneer
Peshtigo Times
Shawano Journal
St. Paul (Minn.) Pioneer

Special Issues of Newspapers

    Marinette Eagle-Star, 26 June 1971
    Peshtigo Times, 6 October 1971
    Peshtigo Times, 4 October 1989
    Peshtigo Times, 7 October 1998

Articles, Pamphlets, and Periodicals

Abbe, Cleveland. "How the United States Weather Bureau Was Started." *Scientific American* 114 (1916): 529.

Arnold, Isaac N., and J. Young Scammon. "William B. Ogden." Fergus Historical Series, No. 17. Fergus Printing Company, 1882.

"Forest Fires in the West." *Harper's Weekly,* 25 November 1871: 1109.

"The Forest Fires of Wisconsin and Michigan in 1871." In *Chicago and the Great Conflagration,* by Elias Colbert and Everett Chamberlin, C. F. Vent, 1871.

Goens, David W. "Fire Whirls." *NOAA Technical Memorandum NWS WR-129.* National Weather Service Office, Missoula, Mont., May 1978.

Haines, Donald A., V. J. Johnson, and W. A. Main. "An Assessment of Three Measures of Long-Term Moisture Deficiency Before Critical Fire Periods." *USDA Forest Service Research Paper NC-131.* North Central Forest Experiment Station, East Lansing, Mich., 1976.

Haines, Donald A., and Earl L. Kuehnast. "When the Midwest Burned." *Weatherwise* 23 (June 1970): 113–19.

Haines, Donald A., and R. W. Sando. "Climactic Conditions Preceding Historically Great Fires in the North Central Region." *USDA Forest Service Research Paper NC-34.* North Central Forest Experiment Station, St. Paul, Minn., 1969.

Hanson, Chad. "The Big Lie: Logging and the Forests." *Earth Island Journal* (spring 2000).

Hayes, Paul G. "Increase Allen Lapham: Wisconsin's First Geologist." *Geoscience Wisconsin* 18 (2001): 1–5.

"The Heavens Rained Fire in the North Woods." In *Historic Fires of America,* pages 60–69. Country Living, 1973.

Lawrence, E. N. "Meteorology and the Great Fire of London, 1666." *Nature* 213: 169.

Martin, Xavier. "The Belgians of Northern Wisconsin." In *Collections of the State Historical Society of Wisconsin* 13 (1895): 375–96.

Miller, Eric R. "New Light on the Beginnings of the Weather Bureau from the Papers of Increase A. Lapham." *Monthly Weather Review* 58, no. 2 (1931): 64–70.

Olson, Kris Beisser. "The Great Fire of October 1871: A Nation Responds." *Voyageur* 13, no. 2 (1997): 10–17.

Pendowski, Paul. "When Peshtigo Burned." *Wisconsin Conservation Bulletin* 36, no. 4 (1971): 8–9.

Phillips, Donna Potter. "Peshtigo, Wisconsin: The 1871 Fire." *Heritage Quest* 68 (March/April 1997): 87–89.

"Private Gardens in Chicago." *Prairie Farmer* 7 (September–October 1847): 276–77.

Pyne, Stephen J. "Fire Policy and Fire Research in the United States Forest Service." *Journal of Forest History* 25, no. 2 (1981): 64–77.

———. "Firestick History." *Journal of American History* 76, no. 4 (1990): 1132–41.

———. "Flame and Fortune." *The New Republic*, 8 August 1994; revised and reprinted on www.public.asu.edu/~spyne/FLAME.html

———. "Indian Fires." *Natural History* 92, no. 2 (1983): 6, 8, 10–11.

———. "The Political Ecology of Fire. Thoughts Prompted by the Mexican Fires of 1998." *International Fire Fighters Newsletter* 19 (September 1998): n.p.

———. "Sky of Brass, Earth of Ash: A Brief History of Fire in the United States." In *Global Biomass Burning, Atmospheric, Climactic, and Biospheric Implications*, edited by Joel S. Levine, pages 504–11. MIT Press, 1991.

———. "Smoke Chasing," www.public.asu.edu/~spyne/smokechasing.htm

Roberts, Paul. "The Federal Chain Saw Massacre." *Harper's Magazine*, June 1997.

Rohe, Randall. "Life in Peshtigo Harbor 1867–1895." *Voyageur* 7, no. 2 (1991): 28–43.

Schaefer, Joseph. "Editorial Comment: Great Fires of Seventy-One." *Wisconsin Magazine of History* 11 (September 1927): 96–106.

Stearns, Forest W. "History of the Lake States Forests: Natural and Human Impacts." In *USDA. Lake States Regional Forest Service Assessment: Technical Papers, General Technical Report NC-189*, edited by J. Michael Vasievich and Henry H. Webster, pages 8–29. North Central Forest Experiment Station, St. Paul, Minn., 1997.

Steuber, William F. Jr. "The Problem at Peshtigo." *Wisconsin Magazine of History* 42 (autumn 1958): 13–15.

Titus, Stephen. "Dispatches. News From the Field." *Outside* (September 2000): 36–41.

"Top Five Deadliest Disasters in U.S. History." United States Geographical Survey. www.usgs.gov

Vogel, Walter. "Forest Fires in Manitowoc County—1871." *Occupational Monograph 58*, 1986 Series. Manitowoc County Historical Society, n.p.

Ward, Christina. "100 Years Later: Remembering the Great Hurricane of Galveston." The American National Red Cross. www.redcross.org/news/galveston/overview.html

Whipple, Dan. "Fire Storms." *Weatherwise* 52 (July/August 1999): 20–27.

Wildland Fire Assessment System Website. USDA Forest Service, Rocky Mountain Research Station. www.fs.fed.us/land/wfas

General

Brinkley, Alan. *The Unfinished Nation: A Concise History of the American People.* Vol. 2. *From 1865.* McGraw-Hill Higher Education, 2000.

Caiden, Martin. *The Night Hamburg Died.* Ballantine, 1960.

Casey, Robert J., and W. A. S. Douglas. *Pioneer Railroad: The Story of the Chicago and North Western System.* McGraw-Hill, 1948.

Cashman, Sean Dennis. *America in the Gilded Age: From the Death of Lincoln to the Rise of Theodore Roosevelt.* 3rd ed. New York University Press, 1993.

Clark, James I. *Farming the Cutover: The Settlement of Northern Wisconsin.* State Historical Society of Wisconsin, 1956.

Clark, James I. *Wisconsin Agriculture: The Rise of the Dairy Cow.* State Historical Society of Wisconsin, 1956.

———. *The Wisconsin Pineries.* State Historical Society of Wisconsin, 1956.

———. *The Wisconsin Pulp and Paper Industry.* State Historical Society of Wisconsin, 1956.

Clevely, Hugh. *Famous Fires.* John Day, 1957.

Costello, John. *The Pacific War 1941–1945.* Quill, 1982.

Cromie, Robert. *The Great Chicago Fire.* McGraw-Hill, 1958.

Current, Richard Nelson. *Pine Logs and Politics: A Life of Philetus Sawyer 1816–1900.* State Historical Society of Wisconsin, 1950.

Davis, Kenneth P. *Forest Fire Control and Use.* McGraw-Hill, 1959.

Dower, John. *War Without Mercy: Race and Power in the Pacific War.* Pantheon, 1986.

Eicher, David J. *The Longest Night: A Military History of the Civil War.* Simon & Schuster, 2001.

Frank, Richard B. *Downfall: The End of the Imperial Japanese Empire.* Random House, 1999.

Fries, Robert F. *Empire in Pine.* State Historical Society of Wisconsin, 1951.

Gallagher, Winifred. *The Power of Place: How Our Surroundings Shape Our Thoughts, Emotions, and Actions.* Poseidon Press, 1993.

Gates, Paul Wallace. *The Wisconsin Pine Lands of Cornell University.* Cornell University Press, 1943.

Grazulis, Thomas P. *Significant Tornadoes 1680–1991*. The Tornado Project of Environmental Films, 1993.

Guthrie, John D. *Great Forest Fires in America*. USDA Forest Service Bulletin, n.d.

Hanson, Neil. *The Dreadful Judgement: The True Story of the Great London Fire*. Doubleday, 2001.

Hawks, Graham Parker. *Increase A. Lapham: Wisconsin's First Scientist*. Ph.D. dissertation, University of Wisconsin, 1960.

Holbrook, Stewart. *Burning an Empire: The Story of American Forest Fires*. Macmillan, 1943.

———. *Holy Old Mackinaw*. Macmillan, 1938.

Irving, David. *The Destruction of Dresden*. Holt, 1963.

Kerr, E. Bartlett. *Flames Over Tokyo: The U.S. Army Air Forces' Incendiary Campaign Against Japan 1944–1945*. Donald I. Fine, 1991.

Kirkland, Joseph. *The Story of Chicago*. 2 vols. Dibble Publishing, 1892–1894.

Larson, Erik. *Isaac's Storm*. Crown, 1999.

Licht, Walter. *Industrializing America: The Nineteenth Century*. The Johns Hopkins University Press, 1995.

Lyons, Paul A. *Fire in America*. National Fire Protection Association, 1976.

Maclean, Norman. *Young Men and Fire*. University of Chicago Press, 1972.

McKee, Alexander. *Dresden 1945: The Devil's Tinderbox*. Souvenir Press, 1982.

McPherson, James M. *Battle Cry of Freedom*. Oxford University Press, 1988.

Miller, Donald L. *City of the Century: The Epic of Chicago and the Making of America*. Simon & Schuster, 1997.

Misa, Thomas J. *A Nation of Steel: The Making of Modern America 1865–1925*. Johns Hopkins University Press, 1995.

Monmonier, Mark. *Air Apparent: How Meteorologists Learned to Map, Predict, and Dramatize Weather*. University of Chicago Press, 1999.

Murphy, Jim. *The Great Fire*. Scholastic, 1995.

Musgrove, Gordon. *Operation Gomorrah*. Jane's, 1981.

Nelligan, Emmett (as told to Charles M. Sheridan). *The Life of a Lumberman*. N.p., 1929.

Nolan, Alan T. *The Iron Brigade: A Military History*. Indiana University Press, 1961.

Paul, Caroline. *Fighting Fire: A Personal Story*. St. Martin's Press, 1998.

Perry, Bliss, ed. *The Heart of Emerson's Journals.* Dover Publications, 1937.

Pratt, Fletcher. *A Short History of the Civil War.* Pocket Books, 1948.

Pyne, Stephen J. *America's Fires: Management of Wildlands and Forests.* Forest History Society, 1997.

———. *Fire in America: A Cultural History of Wildland and Rural Fire.* Princeton University Press, 1982.

———. *Introduction to Wildland Fire: Fire Management in the United States.* John Wiley, 1984.

———. *World Fire. The Culture of Fire on Earth.* Henry Holt, 1995.

———. *Year of the Fires: The Story of the Great Fires of 1910.* Viking, 2001.

Reimann, Lewis C. *When Pine Was King.* Lewis C. Reimann, 1952.

Riordan, John J. *The Dark Peninsula.* 2nd ed. Avery Color Studios, 1976.

Sargent, Charles Sprague. *Manual of the Trees of North America.* Vol. 2. Dover Publications, 1965.

Sheahan, James W., and George P. Upton. *The Great Conflagration. Chicago: Its Past, Present and Future.* Union Publishing, 1872.

Smith, Don R., and Wayne Roberts. *The Three Link Fraternity — Odd Fellowship in California. An Introduction to the Independent Order of Odd Fellows and Rebekahs.* Linden Publications, 1993.

Smith, Jacqueline. *The Facts on File Dictionary of Weather and Climate.* Checkmark Books, 2001.

Souter, Gerry, and Janet Souter. *Fire Stations.* Barnes & Noble Books, 2000.

Steinberg, Ted. *Acts of God: The Unnatural History of Natural Disasters in America.* Oxford University Press, 2000.

Suavé, Todd D. *Manifest Destiny and Western Canada.* 1997. www.dickshovel.com

Sutherland, Daniel E. *The Expansion of Everyday Life, 1860–1876.* University of Arkansas Press, 2000.

United States Strategic Bombing Report. Office of the Chairman, U.S. Government Printing Office.

Weather. Discovery Books, 1999.

Webster, Charles, and Noble Frankland. *The Strategic Air Offensive Against Germany 1939–1945,* 4 vols. H. M. Stationery Office, 1961.

Whitnah, Donald R. *A History of the United States Weather Bureau.* University of Illinois Press, 1961.

ACKNOWLEDGMENTS

We are indebted to many people who gave generously of their time, knowledge, special skills, or in any number of other ways helped us in this project.

During our trips to Peshtigo we benefited from the knowledge of Robert "Cubby" Couvillian and Joe Race, historians of and guides to the great fire. Mayor Dale Berman took time to sit and talk with us, as well as share his own collection of information about the fire. Leo Pesch and Mary Ann Gardon of the *Peshtigo Times* dug through their files to provide us with many of the photographs and illustrations in the book. Rob Becker of the *Marinette Eagle Herald* provided us with the rare photograph of Luther Noyes. Nola Cook of the Menominee Tourist Information Center was a font of information about where to go and with whom we should consult. Becky McGuire of the Marinette County Historical Society provided pictures, information, documents, and questions.

We owe special thanks to many librarians and archivists. We were fortunate to have the invaluable assistance of Ruth Ann

Wesoloski, Jeannie Albers, and Tom Pichette of the Spies Public Library in Menominee, Michigan, and of Carol Brenner and Cathy Menard of the Stephenson Library in Marinette. We are indebted to the staff of the Archives Section of the State Historical Society of Wisconsin in Madison, Brett Barker of the *Wisconsin Magazine of History*, and Debra Anderson of the Cofrin Library at the University of Wisconsin–Green Bay. All of them gave generously of their time and specialized knowledge. Many thanks also to the staff of National Archives Annex, College Park, Maryland, especially Doris Cumberpatch of the Research Circulation Desk, and to the staff of the Chicago Historical Society. And very special thanks to Elizabeth Hart and Julie Still of the Paul Robeson Library of Rutgers University, Camden, for their tireless efforts in locating and obtaining copies of books and articles we never thought anyone could locate.

Elizabeth Benchley of the University of West Florida, David Goens of the National Weather Service Office in Missoula, Montana, and Tim Matthewson of the U.S. Weather Bureau contributed the essential pieces of knowledge that we needed to solve the puzzle of the fire.

We are indebted to Louis Aglira of the Philadelphia Fire Department and the staff of the Philadelphia Fire Museum for talking to us about what it means to face a fire, even though no one could ever really understand or appreciate what a fireman faces.

Joseph Piccoli, Jr., and Robert Tartaglione read earlier drafts of the manuscript and contributed comments that made for a stronger book. Special thanks to readers Eric Sauter, Dyanne DiSalvo, Stephen Butler, and Phillip Gerard. In addition to reading and making some really smart comments on the various drafts of our manuscript, Marcy Beller shepherded the manuscript through production. Sandra Fox and Susan Muaddi plowed through library shelves and computer files searching for and finding records, books, and articles.

ACKNOWLEDGMENTS

.

The editorial good sense of Peder Zane of the Raleigh *News and Observer* permeates the book.

To our extraordinary editor, Elizabeth Stein, we can only say thanks, for everything. To our agent, John Wright, also thanks for believing in the project.

INDEX

Abbe, Cleveland, 75–76
Advocate
    see *Green Bay Advocate*
Agassiz, Louis, 74
Albert, Prince, 130
anemometers, 77, 78, 123
Army Signal Service, 16, 71, 76, 93,
    109, 208
army worms, 202–3
Arnot, John, 221
atmosphere, 73, 75, 83, 93, 109
atmospheric instability, 84, 86, 208

backburn/back fires, 34, 101
Bakeman, Henry, 148, 149, 214
Barnes, J. K., 74
barometers, 77, 78
barometric pressure, 51, 72, 82
Bartels, F. J., 180
Bartels, Henry, 148, 149, 214
Beach, Reverend Edwin R., 8, 57, 58
Behnke, Louisa, 218–19
Behrend, Alice Judy, 209, 210
Belanger, John, 2, 68, 108, 132, 156
Belknap, William, 174, 180
Bentley Building, 1, 2, 31
Big Suamica, 52, 53

"Big Woods," 83–84, 90
Birch Creek, 32, 145
Bliss, G. H., 70, 83, 95, 112–13,
    129
blowup, 101, 207, 209
    investigation into cause of, 163
bodies, 132, 147, 148, 166, 167–69,
    170
    identifying, 151
    see also dead/deaths
Brookes, Sam, 16, 82–83, 93, 99–100,
    109, 113, 123, 163
Brussels, 10, 162, 171
Burke, Fred, 187
Burning Bush (Behrend), 209

Cairo, Illinois, 87
Capen, Frances L., 16–17
Casual Phenomena Sheet, 82
Cavoit, Nick, 8, 62
Cedar River, 92, 104, 105
Chandler, C. F., 206–7
charcoal, 61–62, 66
Chicago, 6, 14, 27, 42, 96, 211
    aid to, 135, 158, 159
    damage to, 162, 163–64
    firefighters, 112–13

Chicago (*cont'd*)
 fires, 95–96, 107, 112–13, 129–31,
  132, 135, 141, 154, 163, 164, 181,
  191–92
 firestorm in, 113, 114, 122, 125, 207,
  208–9
 fronts meeting, 88
 insufficient water, 192
 Ogden and, 18, 21–24, 28
 Register of Meteorological
  Observations, 16
 topography, 86
 weather forecasting from, 78, 80
 weather obervation site, 82–83, 87
 winds striking, 99–100
Chicago, St. Paul & Fond du Lac
 Railroad, 24
Chicago & Northwestern Railroad,
 24, 68
Chicago Fire Department, 95, 107
Chicago Relief Committee, 180
Chicago River, 96, 129
children
 dead, 133, 171–72, 224
 fevers and coughs, 65
 survivors, 143, 144, 178
Chippewa Indians, 94–95
chore boys, 5–7
Cincinnati, Ohio, 87
Civil War, 15–16, 17, 24, 25–26, 71,
 133, 157–58
Clark, Charles, 2, 110
Clark baby, 121, 145, 146
Clarksville
 see Peshtigo
Clements, J. G., 62, 143–44
climate, 73, 74
Climate of London (Howard), 109
cloud classification, 109
clouds
 cumulus, 83
 mammatus, 113
Colwell, H. J., 66
communication, disabled, 14, 52
Congregational church (Peshtigo), 8,
 48, 167

Conn, A. C., 44
convection columns, 86, 102, 206
Cooke, Jay, 24, 27
cranberry bogs, 27, 28
crown fire, 101, 117
Crozer, J. A., 30, 66–67
Curtiss, William, 214
cyclones, 84, 85
cyclonic patterns, 71–72
cyclonic storm(s), 96, 100–1, 125

Dahl, Herr, 217, 218
Diedrich, Christ, 172
drought, 93
dead/deaths, 70, 161–62, 171–72
 burying, 170
 Door County Peninsula, 164, 211
 number of, 164, 211–15
 in Sugar Bushes, 164, 171, 211, 212,
  213
 see also bodies
Department of Forestry, 208
Door County, Wisconsin, 10
Door County Peninsula
 death toll, 164, 211
Doyl, Pat, 212
Drew, Samuel Peter, 104–5, 120
dry lightning, 109
dry spell, 14, 32, 35, 42, 43, 93
Dunlap House, 2, 68, 108–9, 133, 134
 victims in, 132, 146, 148, 149,
  160–61

Eagle
 see *Marinette and Peshtigo Eagle*
Eagle Printing Company, 222
Eames, Phineas, 108, 116, 123–25, 207
Ellis, William A., 27, 35, 51–56, 60, 61,
 135–36, 187, 195
Emerson, Ralph Waldo, 2, 6, 19, 20,
 74, 109
Emery, Temple, 27, 187
Erie Railroad, 21
Escanaba, Michigan, 43–44, 196, 200
Espy, J. P., 72–73
 Law of Storms, 74, 84–86

Fairchild, Frances "Frank," 158–59, 160, 173
Fairchild, Lucius, 15, 135, 154, 156–58, 159, 162, 173–77
  plea for aid to victims, 174–76, 181
  and relief efforts, 133–34, 180, 183
fall streaks/virga, 109, 113
Farnsworth, William, 94
fire, 11–12, 21, 86
  attitude toward, 71
  controlled, 101
  dynamics of, 85–87
  fear of, 41
  old paradigm regarding, 80
  telegraphic communications defense against, 88
  and weather, 208
fire alarm, 49, 51, 59
fire chemistry, 71–72
fire devils, 52, 101
fire tornadoes, 86, 87, 162, 163
fire whirls, 86–87, 101
firebrands, 117, 121, 122
firebreak(s), 34, 95
fires, 39, 44–45, 66, 82, 163
  atmospheric instability and, 84
  behavior of, 83–84, 90–91, 101, 207, 208, 209
  burning beneath ground, 33, 54
  fleeing to escape, 68–69, 112
  in forest around Peshtigo, 5–6, 7
  around Green Bay, 53–55, 96
  in land clearing, 23
  Lapham's papers on, 74
  news of, 31, 48
  as punishment, 58
  started to clear right of way for railroad, 28
  topography and, 86–87
  in weather reports, 17–18
  see also Peshtigo fire; and under place names, e.g., Chicago, fires
firestorm, 86, 162–63, 192, 206–7
  breathing in, 120–21
  in Chicago, 113, 114, 122, 125, 207, 208–9

damages from, 209
effects of, 190
mystery of anatomy of, 205–9
Peshtigo, 101–2, 113, 117, 119–20, 169, 204, 207, 224
Peshtigo Fire as model of, 101, 208
railroad crews blamed for, 189
victims of, 224
flamethrowers, 117
flies, 203, 205
forest fires, 70–71
  storm systems and behavior of, 85
forests
  owned by Ogden, 24
  Peshtigo, 5–7, 18
Fort Howard, 52, 53
front(s), 87
  warm and cold meeting, 88

gale(s), 84, 87, 92, 99, 100, 114, 123
Galena & Chicago Union, 23
Galveston, Texas, 84, 87
gas, combustible, 112, 116, 205, 206
George L. Newman (schooner), 120, 173
gg (great gale) winds, 84, 87
Gould, J. W., 51–52
Granger, Achille, 51
Grant, Ulysses S., 16, 180
Gray, Asa, 74, 222
Great Barbecue, 208
Great Fire of London, 101, 164
Great Lakes, 26, 73
Greeley, Horace, 42
Green Bay, 12, 18, 44, 92
  fire jumped, 120
Green Bay (town), 14, 26, 46, 52, 68, 91, 102, 134
  atmosphere, 141
  bedlam in, 154
  fire department, 42–43
  firefighters from, 113
  fires around, 53–55, 96
  injured brought to, 173
  news of Chicago fires in, 130–31
  plan for canal, 48, 49
  railroad to Menominee River, 27

Green Bay (town) (*cont'd*)
  relief committee, 177–78, 180, 181
  relief efforts, 179–80, 181
  survivors arriving in, 178
Green Bay Advocate, 14, 42, 84, 96, 103,
  130, 165, 178, 194–95, 213
Green Bay and Marinette Steamboat
  Line, 91
Green Bay Relief Committee, 183,
  184
Green Island, 120
  lighthouse, 104–5
gustnadoes, 101, 207

Hale, Levi, 36, 37, 52–53, 112
Hall, Dr. Ben, 160
Hall, Edward, 224
Hall, Dr. Jonathan Cory, 59, 132
Harmony, Wisconsin, cemetery,
  223–24
Hawley, Captain Thomas, 91, 102,
  134, 135, 141, 153–54
Hay, T. "Tommy" A., 8, 42, 60, 62,
  116
Henry, David, 51
Henry Joseph, 74, 75, 77, 93
Holmes, Oliver Wendell, 19
hospitals, 160, 161
Howard, Luke, 109
Howgate, General Henry W., 69, 77,
  78, 80, 87, 88
Huebner, Reverand Charles, 58

Illinois, 23, 93, 162
immigrants, 9–10, 13, 34–35, 36, 41,
  65, 74, 92, 212
  in firestorm, 102, 104
  stopped coming to Peshtigo, 196
Indians, 10, 31, 92, 94
  intermarriage with whites, 94–95
Ingalls, Eleazar, 2, 11, 31–32, 146
injured (the), 154, 160–62, 173
  treatment for, 161–62
iron manufacture, 66, 67
isobars, 75, 99, 113
isotherms, 75

Jackson, Andrew, 21
Jacobs, John, 10, 94

Kansas, 93
Kewaunee, 105, 106
Kewaunee County, 96, 180
Kilborn, Byron, 73
Kirby, Carpenter & Sons, 10
Kirby-Carpenter Dock, 91
Kirby House, 160
Kuchenberg, Adolph
  stagecoach, 12

Lamb, Willard, 105–6
Lamp, Fredricke Tackman, 36–39, 69,
  219
  and firestorm, 111–12, 121–22
  grave, 217, 218
Lamp (Lemke, Lern, Lempke),
  Charles (Karl), 34–39, 69
  and firestorm, 111–12, 121–23
  in hospital, 162, 178–79
  injured, 147, 148
  post-fire life, 216–19
Lamp family, 69
  children, 36, 37, 38, 217, 218, 219
land, 46–47
  buying and settling, 21, 22
  clearing, 23
Land Office, 21, 22, 46–47
Langworthy, Captain A. J., 182–83,
  185, 192, 205, 210, 213
  report to governor, 211
Lapham, Increase Allen, 75, 76, 86, 99,
  109
  Casual Phenomena Sheet, 82
  death of, 221–22
  investigation of firestorm, 163, 165
  mechanics of the firestorm, 192
  report on firestorm, 205–6, 207, 208
  as scientist, 73–74
  as visionary, 73
  and weather agency, 77–79
  as weather observer, 16, 51
  wind patterns, 93
Lapham, Julia, 78–80

large atmospheric circulation systems, 85
Law of Storms, 74, 85–86, 208
Lawe, John, 94
Lawson, G. A., 105, 107
Leavenworth, Kansas, 87–88
lightning, 86
Lincoln, Abraham, 16–17
Linnaeus, Carolus, 109
Little Sturgeon Bay, 151, 152
Little Suamico, 44–45, 52, 53
loggers, 8, 9, 32, 49, 102, 103, 168, 212
logger's pox, 9
logging camps, 14, 27
Loomis, Elias, 72, 73, 74
Louisville, Kentucky, 87
Ludington, Nelson, 25
lumber
  burned, 53
  transporting, 27
lumber barons, 7, 8, 15
lumber business of Ogden, 44, 123, 135, 200
lumber industry, 7, 8, 10–11, 26, 32
lumberjacks, 7, 9, 32
lumbermen, 49, 106

Mac, Sandy, 136–40, 214
McDonald, D. R., 51
McDonald, Donald Roy, 169
McGregor, James, 51
McGregor, John, 45–48, 57, 68–69, 104, 112, 131, 214
  death of, 132
McGregor, Mary, 45–48, 57, 68–69, 104, 112, 115, 131, 132
Manitowoc
  fire in, 52, 53
Manitowoc County, 180
Mann Gulch, Montana, 209
Marinette, Wisconsin, 1, 2, 10, 11, 12, 14, 15, 16, 17, 31, 42, 49, 52, 62, 65–66, 105, 107, 134, 167, 205
  aid to, 180
  aid to Peshtigo, 133, 135, 141
  blast furnaces in, 66

churches, 57, 204
damage to, 131–32, 144–45
distracting from fires, 67
fires in, 60, 83, 90–91
hospital in, 149
injured housed in, 160
lack of rain, 30
K. Lamp in, 216–17
new presbytery in, 92
population, 13
railroad line to, 68, 188
smoke in, 41
Stephenson in, 24, 25, 26
survivors in, 210
tornado and fire, 120
volunteer fire company, 59
winds striking, 99
Marinette and Peshtigo Eagle, 1, 13, 15, 16, 30–31, 43–44, 48, 52, 60, 66, 68, 72, 84, 91, 100, 108, 165, 189–91, 195–200, 204–5, 209, 213
  circulation, 69
mass transit by rail, 188, 191
May, Dr. Jacob, 149, 160–61
medicine, 72
Medill, Joseph, 191
Menekaune, 99, 113, 135
Menominee, Michigan, 10, 11, 24, 30, 91, 104, 205
  aid to, 180
  blast furnaces in, 66
  distracting from fires, 67
  fire in, 134–35
  injured housed in, 160
  railroad line to, 188
  survivors in, 146
  tornado and fire, 120
Menominee Indians, 10, 31, 94
Menominee River, 10, 14, 25, 26, 134
  bridge, 11
Merrill, Byron J., 152, 153
Merrill, Elbridge West, 31, 32, 33–34, 67, 110, 120–21, 145–46
Merryman, A. C., 67–68, 184
  boardinghouse, 160, 183

meteorology, 51, 72, 75–76, 77, 80,
    109
Michigan, 23, 73, 84, 162
Milwaukee, 14, 42, 99
    firefighters from, 113
    Lapham in, 78, 79, 80
    relief committee, 180, 181
    the storm in, 113
    temperature, 163
    weather reports from, 87, 88
Minnesota, 73
    fires, 23, 83–84, 86, 87, 90–91,
        130
moisture, 85, 86
Moscow, burning of, 164
Muir, John, 19
Mulligan, John, 27, 45, 102, 104,
    131–32, 134
Myer, Colonel Albert J., 71, 74–75,
    76–78, 80, 83, 87, 93, 163

Napoleon, 164
New Franken, 96, 99, 105–6, 114
    survivors from, 178
New York State Legislature, 21
Newbery, Walter, 94, 214
Newberry, William, 147–48, 214
Newberry family, 215
newspapers
    weather records, 16–17
Northwest Pacific & Union, 24, 27
Northwestern Railroad, 27
Noyes, Frances (Belle), 1–2, 70
Noyes, Frank E., 1–2, 16, 70, 91,
    222
Noyes, Luther, 1–2, 28, 59, 62, 91,
    202
    aid to Peshtigo, 132–33
    civic booster/optimism, 14–15,
        41–42, 189–91, 195–200
    in Civil War, 15–16
    death of, 222
    on fires, 59–61
    on inspection committee, 165,
        167
    letter to Fairchild, 156–57, 158

newspaper, 13–15, 16, 17, 30–31, 41,
    43–44, 48, 49, 52–53, 66–68, 84,
    100, 108, 165, 186–87, 189–91,
    192, 209
newspaper: editorial, 204–5
    personal success, 69–70
    and rebuilding Peshtigo, 195
    "red eye," 65
Noyes, Minnie, 1–2, 70

Oakes, W. C., 52
Oconto, 14, 65, 92
    fires in, 44, 48, 52
Oconto County, 11, 34, 117, 125
Ogden, Abraham, 19, 20
Ogden, Mahlon D., 23, 61, 164
Ogden, Marian Arnot, 221
Ogden, Sheldon & Company, 21
Ogden, William Butler, 18–24, 27–28,
    51, 61, 74, 96–97
    death of, 221
    and destruction in Chicago, 141,
        162, 163–64, 165
    lumberyards, 44, 123, 135, 200
    plan for canal, 48
    and railroad extension, 27, 28,
        43–44
    and rebuilding Peshtigo, 186–89,
        197–200
    and Stephenson, 24, 26–27, 28
    summer home destroyed, 167
    visionary, 73
Ogden Grove, 23, 97, 141, 164
Old Peshtigo Road, 104, 120
Omaha, Nebraska, 87
Osgood, Minerva, 15

Paine, Henry H., 72–73, 74–75, 76
Palmer Drought Severity Index
    (PDSI), 93
Pernin, Father Peter, 8, 49, 50–51, 52,
    53, 58, 59, 60, 91–92
    aftermath of fire, 141–45
    and firestorm, 104, 105, 112, 114,
        115–16
    rebuilding churches, 204

Peshtigo, 7–11, 12, 13, 14, 16, 17, 31,
    49, 65–66, 91–92, 96, 107
  aid to, 132, 135, 141–42, 144,
    156–59, 160, 173–78, 179–85
  army worms invasion, 202–3
  churches, 8–9, 57–58, 204
  damage from fire, 131–40, 141–45,
    154, 162, 164, 167–72, 185–86,
    190–91
  death toll, 211
  distracting from fires, 67
  destruction of, 140, 154
  firestorm, 101–2, 113, 117, 119–20,
    169, 204, 207, 208, 224
  forests around, 5–7
  fronts meeting, 88
  inspection committees and burial
    parties, 164, 165–72
  lack of rain, 30
  marker of fire, 223
  mood in, 190–91, 195
  Ogden and, 18, 28
  rebuilding, 186–89, 195–200,
    217–18
  refugees from, 54
  sawdust, 31, 32
  smoke, 41
  topography, 86
  tornado, 117, 120, 165, 166
  victims from, 156
  winds striking, 99, 100
  wood from, 24
Peshtigo Company, 8, 18, 27, 34, 35,
    43, 60, 61, 94, 195, 217
  boardinghouse, 28, 36, 37, 142, 169
  and proposed canal, 48–49
  rebuilding, 196
  woodenware factory, 8, 18, 27, 43,
    44, 51, 60, 142
  woodenware factory not rebuilt,
    198–200
  store, 59, 100
Peshtigo Court, 96, 123
Peshtigo fire, 47, 49, 51–52, 58–62, 83,
    90–91, 101, 103–5, 117, 119–20,
    133, 165, 208–9

  blamed on railroad crews, 188–89
  damage done by, 131–40, 141–45,
    154, 162–64, 167, 185–86, 190–91
  death toll, 211–15
  downplayed in Noyes's newspaper,
    41–42
  losses from, 185–86
  as mode of firestorm, 101, 208
  newspaper reports of, 181
  survivors' accounts of, 209–10
  see also firestorm
Peshtigo Harbor, 12, 18, 27, 42, 48–49,
    102
  expanding, 187, 200
  mill at, 90, 169–70, 199–200
  spared from fire, 169
Peshtigo House, 102, 107
Peshtigo Paradigm, 204, 209
Peshtigo Relief Committee, 182
Peshtigo River, 7–8, 9, 14, 18, 27, 48,
    51, 119, 136–37
  dead in, 162
Peterson, Peter, 51
Phillips, Dr. B. T., 183–85
Phillips, Ben, 170
Place, Abram, 93–95, 110, 147, 149,
    162
Place, Anton, 134
pneumothorax, 120
preachers, itinerant, 45, 47–48, 57,
    69
Prestin, August, 39, 111, 217
Prestin, Sophia, 39, 111, 217

Race, Almira, 69, 103–4, 110, 111, 148,
    162
Race, Harley, 103, 104, 148, 149
Race, Lorenzo, 103, 104, 148–49
Race, Martin, 103, 104, 110–11, 148
railroad crews
  fire blamed on, 188–89
railroads, 48
  Chicago, 22, 23, 24
  expansion of, 43–44, 49, 68, 187,
    188–89, 190
  Ogden's plan for, 27, 28, 43–44

rain, 42, 109, 154
 fire and, 86
 lack of, 6, 7, 14, 30, 32, 57, 93
rainstorms, 84, 85
Reed, Lovett, 214
relief efforts, 173–85
 criticism of, 180, 181, 182–84
 transportaion problems, 182
Report on the Disastrous Effects of the
 Destruction of Forest Trees . . .
 (Lapham), 79
Robinson, S., 70–71, 80, 83, 87, 88
Rockstead, Helga, 116–17

sawdust, 31, 32–33, 57, 58
sawmills, 10, 53
Scheelke, August, 218
Self-Help (Smiles), 191
Shephard, William, 59
Sheridan, General P. H., 180
Sinclair, Jefferson, 25
Smiles, Samuel, 191
smoke, 28, 35, 39, 41, 43, 47, 57, 59,
 87, 90, 92, 102, 146, 154, 166
 Peshtigo, 104
smoke inhalation, 54, 107
snowstorms, 84, 85
soil, 71–72, 93, 185–86, 192
sound (of the fire), 108, 115
Stanton, Edwin M., 71
Stephenson, Isaac "Ike," 11, 18, 24–27,
 42, 59, 61, 72, 97, 157, 192
 autobiography, 199
 death of, 221
 and Ogden, 24, 26–27, 28
 and Peshtigo fire, 131–32, 133–34,
  135–36, 144
 plan for canal, 48–49
 plea for help, 154, 158
 and railroad extension, 43–44
 and rebuilding Peshtigo, 186,
  187
 and relief effort, 177
Stephenson, Margaret, 72, 192
Stephenson, Robert, 11, 25, 59, 132
Stephenson, Samuel, 11, 25, 59,
 132

storm (the)
 and fire, 108–25, 169
 see also firestorm
storm cellars, 92
storms, 73, 77, 83, 84, 87
 Lapham's studies of, 74
 predicting, 84
 types of, 84–86
Strong, General Moses, 27, 187, 188
Sturgeon Bay Canal, 48–49, 72, 97
Sugar Bush(es), 9, 14, 50, 99, 190
 army worms, 202–3
 burial parties, 170
 death toll, 164, 171, 211, 212, 213
 fire, 34, 140
 Lower Bush, 9, 34, 45
 Middle Bush, 9, 103
 rebuilding in, 219
 the storm in, 114–15
 survivors in, 146–48
 Upper Bush, 9, 165, 171
 victims from, 156
Surgeon General's Office, 71
survivors, 108, 109, 113, 116–17, 144,
 149–54, 162–63, 165–67, 168, 170
 aid to, 185
 arriving in Green Bay, 178
 Birch Creek, 145–46
 deaths of, 161–62
 medical attention, 183
 Peshtigo, 142–44
 scars, 210
 searching for relatives, 193–95
 stories of, 165, 209–11
 Sugar Bush, 146–48

telegraph, 53–54, 71, 113
telegraph lines, 129
 down, 14, 16, 83, 88, 134, 136, 157
 fire destroyed, 52
 restoring, 187
telegraphic communication
 first line of defense against fire, 88
temperatures
 records of, 82, 85
Thoreau, Henry David, 19, 20
thunderstorms, 85, 113

Tilden, Samuel, 26, 27
Tilton, Benjamin Franklin, 14, 15, 42,
    44–45, 53, 54, 84, 96, 131, 154,
    165, 194, 212
  editorial on the fire, 192–93
  on losses, 185–86
  on relief efforts, 178, 181
  sky observation, 109
topography, 84, 208
  change in, and fire, 86–87, 124, 192,
    207
tornado(es), 83, 84, 85, 92, 93, 113
  Peshtigo, 117, 120, 165, 166
  evidence of, 169
  and fire, 169, 207
  Wisconsin, 208
Towsley, C. R., 100, 119–20
trade winds, 72
trains, underground, 97
trees, 6, 9, 44
  charcoal content of, 61–62
Trudell, Mrs. Theodore, 62, 143

Union (steamer), 12, 68, 91, 102, 134,
    153–54, 173
United States
  vulnerability to weather patterns,
    88
United States Department of
    Agriculture, 96
United States Forest Service, 208
United States Weather Bureau, 208

victims, 156, 162, 213, 224
  help for, 132
Victoria, Queen, 130
vortex (vortices), 86–87, 117, 125

wall cloud, 114, 115
Walton, New York, 18, 19, 20
War Department, 208
Washburn, Cadwallader, 176, 184
water supply, 14
Watson, George W., 105–7
weather, 71–72
  fire and, 208
  old paradigm regarding, 80

weather bulletins, 16–17, 75, 76, 87
weather forecasts, 77–78
weather map(s), 75, 77, 96, 99
  conditions before Peshtigo Fire,
    208
weather observation sites, 87–88
weather observers, 16, 82–83, 87
weather service, 74–75, 77
Weld, William, F., 23
well(s), 112
  dead in, 172
  dried up by fire, 186
Wells, Robert, 62
Wenzel, Charles, 51
West Indian cyclones, 84, 85
Williamson, John, 117, 151–52
Williamson, Maggie, 117, 151
Williamson, Margaret (Maggie),
    117–18, 150–51, 152–53, 215
Williamson, Thomas, 117, 149–53,
    209, 215
Williamsonville, 10, 96, 99, 113,
    114
  death toll, 215
  fire, 117–18
  survivors from, 178
wind(s), 14, 43, 50, 51, 68, 90, 92, 163,
    208
  cycle with fire, 85, 86–87, 192
  direction and velocity, 74, 82–83
  drying the land, 93
  in firestorm, 101, 102, 111, 113–14,
    120, 123, 125, 133, 165, 205,
    206
  northeast, 85
  shifts in, 52, 58–59, 87, 99–100
  varieties and movement of, 84
wind shear, 124, 207
Wisconsin, 28, 73, 84
  as Eden, 11–12
  fires in, 23
  firestorm, 162
  tornadoes, 208
  wind patterns, 14, 26, 93
Wisconsin, Its Geography and Topography
    (Lapham), 74
Wisconsin Assembly Journal, 1873, 211

ABOUT THE AUTHORS

Denise Gess, the author of two critically acclaimed novels, *Good Deeds* and *Red Whiskey Blues,* is the Visiting Assistant Professor of Fiction Writing at the University of North Carolina, Wilmington. William Lutz is a professor of English at Rutgers University, Camden, and the author of fifteen books, including the best-seller *Double-speak.*